DISCOVER THE OUTDOORS

DISCOVER
THE
OUTDOORS

BY ROBERT ELMAN

THE LION PRESS

Publishers, New York

*To my parents, who first showed me the mysteries
and laughter at the water's edge; to my wife,
who shares all the joys of the wilds with
me; and to my children, Natalie and
Thomas, who discover new trails
each day.*

TABLE OF CONTENTS

The drawings in this book are by Michael Cassidy. The author also wishes to thank the following individuals and organizations (listed in alphabetical order) for generously contributing photographs and other illustrations:

Aluma Craft Boats; Roy Attaway; Eddie Bauer Expedition Outfitters; L. L. Bean, Inc.; Bear Archery, Inc.; Bicycle Institute of America; Howard Brant; British Columbia Government; Buck Knives; Canadian National Railways; Russell Carpenter; Coleman Company, Inc.; Colorado Outdoor Sports Corp.; Crosman Arms; Daisy-Heddon; Dant Cable Saws; Dave Elman; John R. Falk; Florida Game & Freshwater Fish Commission; Gerry Mountain Sports; Gulf American News Bureau; Kaiser-Jeep; Nicholas Karas; Larry Koller; Sid Latham; George Laycock; Gerald Lynas; Marlin Firearms; Montgomery Ward; New Mexico Dept. of Game & Fish; New York Public Library; New York State Dept. of Commerce; Normark Corp.; Ontario Dept. of Tourism & Information; David Petzal; Plastics Research & Development Corp.; Primus, Inc.; Remington Firearms; Louis D. Rubin; Leonard Lee Rue; John Samson; Savage Arms; 10-X Corp.; Tennessee Game & Fish Commission; Texas Game & Fish Commission; Thermos Division of King-Seeley; True Temper, Inc.; U.S. Fish & Wildlife Service; U.S. Forest Service; The Walters Art Gallery; Mason Williams; Winchester News Bureau; Wisconsin Conservation Dept.; Worth Lures; Bob Zwirz.

By searching right near home, you can sometimes find friendly and curious wild animals. This is a baby opossum

1

RIGHT AT YOUR DOORSTEP

Famous outdoorsmen like Kit Carson, Theodore Roosevelt and even the man who founded the Boy Scouts, General Robert S. Baden-Powell, had to learn most of their woodland skills by trial and error. This book will give you a headstart by teaching you some of the needed skills and showing you how to acquire others. Hiking, camping, swimming, fishing, tracking, exploring—all the outdoor activities—are greater adventures when they are done safely and well. And they are all the more fun for a boy or girl who understands that nature holds endless wonders to be discovered in the woods and waters, earth and sky. When you come to know the plant and animal wildlife, you can have adventures that would otherwise be impossible.

There is no book that can teach you everything there is to know about outdoor skills or about the secrets that can be discovered in nature. Even a whole library of books could not hold all the nature lore and camp crafts that outdoor enthusiasts have learned. In fact, the woods hold many discoveries that you must make for yourself. But this book will teach you the most important things about getting along in the wilds, and will show you how to make those other discoveries for yourself.

If you walk slowly through an ordinary field, you can discover many flowers and other plants, as well as a wide variety of small animals

No matter where you live, there is a great secret hidden right outside your door. The secret is that the world of nature—a home for billions of strange and beautiful living things—is in front of you and under your feet and above your head and all around you. Some of these things are invisible but most of them can be detected if you know how to search for them. At first you may not see much, but the outdoors will begin to reveal a vast number of exciting treasures as you sharpen your senses of hearing and sight, touch and smell.

Learning how to discover the outdoors takes a little practice, but it's easy and fun. Begin anywhere—indoors will do—by playing detective. Like Sherlock Holmes, you must realize that a room is not just a space but a collection of things, some of which are not usually noticed. On a sheet of paper write down all the things you see and hear in a room: a rug (what color is it?), paint or wallpaper, three pictures, seven books on a table, two chairs, four finger smudges on the door jamb, an empty candy dish in the shape of a maple leaf, curtains on the windows, the sound of a clock ticking in the corner and an automobile passing by outside.

Good; now you're learning to be alert, and you may add odors to the list of things you detect—perhaps the smell of chocolate cake wafting from the kitchen, or the fragrance of flowers in a vase. If your list has less than twenty items that you can see or hear or smell, you need to practice. And outdoors, there are many, many more things that you must notice, if you are to discover nature's mysteries.

When you step outside, be as alert as if you were looking for a lost coin. Exercise your physical senses in a definite order: start with watching and listening at the same time, because you never know whether you will first see or hear a bird, animal, insect, rustling plants or chuckling water. Next, take a deep breath every once in a while; smelling is pretty much automatic, but the fragrance of a wild plant or freshly-dug earth where an animal has burrowed may be quite faint.

When you find something safe and interesting to examine, touch it. You can learn a lot about how a thing is made by how it feels. Of course, it would be stupid to touch poison ivy or a wasp, so that word "safe" is important. Later on, we will discuss how to recognize the few harmful things as well as the many friendly things to be found in the wilds.

When you wander outdoors, just what are you looking for? Almost anything. Few people realize what an amazing variety of wildlife surrounds them, even in cities. A naturalist named R. S. R. Fitter once counted seventy-four species, or varieties, of birds living in London throughout the year, plus twenty-six species that nest there during the summer, forty-five that are winter visitors and forty-one more that pass through as they migrate to other places. Imagine a total of one hundred and eighty-six different kinds of birds in a city like London! And Mr. Fitter also found one hundred and twenty-six kinds of flowering plants and ferns in vacant lots.

A curator at the American Museum of Natural History once collected almost fifteen hundred varieties of insects in his small backyard, which was only a block from the railway station in Ramsey, New Jersey. Wildlife turns up in unlikely places, if you know how to find it. Certain animals, like opossums and raccoons, enjoy rummaging in suburban trash cans at night. If you hear a rattling out there, take a flashlight and see if you can spot a pair of eyes or a fat little form scurrying away.

In the fall of the year, I've stood on the western edge of New York City's Central Park and watched flocks of majestic Canada geese and snow geese fly past on their way South. Most New Yorkers don't know that these wild birds can be seen in the city—but they can, if you know when to watch for them. On cold fall days, when the sky is very dark and grey or when a storm is brewing, geese fly low and stay as close as they can to water (in this case, the Hudson River and New York Harbor). If you are at such a place at such a time, look up and you may see them.

In Central Park I've also seen cottontail rab-

The mother opossum carries her young on her back

In a city park this boy has found specimens of sweetgum, honey locust, hazel, several other plants — and even a pheasant feather

bits, though most people think that rabbits have been gone from the park for many years. Look for these animals at the edges of thick briar tangles and undergrowth. Like most such areas, the same park also has many wild trees and other plants that might surprise you— sweetgum, honey locust, hazel, haws, sticktight, gingko, even Osage orange (a relative of the mulberry which was originally found only in the Southwest). And along the New Jersey cliffs that line the lower Hudson River, you can find wild apple and dogwood blooming in the spring.

Another New York wildlife haven is Van Cortlandt Park. There, in the summer, you can find raccoons, opossums and painted turtles, especially in the little swamp. If you ever go there, look for a small wooden bridge; it marks the edge of the swamp. Then walk very quietly along the wet places—you should be wearing waterproof boots—and search the ground. You will find animal tracks and perhaps a few of the animals themselves. A later chapter will help you learn to identify some animal tracks, and you'll learn about others for yourself by following them until you discover what made them. Birdwatchers also like to roam Van Cortlandt Park or make a trip to New York's Jamaica Bay, a sanctuary where herons and all sorts of other wild birds flourish.

Canada geese can sometimes be seen flying over New York's Central Park. Here they are shown resting on their way South

These examples show that wildlife is all around, even in large, crowded, almost treeless cities where you might not think to look. And out in the country, of course, the wealth of nature is far greater. The poet William Blake understood that there was more to hiking than breathing clean air, more to fishing than catching your own lunch. Knowing that the wilds hold thrilling mysteries, he advised those who love the outdoors:

> *To see the world in a grain of sand,*
> *And a heaven in a wild flower;*
> *Hold infinity in the palm of your hand,*
> *And eternity in an hour.*

In getting acquainted with the outdoors, always remember to look down as well as up. You will find beautiful plants and rocks—you might want to start a mineral collection—and you can go on an insect hunt. Insects are wonderful creatures, most of them beneficial rather than harmful, and they are fun to study. What's more, certain caddis flies and "worms" of the caterpillar type will make wonderful baits when you go fishing.

Ask yourself questions about all the things you see: What is a bee doing in that flower? Where will it go next? Can it see, hear, smell? Do certain colors and scents seem to attract it? How far can it fly? Watch carefully and you will learn the answers, or most of them.

Look into flowers, among the blades of grass, under stones, along the edges of ponds and puddles, along the cracks of tree bark. Have you seen ants scuttling about carrying what looks like rice? They are really carrying their eggs to a safe place. Sometimes in a garden or in the woods, you will notice what looks like dots of saliva on the plants, but you know that no one has been there for days. You are really seeing a protective covering secreted by an insect called the spittle bug. Other oddities will reveal themselves to anyone who is curious.

Raccoons often invade the suburbs, looking for food scraps. This one is washing his dinner at the edge of a stream

When you find an insect or animal that particularly interests you, get a book from the library about that species. You will find many fascinating things about each creature. Take fireflies, for example. Did you know that they are really flying beetles and not flies? The ones that flash during flight are almost always males, and they are flashing signals to the females, who generally answer from the ground or from a perch among the leaves. This is the way they go courting. If you watch them carefully in the evening, you can time the flashes and imitate them with a flashlight. This will often attract them to you.

Insects are heard as well as seen, and another fascinating species is the musical but rather noisy cricket. Most people like the sound made by crickets at night. These harmless insects get along so well with man (remember the cricket on the hearth?) that they've gained a silly reputation for bringing good luck. Some animals and birds make sounds with their vocal cords, or by inflating and deflating air sacs in the neck to make a drumming noise, or by beating the air with their wings. It is widely believed that crickets produce a noise with their back legs, but the musical instruments are really their wings, which have edges resembling a file.

A girl and boy examine a mushroom growing from a forest log. They don't know what it is, so they'll look but won't touch

A bluejay feeds the babies in the nest

To play its song, a cricket rubs its wings together incredibly fast—like a country fiddler who has gone berserk. The sound is usually described as a chirping. That may be close, but it isn't exact. Many insect sounds (buzzing, whirring, clicking, chirping) cannot be described precisely, and this is one reason among many others to explore the outdoors with an older, more experienced person. When you hear a new sound, ask what makes it. Once you've identified it, you probably won't forget it.

As you begin to learn about the living things in the outdoors, you may want to specialize in hunting and studying one particular type of small creature. That way you can learn a great deal in a short time, and finding out about one creature always leads to discoveries about others. Spiders, for example, are among the easily hunted creatures because they are so abundant, and there are thousands of different kinds. A single grassy acre in England once turned up more than two million spiders for a curious scientist.

Of the many varieties in the United States, a few can hurt—like a wasp—if they bite (which they generally do only in self-defense) but just

This hammock spider makes its home on the side of a house, where it traps and eats small insect pests

engineering. One of the pictures in this book shows a hammock spider which I found investigating a gas meter on the side of a house. Its name comes from the shape of its web. Another picture shows an orange garden spider that I found in a milkweed patch at the edge of some Vermont woods. Golden and black, striped almost like a tiger, it looks both beautiful and ferocious but it is really quite harmless. When I discovered it, this spider was climbing a thick silken ladder constructed along the lower part of its web; it was approaching a fly which it had caught in the web for dinner, and the sticky strands had also trapped a wasp. Spiders are extremely beneficial, for they eat millions of crop-destroying and biting insects.

Still another strange creature—and one that you must learn to hunt if you are going to become a good fisherman—is the common earthworm. There are about 2,000 species wiggling around the world, including a twelve-foot Australian giant and a tiny variety that glows like a firefly. The common four-inch kind that is abundant in Europe, Canada and the United States can be found almost wherever there is dark rich earth. This animal is food for many birds and some animals. The worm also helps plants grow by digging burrows that aerate the soil. An earthworm has no ears or eyes, but can sense even the dim light of dawn with delicate nerves beneath its skin. It has five pairs of hearts and two sets of powerful muscles, one going around it and one going lengthwise. It eats tiny bits of earth, nourishing itself with the organic matter, and secreting the earth, now chemically treated, in a form that is more nourishing for plants.

If you ever hunt the American game bird called the woodcock, look for round holes that have been drilled in the soft earth around alder thickets; the woodcock lives almost exclusively on worms and he drills those holes with his long needle-like beak to pull out his dinner. If you catch a frog and keep it as a pet for a while, you can feed it bits of earthworm, as well as mealworms, small insects and dried daphnia (a tiny shrimplike water creature that is dried and sold

two, the black widow and the brown recluse, are seriously poisonous. The black widow is found mostly in the South. This species is easy to recognize, because it has a brownish-grey or black body with a red marking in the shape of an hourglass on its abdomen. The brown recluse, found in the South and Midwest, has a fiddle-shaped marking on its back. In fact, it has been called the fiddler spider.

True insects have six legs. Spiders are not insects. They have eight legs, as well as a number of other differences of anatomy that set them apart from insects. Most spiders also have eight eyes, though some species have two, four or six, and a few are blind. One kind, called the crab spider, can change color from tan or yellow to white in order to blend with its surroundings.

These strange creatures weave several different kinds of webs, and each type is a miracle of

An orange garden spider climbs the ladder of its web, built among milkweed and goldenrod stems at the edge of a Vermont forest

by pet shops as food for fish, reptiles and amphibians). You can see that the earthworm has a variety of uses besides being excellent bait for many kinds of fish.

When you begin discovering the outdoors by hunting for birds, plants, insects and animals, you will continually see new things. It will be very helpful to buy some of the pocket-size books called field guides. These little books describe and picture the things you may find, and will enable you to identify what you see. Among the many excellent ones are the Golden Nature Guides, which cost about a dollar each and cover such subjects as trees, flowers, mammals, sea shells, rocks and minerals, birds, insects and reptiles. Pick a couple that interest you most and put them in your pocket when you go exploring. Or carry paper and a pencil to write notes about what you see, and when

you get home you can compare your notes with the pictures in the field guides.

Another important bit of advice is to be very quiet and move slowly when you find a wild creature; you won't be able to watch it if you frighten it into fleeing. When you have become skilled at finding and watching the small wild things that are all about you, it is time to prepare for a real hike that will give you a chance to search for bigger game, from rabbits to deer. Part of your preparation is to know about certain equipment and how to use it to make outdoor life easier; you will also want to know how to plan a hike or camping trip, and even how to forecast the weather. But first you may be interested in finding out about the adventures of some famous outdoorsmen who learned all these things and put them to thrilling use. The next chapter will give you a few examples.

Leonard Lee Rue examines a Cape buffalo calf in Africa. Mr. Rue is one of America's outstanding modern woodsmen

2

SOME FAMOUS WOODSMEN AND WHAT MADE THEM GREAT

Fortunately, there is no longer any need to repeat some of the exploits of outdoor adventurers who lived more than a century ago, and we should be glad this is so. The woods conceal no hostile savages who must be outwitted, as was done by Kit Carson, Daniel Boone, Davy Crockett and Buffalo Bill Cody. The Americans are not at war with the Mexicans, as they were when Davy Crockett lost his life at the Alamo, nor is the Union fighting the Confederacy and desperately searching for volunteers like Kit Carson and William F. Cody. For those who understand the ways of nature, the wilderness is no longer a dark place of danger. However, the great woodsmen of the past shared certain wonderful abilities and traits which can be imitated by today's young outdoor adventurers, and even now there are woodsmen who are achieving greatness.

Among the traits shared by all of the famous woodland wanderers was a loving understanding of nature. They did not try to "conquer" nature; they simply got along well with her. Another common trait was a keen alertness to everything that went on in the wilds. And still another was an early mastery of the skills needed in the outdoors. Most pioneer men and women began exploring the wilderness when they were from ten to fourteen years old, and some began when they were younger. They

A typical outdoorsman of the 19th century

From these old drawings, you can visualize the appearance of early woodsmen like Davy Crockett and Kit Carson

spent long hours in the woods and fields, just watching and listening, observing nature's activities. They memorized the wild plants that could be used for food, shelter, clothing or medicine, and they learned to know the tracks of all the animals. At an early age, they became accomplished hunters, fishermen and campers.

Davy Crockett could foretell the weather or stalk a deer when he was just a boy. Born in 1786 on the Tennessee frontier, he was brought up in the backwoods. Before he was in his teens, he was a skilled trapper, hunter and marksman. To keep from going hungry, he had to learn to shoot well, for in those days the only guns available were muskets or Kentucky-style long rifles. These old flintlock arms held only a single shot, and they took a long time to load. If a hunter missed his game, the animal would disappear before it was possible to pour more gunpowder down the barrel, followed by a bullet wrapped in a patch to keep it tightly in place, and then pour an extra bit of powder on the priming pan, and then cock the jaw that held the flint that struck the steel that sent sparks into the priming powder that ignited the main charge of powder that—finally—fired another shot.

But Davy seldom worried about dinner walking off while he was preparing to shoot. With his gun ready, he could stalk silently over the forest floor, a skill you can develop only with practice, until he was close to a deer, bear or wild turkey. And then his shot was true. He could also go to the streams for his food, fooling a fat trout with a worm, or a bit of wool and feather on his homemade hook, fashioned to imitate an insect and dropped where it would gently drift beneath an overhanging bank. The same methods work well today.

Davy soon earned so great a reputation that many young frontiersmen came to him for lessons. In 1813 when he was twenty-seven, he served under General Andrew Jackson in an expedition against the Creek Indians, who had gone on the warpath. Later he became a member of his state legislature and then served in the national House of Representatives. He was known for telling tall tales which were funny, and which might have seemed absurdly boastful except that no one could be sure they weren't true. After all, he had listened to the cougar and learned to imitate it; perhaps he really could roar louder than a lion and scare the other lions into the trees. In 1835 he went to Texas, which was then fighting for its independence from Mexico, and a year later he became one of the brave defenders of the Alamo. He died there, holding the fort against the attacking Mexican army.

Another heroic woodsman was Daniel Boone, who was born in Pennsylvania in 1734. When he was fourteen, his family moved to the banks of the Yadkin River in North Carolina, an even more remote wilderness than the forests of Pennsylvania. By that time, fortunately, he could take care of himself in any wilderness. He had gained a reputation as an expert rifleman, and his extended hikes through the woods had made him not only physically fit but exceptionally strong. Stories were told about what a wonderful long-distance runner he was.

During the French and Indian War he became a soldier, and afterward he led explorers and settlers into the unmapped Kentucky Territory, where he established a settlement called Boonesboro. During his youth, he was forced to spend much of his time battling hostile Indians who continually attacked the settlers. But as he grew older, the Indians began moving West, and those who stayed behind made peace with the white men. In safety and leisure, he was then able to give shooting lessons to younger men, and also to serve as a state legislator and a militia colonel. When duty did not keep him at home, Daniel went on long hunts accompanied only by his dog, his gun and sometimes a horse. At the age of eighty-two, he went West, exploring; no one knows for certain where he roamed, but it is believed he wandered as far as Nebraska or Wyoming before returning to live in Missouri. When he was almost eighty-six, he died peacefully, sitting under a tree with his dog.

Christopher Carson—Kit to his friends and eventually to the world—was born in Kentucky in 1809 and was raised on the Missouri frontier. His two heroes were Daniel Boone and Davy Crockett, and he roamed the woods learning the skills that had made those woodsmen famous. By about 1826 he was a professional trap-

The pioneer hero, Daniel Boone, with his hunting knife and flintlock rifle

Colonel William Frederick Cody — Buffalo Bill — poses with a Winchester lever-action rifle and one of his favorite horses

per, hunter and guide. Then he became an explorer, going on expeditions with John C. Frémont for the United States Government. In those days, most of the land west of the Mississippi was a vast unexplored wilderness, but by 1845, Carson's expeditions had gone all the way to California. He fought for his country in the Mexican War, and then, in 1854, became an Indian agent in New Mexico. Having learned the languages and customs of the Indians, he was able to keep the warlike Apaches and other tribes from going on the warpath time and again. He fought on the western frontier during the Civil War and rose to the rank of brigadier general. After the war, he worked again as an Indian agent and Army guide until he died in Colorado in 1868.

One of the most famous outdoorsmen of the nineteenth century was William Frederick Cody—Buffalo Bill. Born in Iowa in 1846, Bill Cody started working as a wagon driver when he was about fourteen, and a few months later he became one of the first Pony Express riders. While working for the Pony Express, he set a record that has never been broken: switching to a fresh horse at each relay station along the trail, he rode three hundred and twenty-two miles in twenty-one hours and thirty minutes. To accomplish such a feat, he had to be a superb horseman.

He fought for the Union during the Civil War, and shortly afterward was hired as a professional hunter by the Kansas Pacific Railroad. Game was needed to feed the construction crews while the railway was being extended westward. Bill proved to be so good at hunting bison in order to supply this meat that he soon earned the nickname Buffalo Bill. A popular frontier song of the late 1860's went like this:

Buffalo Bill, Buffalo Bill,
Never missed and never will;
Always aims and shoots to kill,
And the company pays his. . .buffalo bill!

He hunted many bison for the railroad workers, but he was not among those irresponsible "market hunters" who almost exterminated the huge buffalo herds, taking only their skins to sell as robes and leaving most of the meat to rot on the prairies. Because of such men, the bison nearly became extinct. Buffalo Bill, on the contrary, was a determined conservationist. In his later years, he toured the United States and Europe with his famous Wild West Show, in which he and other performers demonstrated their riding and shooting skill. The show was discontinued when he died in 1917.

Having mentioned both buffalo and conservation, it's fitting now to talk about Teddy Roosevelt, a man who helped to save the bison from extinction, and who helped to start conservation programs on a national scale. Born in New York in 1858, Theodore Roosevelt had the misfortune of being a sickly child. He showed an early interest in nature, and he strengthened his weak body by pursuing outdoor activities—hiking, camping and hunting. By the time he reached manhood, he had made himself healthy and strong. Most people know about his colorful career—or rather, several careers—as a police commissioner, rancher, writer, Assistant Secretary of the Navy, soldier (in fact, leader of the Rough Riders in the Spanish American War), Governor of New York, Vice President and, finally, President. Somehow, while engaging in all these endeavors, he found time for long camping trips and big game hunts, both in the United States and in Africa. By the time of his death in 1919, he had also spent a great deal of time and energy promoting conservation efforts, including the establishment of wild areas as national forests and parks so that there would always be beautiful woods, mountains, streams and wildlife, no matter how large the cities might grow.

At the turn of the century, working with a few sportsmen and conservation organizations, and in cooperation with the Canadian Government, he helped to locate, protect and maintain herds of buffalo. Because of the wanton slaughter of the animals, there were then fewer than one thousand left on the plains of the United States, but grazing land was found for them and

This photo shows Theodore Roosevelt, 26th President of the United States, in the clothing he wore when hunting western big game

Robert Elman (left) and Wyoming rancher Gary Marquiss inspect bison hunted by author with old-time buffalo rifle. Thanks to conservation efforts of outdoorsmen, bison are no longer in danger of extinction; they can even be hunted on a limited basis

the herds began to increase again. Today, thanks to these efforts, there is a good population of bison in Canada and the United States. In fact, there are places where some of the animals must be periodically hunted because there is not enough land to provide grass for all of them to eat. I once shot a buffalo myself, in Wyoming, and I can tell you that bison steak broiled over a campfire is delicious. The railroad workers must have eaten well while Buffalo Bill worked for them.

You might think, in this age of machines and big cities, a boy or girl can no longer follow the trails of the men I've described, learning the ways of the wilderness. This is not so. Leonard Lee Rue, who took some of the pictures in this book, furnishes ample proof that it is possible even today to become a great outdoorsman. Born forty-three years ago, Len was raised near Belvidere, New Jersey. Few people realize that a state so near New York and dotted with so many crowded towns and cities has vast woodlands, yet New Jersey has hundreds of thousands of acres of woods and streams that are inhabited only by wildlife. As he grew up, Lennie spent a great deal of time in such areas, learning about the animals and birds. He is now internationally known as a naturalist, outdoor writer-photographer and lecturer. Traveling throughout North America and in Africa, he has taken countless close-up pictures of animals— including animals that are dangerous when approached without great skill. He has photographed eagles, bears, lions and alligators from only a few feet away. He can glance at tracks and tell you what animal made them and how long ago. He can examine a bird that has been killed by an enemy and tell you whether it was slain by a fox or an owl. Even today, it is possible to learn such secrets of the outdoors.

3
BASIC TOOLS AND SKILLS

Wild creatures could not survive if nature had not provided them with the protection of fur, feathers or scales. These protective coats are actually waterproof on many species that spend a large portion of their lives in or on the water. For further protection from the elements and from hungry predators, a number of animals dig burrows, build nests, take up residence in hollow trees, live in caves or occupy abandoned dens that have been built by other animals.

Have you ever seen a pile of dead leaves high in a tree and wondered how they accumulated way up there where they could not have fallen from higher branches? That pile was probably a squirrel nest. Squirrels build nests of leaves and twigs when they can't find a handy hole in a tree—and sometimes they prefer a nest even if there is a convenient tree hole. Some woodpeckers and other birds peck a hole in a tree trunk when they want a place to nest; their sharp, strong beaks are perfect wood-boring tools. A mother cottontail rabbit digs a burrow or shallow hole under thick brush tangles such as briars or wild raspberry. She plucks out bits of soft fur from her underside and lines the nest with them so that her young will have a warm, soft bed, and she covers the top of the nest with a blanket of more fur and sometimes grass and leaves. This not only keeps the babies comfortable but helps to hide them from enemies.

An ordinary claw hammer, pocketknife and rope are very useful outdoor tools

This is a nest of baby rabbits. The mother covers them with a soft blanket of fur — plucked from her body — and grasses

Unlike the animals, human beings have no protective coat of fur or feathers, and there are times when you need a protective shelter in the woods. Instead of fur, of course, you have warm and sometimes waterproof clothing. And instead of building a nest, you can put up a tent. However, neither warm clothing nor a tent will always be protection enough. For this reason, you must learn to use certain tools and materials that will add to your comfort outdoors. Furthermore, it isn't only a question of comfort but of fun, too. You may want to put up a swing or a hammock, build a lean-to or a tree house, carve new tent stakes to replace lost ones, construct a safe fireplace or take on any number of other projects, from whittling wooden tent pegs or a roasting stick for hot dogs to making fire tongs and pot hooks or carving a totem pole.

Practicing with a few basic tools will give you a skill at using your hands which is extremely important around a camp or on a trip in the woods. It also serves another purpose, for working with such tools gives you excellent exercise that will build your body and put you in condition for a vigorous outdoor life.

One of the first tools you should practice with is an ordinary, fairly light claw hammer—the kind with a flat striking head and built-in nail puller. After you've become proficient with it, you may often substitute a camp axe, but nothing beats an old-fashioned hammer for making repairs at a permanent campsite, or building tree houses or elevated deer stands.

Gather some scrap wood, preferably two-by-fours or planks of fairly similar dimensions. Collect a boxful of nails in various sizes, making sure that some of them are long enough to go through the narrower width of a two-by-four and fairly deep into a tree or another piece of wood. For camp use, you don't want headless nails or brads; you want common nails with good, big flat heads that make easy hammering targets and can take a pounding. Practice driving them in, both vertically and at angles. At first a lot of them will bend over before they're all the way in. The secret is to make the hammer come down on an exact line with the nail.

Practice often and you'll soon get the hang of it.

Next you want a saw. There are crosscut, rip and all-purpose saws in several lengths. For work around camp, the blade should be no longer than 24 inches, and a rip or all-purpose saw is best. It won't cut as neatly as a crosscut saw, but it will make the work go faster and will cut across the grain of the wood as well as in the direction of the grain. The important thing is to use smooth, positive strokes, exerting cutting pressure on the stroke down and away from you, not as you pull the saw up and toward you. Practice this, also.

There is a handy tool called a wire saw or cable saw, which you can actually roll up and put in your pocket. It consists of a flexible cutting wire with a ring on each end. To cut with it, you simply put the middle finger of each hand into the rings, get a good grip and pull back and forth. This is a fine tool for cutting small pieces of firewood and doing little odd jobs on the trail or in camp, and it's easy to tuck away in a pocket or pack. For bigger jobs, however, a real saw is needed.

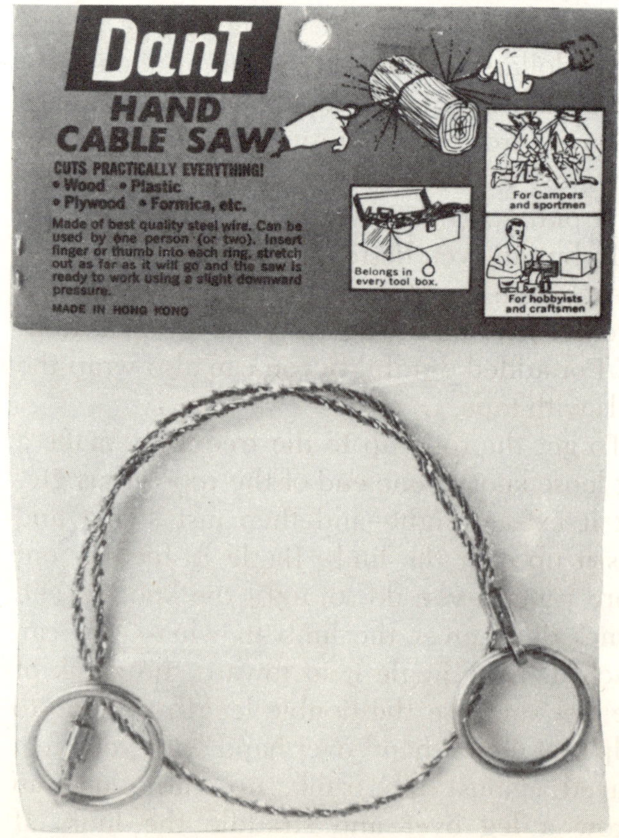

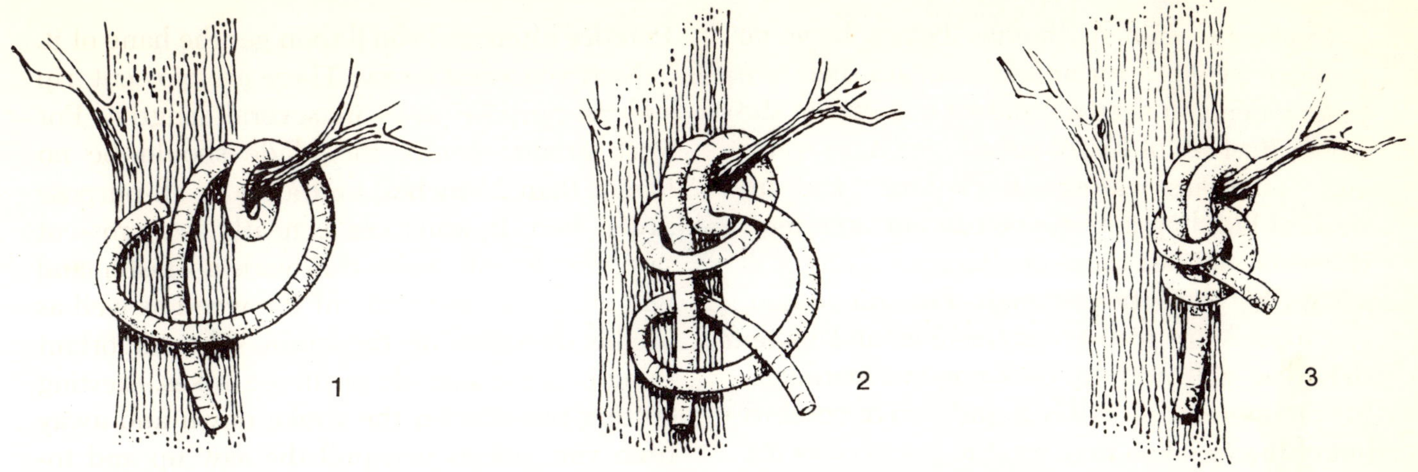

Here's how to tie a fisherman's bend knot, for putting up a swing or any other project that requires a secure rope: (1) loop the end of the rope around a limb in a complete circle and push the end through the loop thus formed; (2) make another loop around the rope itself and push the end through to form a half-hitch; (3) make at least one more half-hitch, pulling the ends tight

With a hammer, nails, saw, some wood and a good length of thick rope, you can put up a swing or a tree house. For a swing, find a slab of wood about eight inches wide and a little longer than the width of your bottom. Then find a tree with a very stout horizontal limb at a convenient height—eight to twelve feet up—and with no branches or brush crossing the space where you'll be doing the swinging. For a couple of dollars you can buy a coil of about fifty feet of half-inch hemp rope, or slightly thinner but even stronger nylon rope. If you use hemp, you must knot the ends, so that the strands don't pull apart. With nylon, you can knot the ends, but an even better way is to hold a match to each end; the strands at that point will melt together without taking away the rope's flexibility. For added durability you can also wrap the ends with tape.

To get the rope up to the tree limb, make a big loose knot at one end of the rope—thus giving it extra weight—and then just swing and toss it up over the limb. Jiggle it, feeding out more rope as you do so, until the knotted end comes down over the limb to where you can reach it. Now jiggle it in toward the trunk of the tree and use the double length of rope to help you climb, hand over hand with your feet braced against the trunk, up until you can throw a leg over and straddle the limb. If you're doing this alone, you should have a second length of rope tied to your belt, because you'll need two of them hanging down to the swing. However, it's faster, more fun and safer to have someone helping you.

The second person stays on the ground. The person in the tree loops the first rope around the limb, at least a foot out from the trunk so that a swinger won't bump the tree. Now tie it securely with a fisherman's bend knot. To do this, you loop the end around the limb in a complete circle, then force the end through the loop, pull it tight and tie several half-hitches. A half-hitch is tied by looping the end around the hanging length of rope and then guiding the end back through the loop thus made. Pull it tight and repeat the loop and pull again until you have several half-hitches. A weight on the other end of the rope will not loosen these knots, so it is safe.

The second length of rope is tied around the limb in the same manner, two feet farther out. Then you can climb down and attach the seat, about two and a half feet off the ground. Make sure you get it level. Before putting it up, drive two long nails, close together, halfway in near each end, next to where you'll tie the ropes. Then you should saw four V-shaped notches, two in the front edge of the seat where the ropes will be tied and two facing them in the rear edge. These will keep the ropes from slipping around. The notches only have to be about an inch deep, and they don't have to be precise—just rough triangles.

Tie the ropes around the swing seat, guided by the notches, with the same kind of knots you used up on the tree limb. Then, with the hammer, bend the protruding nails around the loops of rope to help secure them. Make sure you hammer the nails all the way down so they won't snag your clothing, and you're ready for a swing.

A tree house takes longer to build, but is much easier if two people work together. Find a tree with two horizontal limbs at the same height, preferably protruding from the trunk in the shape of a V. Get a rope up over one of the limbs, as you did for the swing, and climb up. Then use the rope to hoist up wooden planks and tools. A second person stays on the ground and ties on the planks and hammer, then gets out of the way while they're being pulled up and while the work is going on—you don't want a plank or a hammer falling on someone's head.

It's easy to put up a swing in the woods, where there are lots of strong horizontal branches growing at a good height

The planks needn't be very thick but they must be strong enough to support the weight of two people. Half-inch thicknesses of good board will do. They must be long enough to reach across the V so that they can be nailed onto the two tree limbs. Their width doesn't matter, but the wider they are, the fewer you'll need to make a roomy platform. The first plank is hauled up and rested across the narrow part of the V. Then the rope is lowered and a hammer and box of nails are hauled up. Nail the first plank securely to both limbs before pulling up a second one. That way you have no loose boards that may fall. Work outward until you've nailed up enough boards to make as big a platform as you wish.

For added strength, in case you plan to use the tree house for a long time, you can nail a pair of two-by-fours down on top of the outer platform edges along the two limbs that form the V. (You'll need good long nails to penetrate both the boards and limbs.) If you want to build sides and make a real tree *house,* the two-by-fours can form the bottom of a frame. Additional two-by-fours can be nailed upright, and siding boards can then be nailed to them.

If you can find a tree with conveniently located limbs above the platform V, you can use those extra limbs as a railing or top, nailing the siding boards to them. If there's no tree with a pair of thick horizontal limbs in the area where you want your tree house, look for one whose trunk divides into a three-branched crotch. You can nail three two-by-fours across the crotch to form a triangular frame for the platform. And if you want a really large platform, you can find three or four separate trees sufficiently close to each other so that they can serve as corner posts to which you nail a triangular or rectangular frame for the platform.

You can climb up to your tree house and get down again by means of the rope, or you can nail planks into the tree trunk to form a ladder or use two long poles and some short planks to make a ladder. Once it's made, your tree house can be an observation deck from which to scan the countryside. If you're quiet and patient enough you can sit there and watch the woods come alive with wild creatures. The birds will get used to seeing you and will fly about as if you weren't there. Some of them, such as chickadees, will come quite close out of curiosity. If you sprinkle some sunflower seeds about and perhaps a little suet (crumbly fat trimmed away from meat), these birds will come to your tree house to nibble and eventually may eat right out of your hand. Grey squirrels will do the same thing if you sprinkle seeds, nuts or bread.

Animals on the ground tend to look downward because most of their enemies approach them on ground level. They seldom look upward, so if you're quiet, rabbits and chipmunks, raccoons and other species will sooner or later come out of hiding and you can watch them. Afterward, be sure to study any tracks they leave in the dirt or mud.

An elaborate tree house can be built by nailing a floor frame between several tree trunks. Hunters sometimes sit on these platforms to watch for deer

If you know an adult who is a deer hunter, ask him about a good place to put up your tree house. Deer tend to use well-worn paths, taking the same trail again and again between feeding and bedding areas. In the evening, they come down from high slopes to the lowlands, fields, woods and orchards, where they look for food. In the morning they climb up the slopes again to hidden retreats where they bed down for the day. The print of a deer's cloven hoof is more or less heart-shaped, with a narrow space between the two halves and with the point at the

With practice, you can recognize tracks in earth or snow. This one was made by a whitetail doe

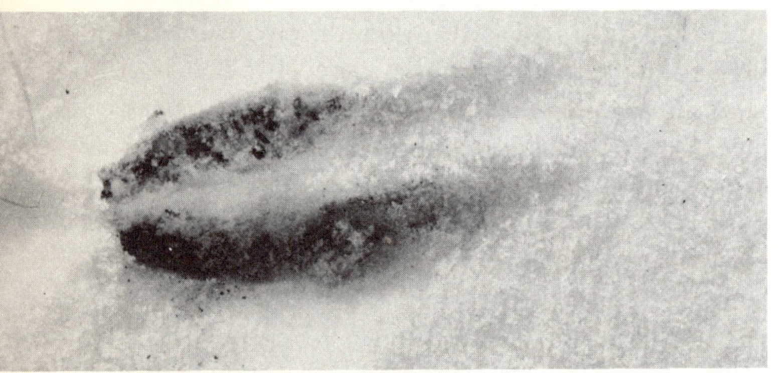

forward end. If you find a deer trail with lots of tracks, don't build your tree house right next to it or the deer will take another route from then on. But if you build it about thirty yards away from the trail, the deer will remain out of sight only for a week or two, until they get used to seeing the new platform in the tree. Then they will begin using the same trail again. Climb up there some day before dawn or late in the afternoon and wait quietly. There is a good chance that you will soon see a deer passing below. During the fall hunting season, deer hunters sometimes sit on such elevated platforms, waiting for a good big buck to come within range. They can then make one careful shot and bring home their venison.

In addition to hammer, saw and rope, you'll need to acquire skill with other basic tools. One of the most important is a pocketknife with several blades that fold into the handle. The official Boy Scout knife is one of the best because it's a combination tool with a cutting blade, screwdriver blade, bottle-cap lifter, can-opener blade and a leather-punch-and-awl for drilling small holes.It has a metal loop called a shackle at one end of the handle, and this can be attached to a belt clip or lanyard (a short cord) if your pockets are full and you want to make sure you knife isn't dropped or lost.

Practice whittling with such a knife and you'll soon be able to cut tent stakes and even carve real wood sculptures. Always hold the wood that you're carving above and behind where you'll place the blade. Get a firm grip on both the wood and the knife. Hold the knife so that your thumb can press down on the dull non-cutting edge of the blade just where it meets the handle. And always carve away from yourself. That's all there is to it.

An easy project that's fun to carve is a miniature dugout canoe. Choose a length of dead tree branch (preferably a soft wood from one of the evergreen trees) about two inches thick and seven or eight inches long. Whittle or saw the ends into points and then split it lengthwise down the middle. Each of the halves will already have the rough outlines of a canoe. You can throw one half away or save it for a second canoe. Round off and smooth the other half until you're satisfied with its shape; then begin slicing away small bits from the top of the flat surface, gradually hollowing it out.

If you watch patiently and silently in the woods, you may see animals like this handsome buck

In addition to doing camp chores, the Boy Scout knife can be used for whittling models such as this dugout canoe

If you want to do a tougher but more realistic job, draw two or three bars with a pencil across the top, where seats would go, and hollow out only the spaces between these bars, working slowly and carefully. Remember, you can always cut more wood away, but once it's cut you can't put it back. When you've finished hollowing it out so that it's a shell with seats, it will look like a real canoe and will actually float. You may find whittling so enjoyable that later on you'll want to get a real woodcarving kit, with chisels, gouges and long-handled knives that can hold interchangeable blades of various shapes and sizes.

All bladed cutting tools must be kept sharpened. You can sharpen a knife with a small whetstone bought at any hardware store. The best kind of whetstone has a coarse surface and a fine surface. You start on the coarse side, and finish up on the fine side. Hold the knife with its cutting edge away from you and at a slight angle to the stone but with the side of the blade almost flat against the stone. Draw it toward you. Repeat this several times on the coarse side with smooth strokes, then finish it up on the fine side.

An axe blade is sharpened a bit differently. Because the blade is so thick, you do some preliminary sharpening with a flat eight-inch-long steel file (called a mill file), working away from you. File first on one side of the blade, then on the other, until the edge is reasonably fine. Then rub a whetstone in a circular motion first on one side and then on the other until the edge is sharp.

By the way, most axes are not ready to use as they come from the store. Before using your axe for the first time, take it to a knife grinder or a hardware store and have the edge sharpened professionally on a grindstone. After this is done once, it never has to be done again unless you damage the blade, but an axe should be periodically sharpened with the file and whetstone.

My favorite kind of axe for most camping is the appropriately named camp axe or one-hand axe (also called a hatchet) which has a short handle and is meant to be held with one hand for light work—though it can be gripped with both hands if the going gets heavy. I prefer the kind with a thick 1¼-pound, single-bladed head and a wooden handle, especially if it is of the old-fashioned design with a thick flat head top for hammering and a nail-pulling notch on the inner non-cutting edge. Such a tool is combination axe, hammer and nail-puller. Many campers prefer the one-piece steel kind, but if an axe has a properly shaped wooden handle about fourteen inches long, it will be light enough and so well balanced that you won't tire quickly when using it. Be sure you have a leather sheath for your axe, and keep the sheath on it at all times when it isn't in use. Otherwise, a good safe tool becomes a thing of danger.

Important woodsman's tools: the hatchet and sheath knife

The sheath should have a safety flap with a thong or snap to keep it securely closed.

When chopping an upright tree (which you should rarely do unless the tree is dead), stand slightly to one side, give yourself plenty of room and practice getting a smooth, accurate swing. When chopping smaller pieces of wood, brace them against a log, a fallen tree crotch or a stump. Keep your legs out of the way and never brace the wood with your foot or you can have a serious accident. But do brace the wood against other wood and not against the ground. Otherwise your last chop will send the blade through the wood into the ground—or worse still, rocks—and damage it. Practice chopping V-shaped cuts, digging into the wood at an angle of about forty-five degrees. A good way to practice is by sharpening stakes. Hold a short, straight dead branch or other length of scrap wood almost upright on a stump or some other chopping block and sharpen the lower end on four sides. A four-sided point will be faster to chop than a round one and will actually be easier to pound into the ground. For the sake of safety, an experienced camper should supervise when a beginner works with an axe. If you use it properly, this will be your most basic and handy camp tool.

Remember that the weight of the axe does the cutting, not the force behind it. If you get a smoothness and rhythm into your swing, the work will go fast and you won't wear yourself out in a few minutes. When you've learned to chop wood well, two suggested projects are making a lean-to and a pine-needle or fern bed with a log frame. You will learn how to make these things in the chapter on overnight hiking.

In addition to your pocketknife and axe, you'll need a sheath knife, or hunting knife as it is often called. As a rule, big ones are badly designed and awkward. Get one with a good steel blade four to five inches long, and try the fit of the handle to be sure you can hold it firmly without slipping. Such a knife can do heavier wood-cutting jobs than the pocketknife, though it can't take on some of the work

A knife or axe is worthless without a fine edge. Honing oil and a sharpening stone will keep your tools sharp

One of the many uses for a hunting knife is whittling pointed tent stakes

an axe is made for. It will stand you in good stead for cutting small firewood, large tent pegs, wooden camp tools and gadgets, in fact all sorts of odd jobs. It can also be used to clean fish, and when you become a sufficiently accomplished woodsman to hunt big game, it will even do the skinning job for you.

Whether you're a boy or girl, you should know how to use all the tools I've just described plus one more set of tools: needle and thread. You'll know how important this is if you ever have to sew up a torn pack, a leaking tent or a ripped pair of pants. In cold weather, it can even be vital to sew a button on your outer clothing.

Buy a sewing kit with moderately large needles which have big enough eyes to make threading easy even in dim light. Replace the thread in the sewing kit with heavy button thread because strength is essential in outdoor repairs. To fix most rips so that they won't pull apart again, use the thread doubled and knotted at the end. An ordinary chain stitch or almost any other stitch will do, but for a fast, strong job it's sometimes best to pull the two edges of the material into a little ridge and spiral your stitches through them. This will leave a small lump which might not meet with the approval of the best tailors, but if you pull the thread tight you will have a strong and nearly waterproof repair. For lighter work, find the stitch that's easiest for you through trial and error, or ask your mother to give you a few sewing lessons. And be sure you learn to use a thimble. For sewing stiff materials such as canvas and thin leather, your bare fingers just

won't do. A thimble will save you time and pain. I sometimes even use pliers to pull a needle through leather.

A famous naturalist, Ernest Thompson Seton, once told about a trick you can do with a sewing needle in case you get lost. Rub the needle on a pocket magnet and then, to oil it, rub it on the side of your nose. Now place it gently in a cup of water or a puddle. It will float and point north. The only trouble with this trick is that you need to have a magnet along when you get lost, and you can carry a compass as easily as a magnet. It does show, however, that a sewing kit has many uses, and the trick is an interesting experiment.

Once you become skilled with a pocketknife, you may want to buy a woodcarving set featuring many interchangeable blades

By using a bird feeder or sprinkling the ground with food, you can attract small birds and animals. This girl has succeeded in coaxing a chickadee to eat from her hand

A

B

C

D

E

(A) A lavender sky in the morning or late afternoon foretells clear weather. (B) Rippled orange clouds against the blue show it will be windy. (C) A few wispy cirrus clouds — fair but breezy. (D) A grey sky in the early morning — fair weather ahead. (E) "Indian red" clouds — rain within 24 hours and perhaps strong winds. (F) Blazing masses of clouds — a chance of rain tomorrow

F

4

HOW THE INDIANS FORETOLD THE WEATHER

In the summer, a breeze feels wonderful ruffling your hair, and it's fun to let cool raindrops patter against your face. However, no one wants to be caught far from shelter when a real storm approaches. That experience can be cold, wet, unpleasant—even downright dangerous. Before going on a long hike or a camping trip, you can read the weather forecast in the newspapers, or tune in a radio or television report. Such precautions are a good idea, but official weather predictions are made for too large an area to tell you exactly how things will be when you actually set up camp. What's more, newspaper forecasts are often based on facts gathered by the weather bureau the day before, even though a weatherfront can move 500 miles in one day, completely changing the conditions in a small area.

Like everything in the outdoors, the weather changes almost constantly but always according to a pattern. It is full of discoveries you can make if you know what to look for, and there are ways to predict its behavior for the next 24 hours wherever you may be hiking or camping.

Fluffy, motionless white clouds in a clear sky indicate clear weather ahead

The Indians rarely began a long canoe trip if a storm was approaching, never moved a camp-site or set out on an overnight hunt if a cold, heavy rain threatened. A brave could "read the weather" when he touched the ground, held a finger up to the breeze, watched the birds and plants, gazed at the smoke of his campfire, stud-ied the sky or looked at the water. And you can read the weather even more accurately, because you can use not only the same methods but also take along a compass to help you.

In the United States and Canada, good weather usually comes with winds from the northwest, west and southwest, while bad weather arrives with northeast, east and south-east winds. (In some parts of the world, good and bad weather may come from directions dif-ferent from those I have listed; whatever coun-try you are in, it is easy to find out about pre-vailing weather directions by calling the local weather bureau. The directions given here apply to most places in the "temperate regions" above the tropics and below the Arctic.)

A compass can quickly tell you which way the wind is blowing. The most common type has a dial printed with the directions, and it has a moving needle which always points in the general direction of north. Hold the compass out flat in your hand or on the ground, and turn it around until the "N" on the dial is di-rectly in line with the needle point. Put one finger up in the air for a few moments to feel the wind, and look at your compass dial to see from what direction it's blowing. Even a very soft breeze—one that you wouldn't notice—can usually be detected if you wet your finger, be-cause it will feel cool on your moist skin.

With the compass needle pointing at "N," if the wind is blowing from the direction of "NE," "E" or "SE" on the dial, bad weather may be coming, but if the wind is from "NW," "W" or "SW," that's a good weather sign.

If it rains during the morning, with winds between northeast and south, and then the breeze begins to shift westward, the rain will soon stop. A cloudy sky with the wind shifting from southwest to southeast means a squall is brewing and you'd better stay in your tent. Even if the sky is clear, shifting winds that vary back and forth between southeast and south-west often mean that rain or wind squalls will come. No wind at all—you can't feel it with a wet finger, and the smoke of a campfire goes straight up—means there will be no change in the weather all day. For this reason, the Indians liked to start a long trip on a windless morning. The only time when a lack of wind heralds bad weather is during the rare calm before a tor-nado, and then the air feels heavy and clammy on your skin.

The Indians, of course, got along without a compass. Long experience taught them to re-member the directions, and they had other ways of reading the weather. For example, they knew that an early morning fog really means there will be no rain for the day. Since dew is also a sign of good weather, another Indian se-cret is to feel the ground in the early morning. Dew turns to frost when the temperature drops low enough on a spring or fall night, so if frost greets you when you crawl out of your sleeping bag, you probably won't have to worry about rain.

In addition to reading these signs, the Indi-ans closely observed certain plants and birds. Rhododendrons, a family of leafy evergreen shrubs that have always been especially plenti-ful in the Appalachian Mountains, are good temperature indicators. Cold air makes the long, narrow, leathery leaves of these plants droop downward (straight down if it gets cold enough) and curl inward. Because the plants are very sensitive to temperature changes, the leaves begin to react before a human being not-ices that the air is becoming warmer or cooler. Indian tribes living in the Appalachians could predict a rise or drop in the temperature by looking at these leaves.

Rhododendrons are easy to recognize be-cause they have hard, smooth, shiny leaves which are long and narrow, but thick from front to back, and these leaves remain dark green even in the winter. When springtime brings blossoms, they have snowy white, pink,

This wide expanse of calm water, with only small ripples, shows that no strong wind is approaching; the sky indicates continued good weather

red or purple flowers that look much like wild roses. One species, called the oleander or rose bay, is poisonous—but looking at this plant certainly can't hurt you. There are various types of rhododendrons in many parts of the world, and there are numerous other plants that react to the weather. If you study those in your area, they will help you forecast weather changes.

Certain birds provide a kind of Indian storm warning because they eat insects, which are among nature's living barometers. Insects tend to fly low before a storm approaches. Apparently, their bodies sense changes in air pressure and they stay close to the foliage and other protective ground cover if the weather is about to become rough. You can't see small insects high in the air, but birds can. You may therefore predict the weather by watching certain birds—swallows, for example—which feed on flying insects. If the birds are soaring high, the weather will continue to be fair. But if they skim low, it is time to seek shelter.

Water is another revealer of secrets. Sometimes you may think there is just a very mild breeze until you look out on a lake or pond and see constant, fast-moving ripples that indicate wind currents. Perhaps whitecaps will be visible—flecks and ribbons of foam on the crests of the little waves. This usually means it will be a day for staying near the campfire, not venturing out onto the water.

The Indians also understood the secrets held in the colors of the sky. Grey in the early morning, like fog at that time of day, foretells fair weather. A faint lavender color with blue higher up above the clouds during the early morning or late afternoon means good weather ahead; so does a rosy sky at sunrise or sunset, but a dull, deep "Indian red sky" at either of those times warns of rain within twenty-four hours, possibly accompanied by strong winds. A golden amber color is another warning of high winds, while pale yellow signals rain within twelve to twenty-four hours. A sunrise above a big bank of clouds indicates a windy day, but even if the sky is darkly overcast, there is little chance of rain.

At first, you may have trouble remembering all the signs, but the pictures in this book should help you. If you practice looking at the sky and predicting the weather every morning and evening for about a week, you'll find yourself becoming so good at it that your friends will be mystified.

This is a mackerel sky at sunset. The long, thin rows of clouds are shaped by strong air currents, indicating that a high wind is on its way

People who make their living by forecasting the weather have given Latin names to different kinds of clouds. In Latin, for instance, *cumulus* means "heap" and *cirrus* means "ringlet" or "wisp of hair." Cumulus clouds are like fluffs of cotton from low in the sky to medium-high. Little white ones in a blue sky are a sign of good weather, especially after a morning frost or dew. High, filmy, curling cirrus clouds that don't have much shape but sometimes lengthen into streamers usually bring an overcast day, but there will be no rain for forty-eight hours if the wind is from north or northeast; with southeast to southwest winds, however, the same clouds mean rain within twenty-four to thirty-six hours.

A sky of cirro-cumulus clouds (a combination of the first two kinds) means fine weather unless the wind is coming from some direction between northeast and southwest—in which case you may be caught in a short, late-afternoon shower. At sunset, a gathering of dark, high cumulus clouds (called thunderheads or alto-cumulus) against a background of glaring white sunlight means rain the next day, just as the dull "Indian red" sunset does. Sometimes the wind pushes clouds into a very definite pattern. You've probably seen a "mackerel sky," which is covered with long rows of cirro-cumulus or alto-cumulus curls like the pattern on the sides of a mackerel. A mackerel sky means the "wind is up" and a real gale may be on the way. If the clouds darken, the gale may turn into a storm.

Low cloud formations, spread out in a long layer, are called *stratus,* from the Latin word for "covering." A *nimbus* cloud is nothing but a dark, high, ragged cumulus cloud—the kind commonly called a storm cloud. Its name comes from the Latin word for rain cloud, and it usually brings showers or thunderstorms unless the wind shifts to the west or northwest. Such a shift will end the rain and bring cooler weather. A changing procession of the four basic cloud formations—say from cirrus to cumulus to stratus to nimbus—is a sure sign of rainy weather.

Sometimes the clouds aren't definitely of one kind or another but a combination. If the sun looks like it's inside a halo and behind a frosted glass of cirro-stratus cloud (or in a cocoon of high stratus clouds alone), you can expect rain within a day. Small, dark stratus clouds usually bring rain by nightfall. With easterly or southerly winds, a congested covering of grey cumulus clouds will bring rains and squalls in the summer, rain or snow in the winter; but a northerly wind shift will clear things up.

If a thunderstorm catches you away from home, there is no need to panic. You'll be safe from lightning in an automobile with a metal top, or if you take shelter in a service station or a house that has ventilator pipes, rain spouts or lead-in electric wiring. However, you must not stand by a fireplace, because lightning can strike a chimney and travel right down it. If you are on foot in the open, do *not* take shelter in an isolated shed, shack or other small, primitive building. You'll be wet but safe if you simply lie prone on the ground because lightning is attracted by tall structures that stick up into the air. This is why experienced campers never stand under tall trees—especially oaks—during a thunderstorm. On the other hand, low trees or bushes are safe, and so is a natural sheltered spot under an embankment or in the mouth of a cave. Whereas oaks seem to attract lightning, beech and birch trees seem to repel it. If you are swimming or in a small boat, you should come ashore immediately and find shelter—as close to the ground as possible. Even a tent or cabin will be all right, if it is in a sheltered spot, but *not* under tall trees. One more warning: stay away from wire fences as these, too, attract lightning.

If you fail to predict a storm in advance, but do hear and see it coming, you can tell how far away it is because you will see lightning flashes before you hear the thunder that accompanies them. Count the seconds between the flash and the sound. Every fifth second marks one mile between you and the lightning. A severe storm can be seen and heard quite a while before it arrives, so you should have time to find a warm, safe, dry place.

5
TRAVELING LIGHT

For anyone who is in good physical condition and is properly clothed and equipped, hiking long distances is surprisingly easy—though it is best to have a goal no more than three or four miles away for your first hike, and to work your way up to longer distances during the next few outings. To be prepared, you'll need proper clothing and equipment but bear in mind that the less you wear or carry, the longer you will be able to walk without getting tired. You can travel light and still not have to worry about staying warm and dry.

Most wash-and-wear clothing is fine for outdoor activities. Wear very light underclothing for summer hikes in hot regions, but wear some; it serves as cooling insulation, absorbs moisture and can be removed if it becomes uncomfortably damp. Quilted thermal underwear (or the lighter kind that looks like netting) is available in sporting-goods stores and is a comfort in winter, early spring or late fall. For mountain hiking, such clothing can even be desirable in the summer because the air may be cold at high altitudes. If you think the weather may change rapidly, or if you're hiking from the hot lowlands to the cold, high country, wear light underclothing and pack a warmer set.

Moccasin-type shoes with good arches and soles that provide traction are sufficient for easy hikes over fairly smooth terrain

When it comes to socks, the most important thing to remember is never to wear mended ones for hiking. Nothing can produce a sore or a blister faster than the lump of a darned place on a sock. I prefer light cotton socks for warm weather and thicker cotton or woolen ones for cold weather. Try wearing different kinds of socks for a few walks to see which type is most comfortable for you. Many hikers wear two pairs at once. They like to have inner socks of a thin, non-irritating material next to their skin: cotton, silk, or one of the synthetic materials like nylon. They wear a thicker, soft outside pair for padding. This is a good idea if you don't do much hiking or if your skin tends to blister very easily. Blisters result from friction, which is usually greatest at the backs of your heels. To help prevent them, you can coat the backs of your heels with a little moist soap, dab your socks with a bit of the same stuff inside the heels and then dust your socks with talcum or foot powder.

New shoes are as bad as darned socks. Don't hike with shoes that haven't been broken in thoroughly enough to be soft and pliable. For short hikes, your everyday walking shoes are fine. On smooth ground, including many forest trails, light high-top tennis shoes are comfortable. But for walking over rough terrain you should have boots with tops from six to ten inches high, and they should be made of pliable but firm leather. Such boots will give you needed ankle support. The soles should be thick, ribbed rubber or composition which will give you good traction. Smooth soles, especially leather ones, will slip.

For long hikes, pack an extra pair of boots or shoes. Changing them will rest your feet and may be extremely important in wet weather. Also pack an extra pair of laces on any hike.

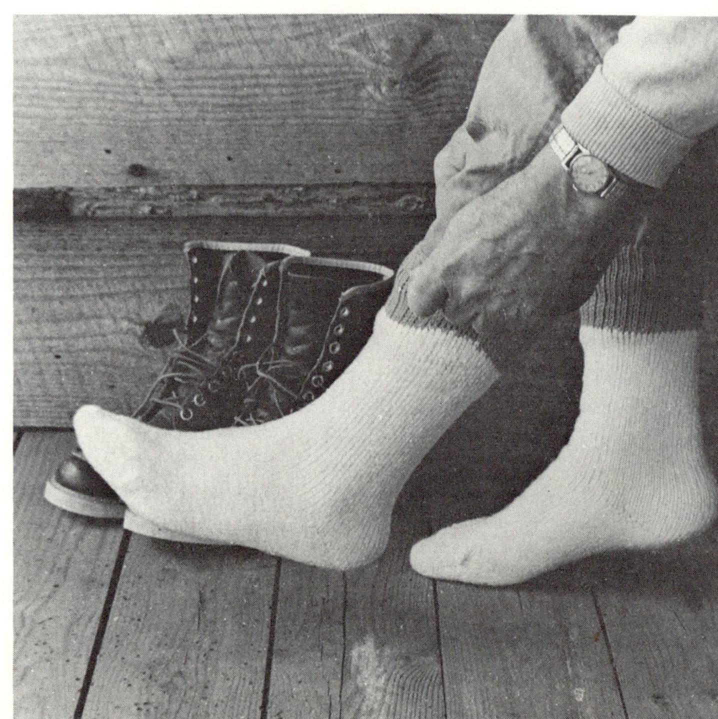

Rough terrain calls for heavy-duty footwear: thick-soled boots at least six inches high and heavy socks for warmth and padding

Tie your laces tight enough to give you support but not tight enough to bind you, and use double knots to keep the laces from coming open. If you wear two pairs of socks, buy hiking shoes or boots half a size larger than you normally would. Too much sock in too small a shoe will cramp you. On the other hand, a thin sock will work its way down into a shoe that's too large. You'll be pulling up your socks continually, and the lumps that they make inside your shoes can give you sore feet.

If your feet become swollen, don't take your shoes off; you may not be able to get them on again. Instead, loosen the laces until you're comfortable—and figure out whether your socks or shoes or both are at fault, so you can prevent the same thing from happening on the next hike.

When leather boots or shoes get wet, let them dry slowly, not near a hot fire. Otherwise, they will become hard or brittle. It won't hurt to stuff them with paper or rags to help them keep their shape as they dry. If they do get hard or brittle, soften them again by thoroughly rubbing in saddle soap and then leather oil. Many kinds of waterproofing oil are now sold at sporting-goods stores. These preparations are good for the leather and should be applied before each hike.

Girls can wear skirts on short, easy hikes, but they'll be more comfortable if they wear slacks for longer journeys, especially where it may be necessary to climb or walk over uneven terrain. Short pants are a good idea for both sexes when the weather is hot and you're traveling in a region where you won't scratch your legs on branches, thorns, stickers or sharp rocks. Of course, anyone who wears short pants and doesn't put insect repellent on his or her legs— plus suntan oil to prevent burning—is not likely to make the same mistake next time.

In most areas, full-length slacks are a better bet. For mountain hiking, they should be warm and sturdy regardless of the time of the year. Brush pants (hunting slacks with reinforced protective facings) are ideal for walking through heavily brushy woods, cactus-choked places or areas where thick tangles of brambles are a hazard. Light, cool slacks are perfect for most regions in the summer. If you think the weather will be changeable, take along both heavy and light slacks. Denims are very sturdy, and old ones that have been washed a number of times are light enough and not too stiff. They should be loose-fitting to permit freedom of movement. Hiking trousers should have no cuffs to snag on roots and underbrush. Do not buy slacks designed to be worn without a belt. A soft, comfortable, moderately wide leather belt can hold up canteens, knives and other gear as well as your pants.

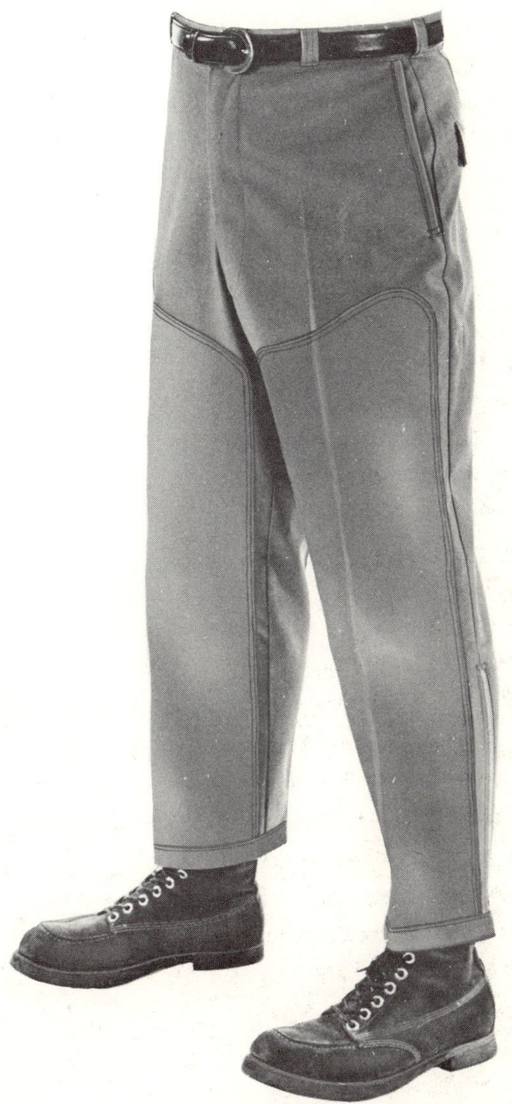

These are brush pants — hunting slacks with protective facings — for walking through scratchy brush, brambles or cactus patches

Pack a second shirt for an all-day hike, and a third one for an overnight excursion. In hot weather, light shirts with short sleeves are fine —if you remember the insect repellent and suntan oil. Under most conditions, you should have a light, medium and heavy shirt for a long hike, and they should have full-length sleeves. Sweatshirts are good for wearing over undergarments or a regular shirt on cool days.

For stalking animals (with a camera, or a gun when you've learned to hunt, or just with your eyes), camouflage-colored clothing is a great help. However, during hunting season, it's safer to wear a bright yellow, orange or red shirt, vest, jacket or cap unless you're in such a remote area that you know there's no one else in the woods. Since most animals are partially color-blind, even a bright red jacket can serve as camouflage, if it's spotted with irregular black and grey patches in a pattern resembling foliage.

Camouflage clothing can be bought for stalking animals with a camera, gun or bow-and-arrows. This archer has even camouflaged his face

In high altitudes or for cold weather, you'll want a fairly light but warm and windproof jacket. Get one with lots of pockets. A really warm, insulated hip-length coat is needed for winter hikes only. You also need mittens or gloves in the winter. Mittens are warmer, so you should generally wear them and pack a pair of gloves in case you want to do some chore that requires the use of your fingers. As a rule, even in the summer you should pack a waterproof jacket, coat or poncho. I prefer a loose, hooded, rubberized coat, designed as foul-weather gear for duck hunters. It offers protection from the head to the knees, is reasonably light and roomy enough to double as a waterproof ground cloth.

Sunglasses are almost always a good idea. Even when the sun isn't very bright, there may be a glare that becomes uncomfortable after a while, and glasses help protect your eyes from the wind and from the glare of snow. If the sun is strong, you should have a brimmed hat, and in cold weather you should have a warm hat. However, the waterproof type is likely to make your head sweat and may therefore be uncomfortable.

I always pack a large candy bar, even on a short hike, because candy is nourishing and tasty, and it gives you a quick way to refuel when you feel tired as well as hungry. The sugar in it is speedily converted into the energy you need. Just bear in mind that if you're thirsty, candy will make you thirstier. An orange can serve the same purpose as candy and can also quench your thirst. On longer hikes, you can take along raisins, nuts, hardtack, wafers, crackers or dried foods for snacks. A sandwich of meat, cheese or both makes a compact but hardy lunch. Another fine idea is to pack hot soup in a heat-retaining jug such as a Thermos bottle. The same kind of jug can also be used to carry milk, fruit juice or coffee with milk and sugar in it. These things can be very welcome by noon. Carry a little extra food, to be saved for emergencies. If you freeze a can of fruit juice and take it along, it will thaw by noon and will furnish a delightfully cool drink.

A hooded rubber coat is a good protection in wet weather, and it can double as a waterproof ground cloth when you camp

Two types of food are particularly good for overnight hikes because they are compact, tasty, nourishing and easy to prepare. One kind is the dried, concentrated soup and stew mixes that come in little packets. You just boil some water, dump in the contents of a packet and simmer it for a few minutes. The other type consists of freeze-dried mixes, which include a wider variety of foods that are equally easy to prepare and are only slightly bulkier (most of them come in small boxes, packets, cans or jars). Cheeses, ordinary dried or smoked meats, powdered eggs, bouillon cubes, small cans of vegetables, packets of flour, cereals and powdered mixes for griddle cakes, corn muffins, biscuits and the like—all of these are excellent foods which can be backpacked easily and won't spoil on the trail or in camp.

A canteen filled with water is essential. You will find that you can relieve thirst better by rinsing your mouth than by gulping down large swallows of water. Besides, water is always precious and should be used up slowly. You can keep your mouth moist with saliva, and thus relieve thirst or a dry throat, by munching raisins or other dried fruit, or even by sucking on a washed pebble to keep your salivary glands working. Another good way is to suck on a piece of lemon occasionally—if you've brought one along.

The safest way to purify water is to boil it for no less than five minutes; then let it cool and it will be safe to drink. Some people not only boil their camp water but then treat it with water-purifying tablets such as Halazone or a chemical purifying and filtering kit. These tablets and kits are available in stores that sell camping equipment. Experienced campers usually carry a few tablets for use when there's no opportunity to boil water. In an emergency, two drops of iodine in a quart of water will make the water safe to drink.

There are a few other items that you should pack or carry on any but the shortest hike. One of these is a pocketknife with several different kinds of blades; the Scout knife described earlier would be a good choice. A knife can come in handy for all sorts of little jobs: for example, snipping and shaving twigs, dry bark and so on for kindling, or even cutting small dead branches for firewood. You may want to peel fruit or cut up some food. Or you might want to whittle a toothpick, or punch a more comfortable buckle hole in a belt or a lace hole in a boot. If you're an amateur botanist, you might also use a knife to cut sprigs when collecting specimens. You can't foresee all the uses a knife may have.

Many hikers hang a knife by its shackle, or lanyard ring, to a belt clip. This has the advantage of keeping the knife literally attached to you so that it can't be lost. However, it's a bother to clip and unclip it. I prefer to carry a pocketknife in the obvious place—a pocket. If you carry a sheath knife, of course, it belongs on your hip, where it's out of the way but easy to reach. The sheath should be a good leather one that can be slipped onto the belt, and it should

A sheath knife should be worn fairly far back on the hip, where it is handy to reach but out of your way

have a safety loop, strap, flap, snap or thong to keep the knife safely in place.

If you're on a short hike, there's no need to carry a pack, but you should at least carry in your pockets some insect repellent, suntan lotion, a couple of adhesive bandages and a small sewing kit with needles, thread and safety pins. It's fun to hike with companions, and every person on a hike doesn't need to carry every item of gear. It will be more comfortable if one person pockets a sewing kit, another a small squeeze dispenser of insect repellent and a third may take a small dispenser of suntan lotion.

There is no reason to weigh yourself down with a backpack except on long hikes. Carrying such a pack can tire you, especially if you're not accustomed to toting one. If your pockets feel overstuffed with equipment, there is an easier way to carry the little essentials. Spread a face towel, undergarment or rain jacket flat, lay the items you're carrying in a compact row on this material and roll it up into a cylinder with the ends tucked in. Tie this roll securely with your extra shoelaces and then secure it with the ends of the laces to the back of your belt. This will be so comfortable that you won't even know it's there.

On an average or long hike, you should have a compact first-aid kit containing adhesive bandage strips, a roll of adhesive tape, squares or a roll of bandage, merthiolate or a similar antiseptic, an elastic bandage for the relief of sprains, aspirin, tweezers for removing slivers or thorns, small scissors for cutting bandage, a tourniquet and a snake-bite kit. It is unlikely that you'll ever need the tourniquet (and any reasonably long strip of material can be used for one; some first-aid kits include a triangular sling that can be twisted into a tourniquet) but people do occasionally get deep cuts even at such "safe" places as the dining room table. Get a Red Cross first-aid manual or similar handbook, and study the instructions before you go afield so that you will know how to use your first-aid items.

Like the tourniquet, your snake-bite kit will probably never be used. There are no poisonous snakes in many areas—in fact, very few in any areas. Moreover, snakes are afraid of human beings and will usually retreat or remain still, hoping they won't be noticed, when a person approaches. If a snake does strike, the foot or ankle is the obvious target, and the fangs probably won't penetrate the leather if you're wearing six- to ten-inch-high boots. Just the same, it is only sensible to follow a few safety rules: if you do hike or camp in an area where poisonous snakes are common, wear high, snakeproof boots; get a field guide to reptiles and memorize the appearance of the venomous species, so that you never make a mistake and approach or pick up a "harmless" snake that turns out to be not so harmless; get a snake-bite kit, read and memorize the instructions for using it, and carry it with your other first-aid equipment. Snake-bite gear usually includes a tourniquet (applied above the puncture to prevent the spread of venom), a sharp, sterile blade to make incisions across the punctures, a suction cup to draw out the venom, and an antiseptic.

It's obvious that you should have matches on a hike or camping trip. They should be the wooden kind, and you can waterproof them by dipping them in paraffin or nail polish. As an added precaution, carry them in a waterproof container such as the screw-top metal cylinder that some types of camera film come in.

Another added precaution is to carry a "metal match." This inexpensive gadget, which is available in some sporting-goods stores, is a small, thin cylinder, usually on a little key chain to prevent loss. When you strike the blade of a knife against it in a downward, slicing motion, it gives off a little shower of sparks. Unlike a cigarette lighter, it never goes dry or needs a new flint. You can start a fire with it by holding it close over a loose pile of tinder, striking sparks and then blowing on the tinder. You can also buy small "heat tablets" which can be dropped into kindling and lit to start a fire.

If the kindling and other available fire material is damp, you'll have difficulty getting a flame started. It is therefore wise to carry a candle. This will remain lit as long as you need it,

A "metal match" is an excellent fire-starter. Just strike a knife blade against it to produce sparks

so you can get the kindling to start burning nicely—and a candle also is a handy source of light in emergencies. Building a safe, efficient fire is a skill, and a detailed lesson will be provided in the chapter on pitching camp.

Even if you plan to be home before dark, it is a good idea to carry a flashlight and extra batteries. Aside from being a safety precaution, it will help you look into interesting dark places such as hollow trees, caves or animal burrows dug in the earth. If you do hike or camp after dark, use the flashlight only when necessary to signal, to light a trail or to see what you're doing with your gear. If you let your eyes become accustomed to the dark, you will see much more, and nature is fascinating at night when nocturnal creatures come out of hiding.

Binoculars can help you identify distant plants, animals, birds and landmarks, and they're fun to use. Five- or six-power magnification is all you need; more powerful field glasses are heavy and bulky.

A camera is another recommended piece of equipment. You will want to record your adventures in the world of nature, and get pictures of many beautiful and unusual things in the outdoors. Be sure to take along extra film. You may also want to record your adventures in words. Carry a pencil and a small notebook so that you can jot down notes about directions, write reminders about camping instructions, sketch trails, landmarks or other items of interest and describe your observations of nature.

Field guides have already been mentioned, and there isn't much more advice that can be given regarding these valuable little books. Which ones you carry will have to depend on where you're hiking and what creatures or plants most interest you.

Finally, it is essential to carry a compass in any unfamiliar area, and sometimes you will also need a map of the vicinity where you hike or camp. In Chapters Six and Seven, you will learn more about maps and compasses. Chapter Eight will deal with the art of backpacking.

6
THE FIRST REAL HIKE

You must not only be properly dressed and equipped but properly conditioned for enjoyable hiking and camping. Part of your basic training as an outdoorsman is therefore to keep your legs, feet, lungs—in fact, your entire body —in shape by walking and running every day. If you've been getting lots of exercise, you can walk much farther than you might imagine before you become tired. You probably walk several miles each day, without realizing it, as you go about your normal activities. You don't notice how far your legs are carrying you because your mind is on more interesting things. Besides, you don't do all your walking in one long session but in many short ones, interrupted by other activities that provide rest periods for your feet, legs and back.

Similarly, a good hiker's mind is on more interesting things than how much work his or her legs may be doing. You will be observing nature and sometimes chatting with fellow hikers. And when you reach a particularly scenic or interesting spot on your walk, you should stop and rest. During one or two of these halts, have a light snack or bite of candy to renew your energy. You will also stop for lunch. After eating a meal, don't resume your hike immediately but rest for another 15 minutes to half an hour. The first stages of the digestive process use up energy. If you rest for a short time after lunch, your digestion will be better and you will not tire as quickly. Too much exertion right after a meal can even cause cramps.

A raccoon searches the river's edge for food

This girl's fully loaded backpack weighs nearly 20 pounds, yet she has climbed mountains without tiring because she has paced herself properly and has taken frequent rest stops

The distance covered on a hike may depend on many factors—your age, physical condition, whether the ground is flat or hilly or mountainous, how much time you and your companions want to spend outdoors, and whether the day is hot, cold or pleasantly cool. As mentioned earlier, a first hike should have a goal no more than three or four miles from the starting point. You can walk four miles in just over an hour and a half without rushing, even though you take a five- or ten-minute rest stop every half-hour. An adult, walking at an average pace, can cover almost four miles an hour over level, unobstructed ground, although that's a little too fast for long walks without fatigue. About three miles an hour is a good speed for hiking over level ground by both youngsters and adults. In planning a hike, bear in mind that it takes two or three times as long to get over steep inclines, and that you will tire faster if your path crosses many high slopes.

The four-mile limit, with rest stops along the way, will not be tiring. This is also a good distance because a longer walk may begin to bore any very young children in the hiking group. Hiking is more fun if you have an interesting goal—an especially scenic spot, some historic site, a fishing hole, or maybe just good grounds for camping or cooking or having a picnic. Your starting point doesn't have to be your home, of course. There may be no interesting goal at the right distance from your home, and you may not even live in a good hiking area. Plan where you want to hike, and then go to the starting point by car, bus or train. Be sure to leave home early in the morning so that you will have lots of time to enjoy yourself and will not be rushed.

Obviously, you must plan your route in advance, unless you're very familiar with the area and know just where you want to hike. In the United States, the national parks and most of the national forests and state parks have spectacular nature trails. The authorities in these parks and forests will be happy to suggest routes and can even supply maps where necessary. In the United States, Canada, Mexico, the British Isles and many European countries, the local, state and national tourism boards, chambers of commerce and conservation departments will furnish maps, descriptive booklets, information about camping and picnic sites, leaflets with hiking directions and lists of suggested hikes, including both short outings and long camping excursions.

Some of the most famous hiking trails stretch through the wilds for as much as 2,000 miles. The Appalachian Trail, for example, extends from Maine all the way down to Georgia, and the Pacific Crest Trail reaches from the Mexican border northward through the western states, along the Sierra Nevada and Cascade Mountains, right up into Canada. Then there's the Hiawatha Pioneer Trail, which winds through Iowa, Illinois, Wisconsin and Minnesota. Such trails are as beautiful as they are long. Many hikers have covered the entire lengths of these trails on long camping trips, but it is more common to pick a convenient spot along the trail as a starting point, and another spot a few miles farther along as a goal for a short or medium hike. Maps of the long trails are available; the addresses of organizations that will supply such maps are listed at the end of this chapter, and lists at the end of later chapters will tell you where to get various other kinds of hiking and camping information.

Nearly every part of the United States has also been mapped by the Geological Survey. Contour lines are marked in brown, and by studying them you can visualize how rough or smooth, mountainous or level the terrain is. Each contour line is twenty feet higher or lower than the one next to it. Wooded areas are indicated in green, and this is also a big help. Best of all, each map shows all the roads and foot trails in the area it depicts. On most of the maps, an inch of space equals one mile of actual land or water, but on some the scale is one inch to only 2,000 feet. The latter type shows the smallest details right down to little clearings and ditches.

To order a map, you first need an index for

the state where you plan to hike or camp. The index is free for the asking (the distribution centers are listed at the end of this chapter) and it shows how the state is divided into sections called quadrangles, with a map listed for each quadrangle. You can then send for the map you want. There will be a very small charge for each one you order.

Other nations have similar map services. Most of the maps have special symbols to indicate swamps, woods, hills, landmarks and so on. A "key" is printed on the map to tell you what the symbols mean, so you can look for landmarks and then consult the map to see exactly where you are.

Even if you are an experienced hiker, it is wise to have at least one hiking companion, unless you are in territory with which you are thoroughly familiar. Some people also like to take a pet. I think the only pet that should be allowed to come is a dog, and then only if he is in good condition and thoroughly trained not to wander away from you. A well-trained dog can add a lot to your fun, especially on a short hike. Because a healthy dog has good hearing and a much keener sense of smell than any human, your pet will often find interesting things along the trail that you would have missed if you were alone. However, it should be added that a dog often frightens away the wildlife.

A good hiking goal might be a camping or picnic site where you can build a fire and eat lunch. To avoid discomfort, rest for at least 15 minutes after eating

If you plan a hike in an unknown area, first procure a map that shows roads and trails, and study your route

An exciting destination for a hike can be the scene of some event or celebration, such as this Wyoming Indian pow-wow

You can play with the dog at rest stops or at your destination, but keep him on a leash while you're walking unless he's trained to stay right at your side at all times. Of course, you must carry food and water for your pet and get permission beforehand to cross any private land or enter any park with a dog. As a matter of fact, you must get advance permission from the owner before you yourself hike across private property.

If you ask politely, you will almost always be given permission to hike on a person's land. Be sure to close any fences or gates after you, and treat another person's property as if it were your own. Don't pick someone else's flowers or fruit unless you have obtained specific permission to do so. And never litter the earth or

Poison ivy sometimes grows as a vine surrounding tree trunks

water with food wrappers, cans, paper or any other trash. One of the first rules of the true outdoorsman is to leave every place as beautiful as when he found it.

There is a definite technique to walking without getting tired. Lean slightly forward from your hips, and swing along rhythmically but with as little sideward or upward movement as possible. Practice walking with your toes pointing straight ahead instead of toeing out. The straight-toed foot placement, called the Indian walk, lengthens your stride slightly; on a long walk, this means you will have to take far fewer steps. The length of your stride depends on your build. Adopt a stride that is comfortable and smooth.

Slow your pace when going uphill to avoid getting out of breath, and slow it again going downhill to avoid slipping. To climb a steep slope, try the lockstep: with each stride, straighten the leg that's to the rear and rest on it for a moment. With the next step, repeat the procedure on the other leg. Don't worry if you aren't covering the three miles an hour previously mentioned; as you hike more, you will find it easier and will be able to go a little faster.

If your legs or feet feel tired or strained, take an extra rest. Lie on your back with your feet propped up against a tree or on a log or rock. In a hiking group, the youngest or least experienced walker should lead, and then no one will fall behind. An experienced hiker should act as the rear guard in case a straggler needs help.

Avoid stepping on logs or rocks, because that can tire you out or even cause a sprained ankle. Hold aside any low branches until the person behind you can grab them. This will keep people from getting their faces whipped with stinging branches. Also warn anyone behind you of holes or obstacles. Most important, learn to look where you're going, even while observing nature all around you. This may take a little practice, but it will prevent accidents. And you can always stop for a closer, longer look at a bird or butterfly, animal or plant.

The most enjoyable trails to hike are the least "civilized," and the easiest terrain is firm or grassy ground. If you have to follow a road for a while, walk single file, with plenty of space between hikers, as far off the actual road as possible and on the side that will allow you to face oncoming traffic. In the United States, that means the left side, but in countries where cars stay to the left you should walk on the right side. Do not walk along railroad tracks or trestles.

Poison oak leaves have a shape somewhat resembling real oak leaves

A combination of common sense and insect repellent will keep you from being plagued with bites and stings. You don't have to be a genius to keep your distance from hornet, wasp and bee nests. If a stinging insect begins buzzing around you, try to stand still until it flies away; frighten it and you'll get stung. If the insect doesn't leave when you stand still, slowly take out your insect repellent, open it and pour or spray some out.

Ticks, like spiders, are eight-legged creatures, but unlike spiders they are all harmful and some even transmit disease. They look like a cross between a small, stubby beetle and a crab. They try to attach themselves to the skin of a human or animal victim in order to suck blood. If one gets on you, get it off by touching it with alcohol or covering it with grease or oil. This will make it drop away. Then kill it.

Scorpions, rare except in the Southwest, should also be avoided. A scorpion looks like a miniature lobster with its tail curved over its back. Most scorpions are no more dangerous than a wasp, but one southwestern variety can be lethal. When camping in the Southwest, never go barefoot. Check your shoes and clothing before getting dressed, shake out your sleeping bag and then roll it up tightly to keep undesirable visitors out.

There are only four dangerous snakes in the United States—the rattler, the cottonmouth, the copperhead and the coral snake. Study their pictures in a field guide. If you see one, stay away. And always carry a snake-bite kit as recommended earlier. Poisonous plants are much more common than venomous snakes, and therefore present more of a problem. Unless you have an allergy to some plants (in which case you should ask your doctor for medication to keep you comfortable while camping or hiking), there are three chief varieties that are bothersome—poison ivy, oak and sumac. Learn to recognize them.

Each poison ivy leaf is composed of three separate, pointed oval leaflets, and fruiting plants have clusters of small white berries. These plants occur as ground vines, climbing

Don't walk on tangles or roots like these; step over or around them to avoid spraining an ankle

vines and shrubs. The stems sometimes have fuzzy fibers which help the vine cling. Poison oak looks much like poison ivy but the stems are usually smoother and the leaves may be slightly longer and sometimes wavy-edged, almost the way true oak leaves look. The leaves of both of these troublesome plants are green, sometimes with a red tinge.

It's fun to plan a three- or four-mile hike to end at a fishing hole. You can add to your enjoyment by taking along a dog — if he's well trained

Poison sumac is less common and easier to recognize. You'll see seven to eleven leaflets, with all but one of them growing out of opposite sides of a red stem and with that last leaflet at the tip of the stem. The leaves are bright green. They are oval in shape. Sumac is a tall shrub or small tree, and it, too, bears loose clusters of small greenish-white berries. True (non-poisonous) sumac has green rather than red stems and bears tight clusters of red rather than white berries.

Poison sumac has light-colored berries, and each stem has 7 to 11 leaflets. (Also see the pictures of poison ivy and poison oak on page 54.)

If you accidentally rub against poison ivy, oak or sumac, the best remedy is an old-fashioned one: scrub your skin with soap and water as soon as possible. Then apply rubbing alcohol, patting it on gently. When you get home, your doctor will give you a soothing and healing lotion such as calamine to complete the treatment. Try not to scratch, as this will just spread the rash. Some hikers carry calamine in their first-aid kits; this lotion also soothes scratches from nettles or thorns.

There are other plants, including some mushrooms and berries, which are harmful—but only if you eat them. Later we will discuss some easily recognized plants of several kinds that are perfectly safe to eat as well as nutritious and delicious. However, if you are an inexperienced woodsman, don't put anything into your mouth without the approval of a very experienced adult camper. Even after looking at pictures in a field guide, it is possible to mistake a harmful plant for a harmless one. A hiking and camping expert named Hugh Grey summed up a safety rule nicely, when he said, "What you don't eat won't hurt you." Most things in the woods are as harmless as they are interesting and beautiful, but you must learn to look and recognize before you touch.

* * *

INFORMATION SOURCES

For trail maps of areas in the eastern United States, write to the Appalachian Trail Conference, 1718 N Street, Northwest, Washington, D.C. 20036.

For trail maps of areas in the western United States, write to the Sierra Club, 1050 Mills Tower, San Francisco, California 94104.

For a map of the Hiawatha Pioneer Trail, write to the Division of Tourism, 57 West Seventh Street, St. Paul, Minnesota 55102 (or to the Division of Tourism at the state capital of Illinois, Iowa or Wisconsin).

For booklets on footwear, hiking and related subjects, write to Wolverine World Wide, Inc., Rockford, Michigan 49341.

For a map index of any state west of the Mississippi River, and for the maps themselves, write to the Denver Distribution Section, Geological Survey, Federal Center, Denver, Colorado 80225.

For a map index of any state east of the Mississippi River, and for the maps themselves, write to the Washington Distribution Section, Geological Survey, Washington, D.C. 20242.

To help you stay on your compass course, you can take sightings on distant landmarks, such as this mountain

7
COMPASS AND MAP

Before setting out on a long hike, you should know how to use a compass and map. Most compasses employ either a free-swinging magnetized needle or a revolving magnetized dial which permits you to figure out directions. When using your compass, make sure there are no iron or steel utensils near it, because such objects will exert a pull on the magnetic parts, preventing you from getting an accurate compass reading.

The long, thin pointer in a needle compass points to magnetic north. This is not the true, or "North Pole" north but a point in northern Canada above Hudson Bay which is determined by the earth's magnetic field. A compass looks something like a wristwatch, with the directions printed on the dial. Clockwise from the top, you'll see North, East, South and West, or N, E, S and W. Sometimes, midway directions between these main ones are also marked; for example, between N and W you might see NW, or northwest. But on most compasses you will see only the four main directions, with lines and numbers between them indicating degrees. There are 360 degrees in a complete circle, 180 in a half-circle (say, from N to S or E to W) and 90 degrees between each main direction and the main direction next to it on either side (say, from S to E or S to W). These

Signs marking trails and areas will help you check your position on your map

degrees help you to keep going in a straight line and keep track of your destination, or spot it on a map when you aren't headed directly for N, E, S or W. Upon consulting your compass and map, you may find that you want to head 20 degrees east of N, for example. This is much more accurate than deciding that you want to go "just a little to the east of N."

A dial compass works the same way, except that a dial instead of a needle swings around to align the letter N with a marking on the compass face. Most people find the needle type easier to use.

Maps are printed with true north at the top, but on trail maps, cross-country maps and topographical maps you will almost always find an angle printed on the margin below the map, with one line pointing slightly to one side to show the difference in degrees between true and magnetic north in the mapped area. Put the map on a flat surface—the ground will do. If a wind is blowing, hold the corners of the map down with rocks. Now put the compass down on the map, just above or below the printed magnetic north line. Turn the compass slowly until its needle points to N on its dial. Lift the compass and turn the map itself until the *magnetic* north line printed in the margin points the same way as the compass needle. After a minute or two of trial-and-error shifting, you will have the compass and map aligned with the terrain where you are, in a north-south direction.

Find your starting point and destination on the map, and draw a straight line between them. That's the exact direction in which you want to go. By laying the compass on the map at the starting point, you can be very precise. Suppose you find that the imaginary line goes through the 20-degree mark on the right side of N. All you have to do is start walking in that north-northeasterly direction, 20 degrees to the right of N. It's a good idea to find a landmark such as a tall tree, mountain peak, valley or other terrain feature lying in your desired direction. Head for it, and stop occasionally to check your compass and make sure you're still

headed 20 degrees to the right of N. When you get to the landmark you're using, find another. It needn't be in the exact direction of your goal; nothing is easier than walking "just a little to the left of that steep cliff up ahead," and this won't throw you off course if you occasionally use your compass to correct yourself.

The difference in degrees between true north and magnetic north is called declination, and it is vital to know about the declination in any region where a cross-country hike takes you far from easily recognized roads or landmarks. If you are hiking over an area with a declination of fifteen degrees west, and you take your bearings with true north as a reference point instead of magnetic north, you will be off your course by fifteen degrees east. After one mile of walking you will be a quarter of a mile off course, and after four miles of walking you will be a full mile off—a good way to get lost.

Printed on the compass dial are the four major directions — N, E, S and W — with the angles between these directions marked off in degrees

Think of true north as simply the top of the world, or the North Pole. This is the ·point where the earth's axis, an imaginary line going straight through the globe from the South Pole to the North Pole, would come out on top. Magnetic north, above Hudson Bay in Canada, is where the compass needle points because the geology of land masses—land altitudes, waters, the density of mountains, even the mineral content of mountains—all influence the magnetic field which attracts a magnetized needle.

Since most cross-country and topographical maps have a line in the bottom margin pointing to magnetic north, you should have no difficulty getting your bearings and hiking in the proper direction. However, in case you must use a map that lacks this marking, you should memorize the approximate declination in your area. (If you are off by a degree or two, the difference won't be great enough to matter on a hike, but a wide declination such as 15 degrees is another matter.) Wherever you hike in the United States, you can figure out your approximate declination from the map printed with this chapter. It has lines showing every five-degree declination east or west from zero, or true north. Bear in mind that as you go *west,* the declination goes *east.*

The declination is zero (meaning the area where true north and magnetic north are the same on a map) from the easternmost point of Georgia, up through parts of South Carolina, North Carolina, Tennessee, Kentucky, Ohio, Indiana and then straight up through Lake Michigan. The declination is ten degrees west from the middle of the New Jersey coast through northeastern Pennsylvania and the middle of New York, and on into Lake Ontario. The declination is twenty degrees west from the middle of the Maine coast straight up toward James Bay and Hudson Bay. The five degree west declination is about midway between zero and ten, the fifteen degree declination about midway between ten and twenty. If you are anywhere east of the zero declination, you can now draw a line straight up and down on your hiking map, and from the bottom of

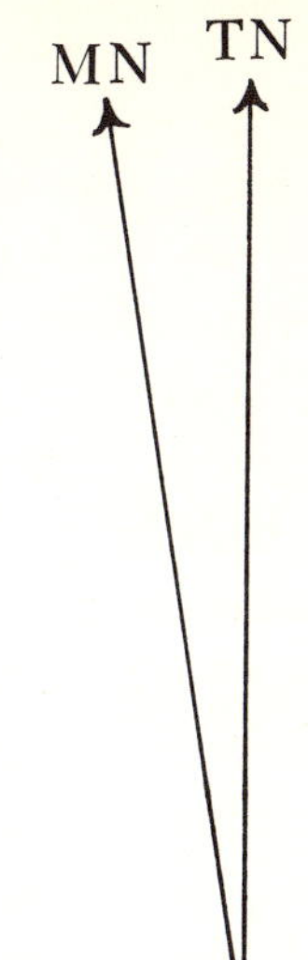

Most cross-country maps have the angle of declination printed in the margin, with one line pointing to magnetic north, and another pointing to true north

this line draw another, angled the proper number of degrees to the left (west). That second line—the angled one—points to magnetic north.

Now let's take the declinations on the. other side of zero. The declination is five degrees east from the western tip of Florida up through parts of Alabama, Mississippi and Tennessee; from there it simply follows the Mississippi River northward. The declination is ten degrees east on a line almost straight up from the middle of Texas to the border between North Dakota and Minnesota, and on through Manitoba to Hudson Bay. The declination is twenty degrees east from the northern border of California up through the middle of Oregon and then curving through Idaho and Montana into Canada. The fifteen degree east declination curves up about midway between ten and twenty degrees, starting at the southwestern tip of California. Therefore, if you are anywhere west of the zero declination, you can now draw a line straight up and down on your hiking map and from the bottom of this line draw another, angled the proper number of degrees to the right (east). That second line points to magnetic north.

Naturally, the direction of magnetic north will differ in other parts of the world. You can find out the proper declination from government mapping agencies and from map and atlas publishers.

Before you begin a long hike, of course, you should know the location of your starting point as shown on the map. You can find this out

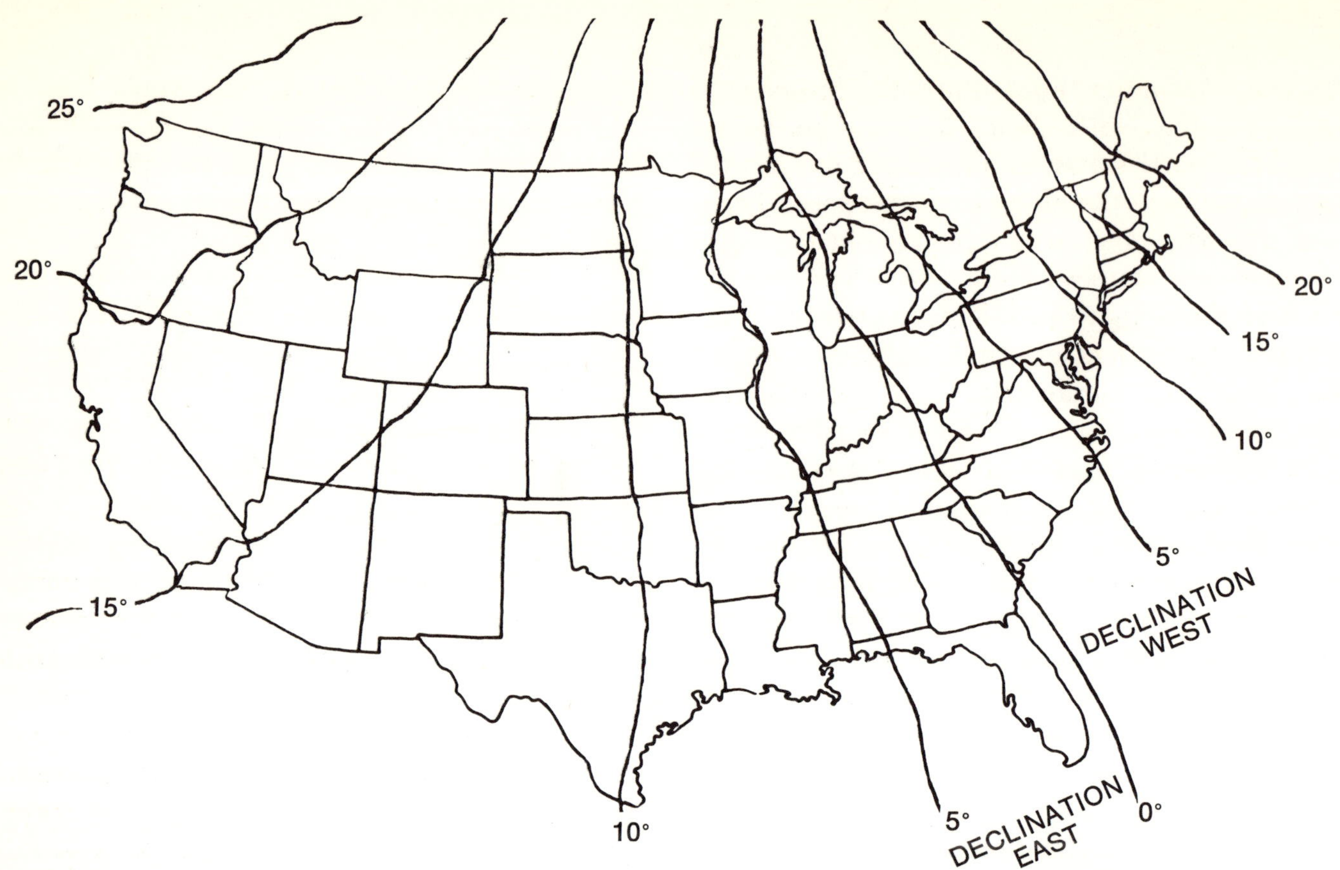

This map shows the approximate declinations east and west in the United States. By studying it, you can judge how far east or west of true north your compass points, depending on what part of the country you are in

from landmarks, road signs and trail markers, as well as by questioning people in the area. Make your first compass and map reading at the hike's starting point so that you'll know which way to go right from the first. A compass merely tells you which way north lies, and where the other directions are in relation to north. Knowing these things will do you no good if you don't take a reading at your starting point. When you're on a well marked trail this is not important—except for practice. But it can be essential when you strike out across unmarked fields and woods.

After you've had some experience, you can even draw maps of your own. You might do this if you discover a good campsite or interesting spot to which you want to return some time, and it isn't clearly marked on your printed map. Mark the general area on the printed map. Then find a big, flat, clear spot on the ground and put down your compass, a sheet of paper and a pencil. Mark the paper with an arrow pointing to magnetic north.

Then sketch in landmarks, taking sightings on them with your compass to get them in the right direction on your homemade map. Write on the map the estimated distances between landmarks. You might, for instance, see a pond to sketch in at the map's northeast corner, a peak to draw at the northwest and a grove of tall trees at the south edge. Suppose you estimate that the grove of trees is one hundred yards, or the length of a football field, from the pond. And the peak is about half a mile away. Write that information on your map. When you return to the area, you should have little trouble again locating the spot where you drew the map.

If you have a compass and map, and have noted outstanding terrain features that indicate where you are, it is unlikely that you'll ever get lost. But if it should happen, there is no reason to panic. A search party will come for you, if you don't show up when and where you're supposed to. But that probably won't be necessary. Sit down and rest for a few minutes, and you may be able to figure out where you are. If that doesn't work, climb a tree and try to get your bearings by finding additional landmarks. If you see smoke, head for it; smoke means people. The same is true of a road. Follow a creek downstream, or follow any power lines you see, and you'll eventually reach civilization.

If night overtakes you, build a small, safe campfire and settle down until morning; there's no sense wandering in the dark. You can, however, check your directions with the stars at night. The constellation known as the Big Dipper is shaped like a long-handled pot, or saucepan. The front edge of this pot lines up with the end of the handle of the Little Dipper, a smaller constellation that also looks like a pot. The star at the end of the Little Dipper's handle is Polaris, the North Star. In different parts of the world, the constellations appear to be in different positions, but with the help of an astronomy field guide, you can memorize the "skymarks" in your area.

If you start walking and aren't sure of your directions, leave a clearly marked trail so that people can find you. Three of anything is the woodsman's signal for danger, a call for help. You can use piles of three rocks, tie together three big clumps of grass, mark your trail with three bent or broken saplings. And you can show the direction you've taken by making trail arrows out of stones, brush or broken saplings. You can even carve arrows into trees. With a map and compass, however, none of this should ever be necessary.

Camping and picnic sites like this one are clearly marked on most trail maps

8
STRIKING OUT CROSS-COUNTRY

Cross-country hikes offer a perfect chance for exploring the edges of streams and trails, where wildlife abounds

On long hikes, it is important to remember that you're not running a race. Find a moderate pace that's comfortable and enjoyable. Toward the end of a hike, however, you may be in a hurry to reach your goal. Perhaps dusk is falling, or maybe you're hungry. In a case like that, you can cover miles rapidly and without getting exhausted by using the Scout's Pace. This consists of an easy, very slow trot or lope for a certain number of paces that you decide on, and then a walk for the same number of paces. The number is generally from thirty to fifty. Keep alternating the walk and the trot. In hardly any time, you'll be at your destination.

After starting with a few short hikes to become accustomed to outdoor walking, you can quickly increase the distance. About twelve miles is considered a good distance for an all-day hike, although some experienced outdoorsmen have no trouble going fifteen or twenty miles in a day.

If you're wearing a backpack, the manner in which you walk becomes all the more important in avoiding fatigue. Lean slightly forward, moving with a comfortable stride and letting your arms hang or swing in a relaxed manner.

This boy is toting an open-topped Adirondack pack basket

If the shoulder straps rub, use a small towel as padding. When loading a pack, put more of the heavy items near the top than near the bottom. This keeps the weight up around your shoulders where it won't be uncomfortable or exhausting. But don't overdo this trick; a very topheavy pack will interfere with your balance and make it difficult to walk. Also, regardless of weight, any items you might need frequently or soon on the trail should be stowed near the top or in a pack's external pockets. You don't want to dig all the way to the bottom for your lunch. Before going on a real hike, you should practice carrying a pack on short walks.

There are conflicting opinions about the maximum weight a pack should have, but everyone agrees that the lighter it is, the better. On an all-day hike, I feel that the most an adult should ever carry is thirty pounds. A young person who hasn't finished growing should carry no more than twenty pounds for any long period, and a small child shouldn't carry more than half that much. Even these weights may impress you as heavy, but you'll be surprised at what a load you can carry easily on your shoulders and back.

Nevertheless, backpacking can be hot, heavy work. When buying a pack, look for one that lets some air circulate between itself and your body. There are several types to choose from. The mountain-climber's rucksack is good for most purposes. Made of waterproof canvas, with a broad bottom and several outside pockets for frequently needed items, it is built over a light tubular steel frame which curves so that you have ventilation between your back and the load. Adjustable webbed straps go over your shoulders and down again to the bottom of the pack, at waist height. While walking, you can occasionally hook your thumbs through these straps to shift the weight and relieve the tension on your shoulders. Such a pack will certainly hold everything you need for an all-day hike, and a roomy one will even hold enough for an overnight excursion— though you'll have to lash your sleeping bag on top.

Still roomier and also comfortable is the open-topped Adirondack pack basket. This is a rigid basket, made of woven ash or willow strips. It is carried the same way as a rucksack, with adjustable shoulder straps. A small one is

These hikers have loaded their packs well, with more of the weight near the top than at the bottom, so the shoulders can bear the carrying strain without undue effort and fatigue

A light, Everest-style pack frame, with a standard, roomy backpack attached

A mountain-climber's rucksack, with outside pockets for frequently needed items

an excellent child's pack, and one of any size makes a good storage box in camp. Because it is rigid, it is good for carrying breakable items or any hard objects like cans or tools which might otherwise dig into your back. Since it has an open top, you can load it extra-full and let a sleeping bag or rolled-up raincoat or poncho protrude from the top. A good place for breakable things is inside the roll.

Probably the most versatile arrangement of all is the Everest-style pack frame, a very light frame of aluminum tubing with adjustable shoulder straps and a web strap that keeps the metal away from the small of your back. Frequently, the bottom of the frame turns out to the rear, forming a shelf. I like this type best. With ordinary rope, you can lash a load of just about any size and shape to this frame. A popular way to use it is to roll some items in a sleeping bag and position the bag horizontally at the bottom, then roll the rest of the gear in a tent or ground cloth and lash that on top, vertically. Such a frame will let you carry equipment for a hike or camping trip of almost any length. One version of this frame, called the Kelty, has a waist strap that lets you bear most of the weight comfortably on your hips.

Sometimes a hiker will attach a head strap, or "tumpline," to his pack (regardless of which type of pack he uses) in addition to the shoulder straps. This lets your neck muscles do some of the work, but is only necessary for long treks with very heavy loads.

To keep the shoulder straps from digging in and making your shoulders sore, you may want to use a light face towel or folded undergarment as shoulder padding. With or without padding, frequent short rests are important.

Even though you follow all of these instructions, a cross-country hike may make your feet a little sore if you're a beginner. If the backs of your heels begin to feel tender, remove your boots and put an adhesive bandage across the sore place to absorb friction. But if a blister has started to form, sterilize a needle by holding it in a match flame and prick the edge of the blister. Apply some antiseptic, and then put on the bandage. If possible, also put on clean socks and change your boots.

When you begin to get tired on a long hike, stop for a rest at the next stream or creek even if you've rested a short time before, and wet your wrists to cool your body rapidly. One of the greatest joys of hiking is to take off your boots and soak your feet in a cool stream. It is not only pleasant but good for your feet. Dry them thoroughly, put on clean socks, get your boots back on and you're ready for the trail again. Another tip about foot care is to trim your toenails fairly short and straight across. The straight trim keeps the corners from digging in and irritating your skin.

During rest stops, at your lunch break and when you reach your destination, you have perfect opportunities for practicing your stalking and tracking. If you move quietly, smoothly and slowly, you can get very close to birds and animals. Instead of speaking to your companions, use signals. You can point to show directions, hold up a hand to make someone stop moving, beckon to make a companion approach, put a finger to your lips for silence. Squirrels, chickadees and some other animals and birds will often come near you, if you sprinkle nuts, bread crumbs or sunflower seeds on the ground. Fish (especially perch, sunfish, carp, catfish and minnows) frequently crowd around for bread crumbs, too. Larger animals are likely to stand still if you creep close very slowly and quietly. If an animal looks your way or seems to be getting nervous, stop moving for as long as you can hold still.

Approach the animal from downwind—that is, from a direction with the wind blowing toward you and not away from you toward the animal. Remember that wild creatures have an extraordinarily keen sense of smell and may become alarmed if the wind blows your scent toward them. Use rocks and trees to conceal yourself as you come closer. Begin approaching in a crouch, and as you come nearer to the animal get down on all fours so that you won't be seen. If you have a camera with you, you may be able to get a close-up photograph, though the click of the shutter will send the animal scurrying away.

Catching frogs is excellent stalking practice, and if you catch one at the end of a hike you

Without wandering far from the trail, you can practice stalking. This fox was photographed from only a few yards away

This brother and sister have found a cluster of frog's eggs during a streamside hike

might want to take it home and keep it as a pet for a few days while you observe it. You can either corner a frog so that its back is to a high bank, or grab it fast, firmly but gently, from directly behind. Frogs can see quite well on both sides and a good way back. They are meat eaters, and you will recall that you can feed one on mealworms, insects, dried daphnia and tiny bits of earthworms.

Frogs (and toads) lead rather weird lives. Called amphibians because they live both in the water and on land, frogs exist in many varieties, from very small ones that are less than half an inch long when mature, to one giant species that can grow to ten inches. Some of the small ones climb trees in search of insects, while others hardly ever leave the water. In spring or early summer, a female frog lays a great many eggs, each one surrounded by a layer of clear, tough jelly. The jelly holds the eggs together in a mass. Some fish eat them (and they have been used for bait), yet many of them survive. If you see a mass of pretty little blue-black spheres, held together in transparent jelly near the edge of a pond or stream, you have found frog eggs.

They develop quickly, becoming longer until they are bean-shaped. The larger end becomes the head, the smaller end becomes the tail—and then it wriggles away as a tadpole. You can watch this strange process of transformation, called metamorphosis, if you take some

This bullfrog was stalked, caught — and brought home from a hike to become a pet

eggs home and put them in water. A large glass jar makes a good container. It should be kept in a shady place. Do not screw a lid onto the jar, but protect the eggs by tying a piece of cheesecloth over the open top.

The tadpole has gills like a fish, but as the little creature grows up these disappear and nostrils form while lungs develop internally. An adult frog breathes air like a land animal, not water like a fish, but most frogs must be kept damp or they will die. Legs sprout, the tail is absorbed into the growing body, and then the frog is an adult.

A frog has a very long thin tongue with a sticky end. To catch insects in flight, the frog flips its tongue out so fast you can barely see it. Except in captivity, this animal does not like to eat anything but live food. A large frog will eat a whole worm. It blinks each time it swallows, because doing so works muscles that push the food down.

Not all species of frogs will thrive when kept as pets. If you take one home, put it in a terrarium (a glass-sided cage sold at pet stores) or in an open-topped box with high enough sides so your pet can't jump out. Put in some dirt and grass, a rock or two and a pan of water. If the animal refuses to eat for more than a day and a half, free it in the woods, near water, or it may die.

People think of frogs as croaking animals. Actually, they make other sounds as well. Some of them trill and some of them make a booming sound by inflating and deflating an air sac in the neck. A frog or toad can sing even underwater. When you think how many flies and mosquitoes and other insect pests they devour, their nighttime singing seems like beautiful music. I have often listened to it contentedly, nestled in my sleeping bag and dozing off as the concert proceeded. Another wonderful thing about frogs is that their legs are considered a delicacy, not only by people but by fish. A small frog makes even better bait than a glob of frog's eggs or a tadpole

Besides stalking frogs and other animals, you should learn to read their tracks. A good way to start is to practice reading the tracks of fellow hikers. Study their footprints. Was a track made by a person running or walking? Could he have been walking backwards to fool you? (If he was, the heel may make a deeper print than the toe, and the prints will be close together and not very evenly spaced.) Was he carrying a heavy load? Was a track made by a youngster or an adult? How long ago did the person pass this way? (New tracks have sharp edges without loose leaves, twigs or other debris in them.) There are pictures in this book to show you how the tracks of some common animals look. You will learn to recognize others from experience, and soon become a skillful woodland detective.

Learning to read tracks is easiest in snow. All of these prints were left by cottontail rabbits

It's fun (and good practice for construction chores around camp) to build a woodland shelter. Such a shelter can be anything from a simple lean-to to an elaborate tepee like this one

9

THE FIRST OVERNIGHT HIKE

On an overnight hike there is more time and opportunity than on shorter hikes for getting acquainted with animals and plants. After dark, for instance, if you shine a flashlight in a frog's eyes, you can catch the animal more easily than by stalking it in the daytime. Many wild creatures become most active at night, and if you arrive at your hiking destination early, you will have time to explore both before and after dusk.

The location of your camp will partly determine the varieties of plant and animal life you can find. Many people like to follow a coastline on their hikes so that they can camp near shore, listen to the beating of the surf at night and collect beautiful shells from the beaches. The creatures that live in and near shallow waters are worth studying, for many of them are strange indeed. Did you know that various starfish species have different numbers of arms and that there is a tiny eye-like organ at the end of each arm so that the animal can see in all directions at once? Did you know that some water plants have built-in bubbles so they can float? Did you know that there is a mollusk (a hard-shelled animal with no internal skeleton) called the "money tusk" which looks like a miniature elephant tusk? It can be found on beaches· from Alaska to California and was valued by the Indians as wampum.

After setting up campsite, two hikers rest by the fire

In other areas you will find different but equally unusual wildlife, and various field guides (as well as your own observation) will reveal enthralling facts about them. Here are a few examples: Many burrow-digging animals enter their dens backwards so that they can face and fight any predator that might attack. The sparrow usually lives about four years. The poorwill, a southwestern bird related to the whippoorwill, is the only bird known to hibernate. A female fly lays its eggs less than a week after it is hatched. In the southern uplands of the United States during the fall, late-blooming red cardinal flowers and velvet lobelias attract female and juvenile hummingbirds, which drink the sugary nectar of the flowers to store energy for their fall migration; the females and young birds seem to need this nectar more than the adult males.

Certain animals are likely to turn up in almost any location. Wherever you camp, there is a good chance of finding turtles of one kind or another. These hard-shelled reptiles are usually divided into three classes: tortoises, which live strictly on land; terrapins, which are very hard-shelled, horny-beaked fresh-water and tide-water animals valued for food; and "true" turtles, which reside partly or entirely in the water, often in the sea.

Some of the larger turtles live up to one-hundred and fifty years. The diamondback terrapin, a type that's easy to catch, is found along the Atlantic and Gulf coasts, and may grow as large as eight inches. It has angular rings on its dull olive top shell and is yellow on the bottom. Painted turtles, found over much of North America, grow about five inches long and have handsome red, orange and yellow markings. A snapping turtle can be recognized by its long neck, powerful jaws and sharp, pronounced beak. It has a long tail with ridges like those on a crocodile and a rough shell with a saw-toothed rear edge. The snapping turtle never feeds out of water because it can't swallow unless its head is submerged. It can, however, inflict a painful bite whether in or out of the water, so avoid this species. Most turtles will eat raw chopped meat, small crabs, bits of fish, worms, lettuce and commercial foods sold in pet stores.

Venomous snakes were mentioned before, but it should be stressed that most snakes are harmless and very beneficial. They are good hunters, and the smaller ones help to control insect populations, while the larger ones eat rodents. A southwestern species called the worm snake is blind. It is about eight inches long, burrows under stones or into the earth during the day, and only comes out at night. A southeastern type called the mud snake or hoop snake is harmless, but there is a ridiculous superstition that its pointed tail can sting and that it can roll itself into a hoop and chase you downhill. A mud snake can move fast, but a racer snake can move even faster and is able to slither up trees with amazing speed. Some species of king snakes will eat poisonous snakes and are immune to venom.

Snapping turtles (above) are easy to recognize and should be avoided, but the diamondback terrapin (below) makes a good pet

Reptile study is an interesting pastime for campers; these Scouts are looking at a garter snake, which is not only harmless but beneficial

Garter snakes are the most common varieties in North America. There are eleven subspecies, some of them little more than a foot in length and others over three times that long. These dark, handsomely striped snakes feed on frogs, and toads and worms. They make nice pets. The young are born alive (rather than in eggs, like some snakes) in the summer. Snakes periodically grow new skins and then shed the old ones, so hikers occasionally find discarded snakeskins in the woods. What strange and fascinating creatures these reptiles are!

Another animal that sometimes frightens overnight hikers needlessly is the skunk. This fat, furry, two-foot-long black and white animal is actually friendly, and will not spray you if you know how to treat it. Skunks like to roam at night. It is not very unusual for one to wander near camp, attracted by the smell of food. Although they feed largely on agricultural pests such as potato bugs, tobacco worms and Japanese beetles, they also look for mice, rats, chipmunks, lizards, fruit and sometimes scraps of food that humans put into garbage receptacles.

There have been instances of young skunks

If handled carefully, skunks are friendly animals; this one has become a good pet

Left, a forest like this holds enough dead branches and fallen saplings to build shelters and make fires without harming the living trees

Above, in a Vermont field near a campsite, vegetation includes thistle, rose bushes and other wild flowers

Below, a sleeping bag can be set up on a soft fern bed held together with notched logs

Left, lengths of running ground pine and tree club moss can be twined into "Indian necklaces" or used for lashings to hold up a lean-to

getting their heads caught in such "traps" as marmalade jars. If you are ever present when that happens, pick the skunk up quickly by the tail and hold it at arm's length. In order to spray its horrible-smelling, skin-burning fluid, it must brace its feet on something and elevate its tail.

It can't do any harm when held by the tail, far enough from your body to prevent it from bracing its feet on you. Carry it away from camp and, with a stout stick, axe or hammer, tap the jar just hard enough to break it off without hurting the animal. Then fling the skunk as far as you can. When it lands it will run off, unhurt, without spraying you. In fact, it uses its spray only as a last resort to defend itself.

In some areas skunks are disliked because they steal duck and pheasant eggs, but in most regions they do no harm and they eat many crop-destroying insects. They are related to the mink and otter, and a skunk is often as playful as an otter, though roughhousing with one is definitely not recommended. With scraps of food, you can sometimes make friends with a skunk, and then you can watch how the animal behaves around camp. A son of wildlife photographer Leonard Lee Rue once tamed a young skunk so nicely that he was able to hold and pet it.

If you do ever get sprayed by a skunk, scrub your skin with carbolic soap and water, or wash with gasoline in severe cases. Wash your eyes with water. Soak your clothes in tomato juice for six hours, or wash them in ammonia or chloride of lime and then hang them in the breeze. Since the scalp is the hardest part of the body to "deskunk," you may have to get a very short haircut if you mistreat one of these animals.

How many natural wonders you see on an overnight hike is determined largely by how observant you are. You should not wander far after dark, but the late afternoon is a cool, pleasant time to ramble through the fields and woods. In a Vermont field one summer afternoon, I found a patch of ground no bigger than five feet wide where I could photograph two kinds of clover, wild roses, raspberries, blooming thistle, milkweed, black-eyed Susans, goldenrod and Queen Anne's lace. I know of a hiker who took a springtime walk in the Great Smoky Mountains of the South, and in just a few minutes found pink trailing arbutus, white hepatica, trilliums, yellow lady's slipper, lily of

the valley and bloodroot. If eaten fresh, lily of the valley (like buttercups and many other plants) is said to cause severe indigestion, but it has been used in making heart medicines. Bloodroot is in the poppy family, and the Indians made a dark red dye from its roots. It's fun to discover flowers that are new to you, find their pictures in field guides and then read about them in books on natural history.

Although you will want to do lots of exploring, your first overnight hike should not be a real camp-out unless you are with older companions who have taught you camping techniques. In later chapters you will learn about fire-making, camp cooking, sanitation and so on, but a first overnight trip need not demand too many skills. If the weather is cool, you may even choose a destination where you do not have to sleep outdoors. Your destination might be a hostel, a rural motel or a lodge in one of the state or national parks. Hostels are supervised shelters, usually with kitchen facilities. Very popular among European hikers, they are becoming popular in the United States as well —especially among bike hikers.

An excellent guide to camping places in North America is Woodall's "Trailering Parks and Campgrounds," a 1,120-page directory with a supplement of sixty-four maps covering the United States, Canada and Mexico. The book's information includes camping regulations and fees, the location of dumping stations and descriptive material. Another excellent reference is the Rand McNally "Guidebook to Campgrounds," which lists more than 15,000 campgrounds in the United States and Canada, with locator maps next to the listings. In the back of this book are dozens of clip-out coupons that entitle you to discount rates at many good commercial campgrounds. (The fees for overnight stops or longer visits at such spots vary but are never expensive.) You can also get pamphlets and guides from the National Park System and from camping organizations.

If you decide to sleep outdoors, you'll need one vital item of equipment in addition to those already described—a good sleeping bag.

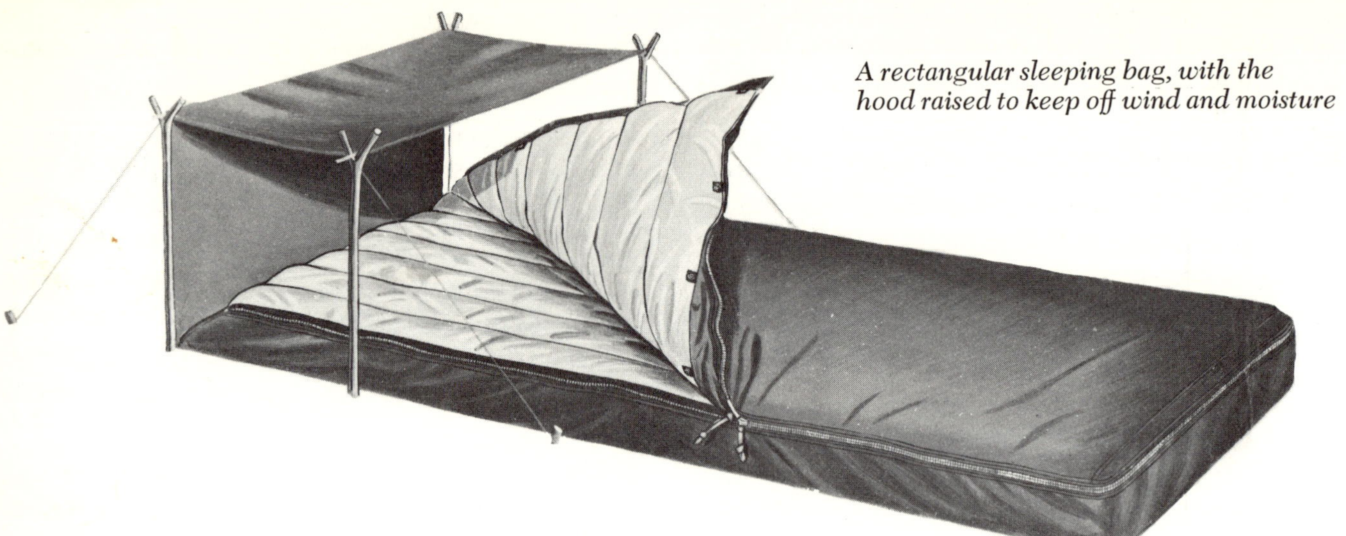

*A rectangular sleeping bag, with the
hood raised to keep off wind and moisture*

Sleeping bags come in many models, but there are two main types, the rectangular design and the "mummy" bag. Many campers, particularly in cold climates, prefer the mummy bag, which actually does look like a mummy when a person is inside it. This is a form-fitting sleeping bag with an adjustable hood that keeps your head warm. Most mummy bags are filled (between the outer covering and inner lining) with good insulating material, and they offer the most warmth and least weight possible. However, this type of bag feels too confining to some people—including me. You can get accustomed to a mummy bag if you don't try to move around inside it but rather let it roll when you roll. Both mummy bags and rectangular ones are available in extra-large sizes for unusually big people, but an oversized bag is expensive.

The rectangular type usually has a long flap with drawstrings at the top end. When you roll the bag up, this flap neatly goes around it as a covering, and can be tied tight with the strings. When you open it for use under the stars—not in a tent—the flap can be propped up as a hood to protect you from rain, dew and wind.

Here's the best way to prop up the hood. After spreading the bag out flat, drive into the ground at the top corners two pointed sticks that are forked at the upper ends. These sticks should reach about a foot and a half above the ground. Lay a straight stick across the forks, in line with the top of the bag. Drive two more

forked sticks into the ground on each side of the bag, about two feet toward the foot of the bag from the first two, and again lay a straight stick across. Now you have a frame for the hood. Pull it up over the top horizontal stick and back toward the foot of the bag over the second stick. You can keep it in place with the drawstrings—by tying them to the second set of forked sticks or by driving small pegs into the ground and tying the strings to those after pulling them taut. You can also tie the strings to a handy sapling.

If you're in a hurry, you don't have to look for forked branches or sticks. Use straight ones and simply slip the edges and corners of the hood over them. But don't pull the hood very taut, or the tops of the sticks may rip the material.

Before buying a sleeping bag, you should check the outer covering, the insulating filler, the lining and the closure. The outer material should be water-repellent, but it must not be waterproof. It has to "breathe" or dampness will collect within it. Some bags have a rubberized bottom. This keeps out ground moisture, but interferes with dry cleaning. A separate ground cloth is a better idea, and you don't even need that if you have an air mattress or a tent with waterproof flooring material.

The insulation is the most important factor. Pure goose down gives the greatest warmth with the lightest weight, but it is found only in very expensive bags. For most camping, dacron insulation is quite warm enough. It, too, is light, and is featured in a majority of bags. The lining is most often flannel and many bags have a second, removable flannel liner that snaps in and out. This gives extra warmth and helps to keep the bag itself clean. The removable liner can be laundered, but the rest of the bag should be dry cleaned.

The best method of closure for a sleeping bag does not consist of snap fasteners (although these will do). Nothing beats a rust-proof, heavy-duty zipper which goes all the way down one side and clear across the bottom. It's simple to open or close even from the inside; it makes the bag easier to crawl into, and it permits you to open the bag out flat and air your bedding. A good idea is to turn your bag inside out and hang it up in the breeze during good weather. This will air it out very well.

As for night clothes, a good sleeping bag keeps you warm enough so that you will generally be comfortable in clean underwear. However, some campers prefer a sweat shirt and sweat pants as outdoor pajamas, because they're warm, soft and cover the whole body. In very cold weather, a long suit of insulated (quilted) underwear is even better—though you may feel like you're roasting if you wear that sort of thing in a good sleeping bag on a warm summer night.

If you sleep outdoors on your first overnight hike, this is a perfect time to try one or two woodcraft projects—making a lean-to shelter and making a fern or pine needle bed. To make the bed, the only tool you'll need is your axe. For the lean-to, you may need no tools at all or you may need your axe and possibly some rope; it depends on the type of foliage where you camp.

The first thing to remember when you undertake this kind of project is that a good outdoorsman almost never chops down a live tree. Doing so is senseless killing, and if enough campers chopped down trees the forests would soon disappear. Sometimes a landowner does what is called "weeding" his trees, cutting down certain scrawny or sick or overcrowded ones so that the others can grow better. A landowner may therefore give you permission to cut down a few unhealthy saplings, but be sure to chop only those that he specifically points out. As a rule, you will be able to find enough fallen saplings, logs and branches to build whatever you wish without damaging live trees. If the wood is not waterlogged or rotten, a structure made from it will be sturdy enough for camping purposes.

A "mummy" sleeping bag, a form-fitting type with an adjustable hood for the sleeper's head

Let's begin with the lean-to, because you may want to put the bed inside it. A lean-to shelter is basically a windbreak, a shed-like structure composed of a sloping roof with one end propped up by trees or poles and the other end resting on the ground. From the side, therefore, it has a triangular shape. A good protected spot for it is with its back to a slope or woods, but it's more important to build it with its back to the prevailing wind so that it will protect you from the gusts.

The size of the lean-to may vary, so you must decide whether you want to put your provisions in it, or have one person or two people sleep in it. A big structure is harder to build than a small one, and takes longer. A good size is usually about five feet high and six feet wide if two people are to sleep in it. Therefore, you begin by finding two straight trees about six feet apart in a good location for the structure. If you are lucky enough to find two that have Y-shaped crotches at about the same height (and no more than five or six feet up) you can simply lay the crosspole—on which the roof will rest—across the two crotches. Otherwise, you can use rope to lash it across at the right height.

Then find two more long sapling poles to form the left and right edges of the roof. Lay them on a slant, with one end dug into the ground and the other resting over the crosspole, just inside each of the two trees. To complete the frame, lay one or two more sapling poles at the same slant at intervals along the crosspole. These should be lashed to the crosspole to keep them securely in place. Sharpen the ends of some shorter branches and drive them into the ground along each side of the frame to form an upright side frame. Now weave still more short branches in among the roof and side frames. The structure can then be covered with a thatch of long grasses or

Here's a sturdy lean-to frame, employing two strong crosspoles lashed to saplings

With its poles dug into the sand, this beach lean-to is good and steady; a piece of canvas serves as a windbreak

The author's wife and son weave a thatch roof into a criss-cross lean-to frame

Projects such as building miniature shelters can be fun for the younger campers

ferns, or with brush. Evergreen brush from pines, cedars, spruce, larch, fir or hemlock is best, because the dense foliage of needles makes a good covering, and the many little twigs catch in the frame, thus keeping the brush in place. Other possible materials are extra blankets or ground cloths, sheets of plastic or strips of birch bark taken from fallen trees.

I built a large, sturdy lean-to in Vermont without even using rope for the lashings. I found two trees with Y-shaped crotches at a convenient height and sufficiently level with each other, and I laid the crosspole through these. Then my children and I gathered lengths of running ground pine and tree club moss (locally known as ground cedar). These are long, strong ground vines that really belong to the fern family but look like flexible ropes of pine and cedar. We used the vines to lash the frame poles in place and then covered the structure with evergreen branches and brush gathered from the forest floor. The leftover strands of running ground pine were braided into Indian necklaces.

The frame of a fern-and-evergreen bed has taken shape here, and is partly filled with a foundation of cedar and spruce branches

The author's daughter has taken time out from camp chores to go exploring—and has found a fascinating land snail

A similar vine is the Oregon spike moss, which grows in Oregon, Washington, Canada and Alaska. It hangs in long, dense mats and can be used both for lashing and for thatching. Most parts of the world have vines or similar plants that can be utilized for tying together parts of structures you build in the woods.

The pine needle or fern bed is a simple framework of four logs placed in a rectangle on the ground, with their ends interlocking so that the bed doesn't fall apart. You fill the space inside the rectangle with a thick mat of pine needles or wide-leafed ferns, cover this with a ground cloth and spread your sleeping bag on top. This gives you a delightfully soft and fragrant bed.

The two logs that go lengthwise should be about seven feet long, and the logs forming the head and foot of the bed should be almost three feet long. With your axe, chop a large, V-shaped notch near each end of each log, about halfway into the wood. Make sure that the two notches in a log face in the same direction. Then position the logs on a flat piece of ground you have chosen as your bedding place, with the notches on the head and foot logs facing up. The notches on the long side logs face down and lock right into the matching head

and foot notches so that nothing can slip. It's as easy as that, and I've slept better in some pine needle beds than at home.

* * *

INFORMATION SOURCES

Woodall's "Trailering Parks and Campgrounds" directory can be ordered for $3.95 from Woodall Publishing Company, 500 Hyacinth Place, Highland Park, Illinois 60035.

The Rand McNally "Guidebook to Campgrounds" is available for $3.95 from book and map dealers or can be ordered from Barcam Publishing Company, Box F, Palos Verdes Peninsula, California 90274.

For information on camping in National Parks, order a fifteen-cent pamphlet called "Camping Facilities in the National Park System" from the Superintendent of Documents, Government Printing Office, Washington, D.C. 20025.

For general hiking and camping information, plus lists of other sources, write to the National Campers and Hikers Association, 7172 Transit Road, Buffalo, New York 14221.

For descriptive literature and details on overnight shelters and campsites in Europe, write to the travel bureaus of any countries where you plan to hike; among the nations that have good hiking areas and encourage this activity are Great Britain, Scotland, Ireland, Belgium, France, Germany, the Scandinavian countries, Switzerland. Each of the Canadian provinces also has a travel bureau that will provide maps and information.

10
BIKE HIKES TO EVERYWHERE

Just about everyone enjoys riding a bicycle, and in areas where there are reasonably smooth trails or roads with light traffic, bike hiking has several advantages. Since it takes you where you're going a lot faster than walking, cycling gives you extra time for outdoor activities when you reach your destination. It also enables you to cover longer distances in a day, or on an extended tour, and it's one of the best methods of exercising to keep physically fit. By planning bike hikes on lightly traveled roads, you can avoid the heavy automobile traffic along the highways. Cycling can therefore be done in perfect safety if you know how to plan—and if you abide by these riding rules:

☆ Obey all traffic signals and regulations—red and green lights, one-way streets, stop signs and so on.

☆ Slow down at all street intersections and look to the right and left before crossing.

☆ When you're on a road used by motor vehicles, keep to the right (or to the left in countries where traffic proceeds on the left side of the road); stay in single file and don't ride close to vehicles ahead of you.

☆ Ride in a straight line; don't weave in and out of traffic or swerve from side to side.

☆ Watch for cars pulling out into traffic and, when passing a place where cars have stopped, watch for opening doors.

There's no danger from traffic along this Florida bike-riding route

Some bikeways are dotted with interesting tunnels and covered bridges

☆ Always signal with one hand when you are about to stop or make a turn. If you get off your bike, make sure you leave it in a safe place, far out of the line of traffic.

☆ Give pedestrians the right of way. In fact, avoid sidewalks whenever possible, and when you must cross a sidewalk use extra care. Sometimes it's a good idea to get off your bike and walk it across.

☆ Never race or do any stunts on a road where there is any traffic whatever. Try to maintain a steady, safe speed.

☆ Never ride two on a bike, and don't even carry any packages that might obstruct your vision or interfere with your control of the bicycle. (Instructions for proper packing, with bike bags or baskets, will be given later in this chapter.)

☆ Attach a loud signaling device—such as a squeeze horn or bell—to your handlebar, and use it to warn of your approach if you think another cyclist, pedestrian or driver has failed to see you coming.

☆ Install or clip a white light on your bike up front, and attach a reflector light or reflector strips (available as stick-on tape) at the rear. If you must ride after it begins to get dark, wear white or light-colored clothing and switch on the headlight.

☆ Be sure your brakes are operating efficiently, and keep your bike in perfect running condition.

You can find scenic routes, outdoor activities, hostels and sometimes even nature trails and camping sites—as well as added safety—by using "bikeways" for most of your bike hiking. Bikeways originated in Homestead, Florida, where they are called Bicycle Safety Routes. They have now spread throughout the United States and across much of Canada and Europe. Bikeways are systems of secondary roads, usually parallel to main streets, and often with roads or trails branching off into woodlands, toward lakes or camping grounds. They are marked with big signs—usually featuring a picture of a cyclist—which not only help to point the way but also warn drivers to slow down and proceed cautiously along those stretches where cars are permitted. Even on the portions of road where automobiles are allowed, few motor vehicles are present because the route is designed to prevent speed.

If you were to bike hike all the way across the United States from Los Angeles to New York City (as Olympic athlete Bob Richards did in 1969), you could probably do about a third of your riding along bikeways. Maps showing these routes are distributed by local bike clubs, chambers of commerce, Boy Scout and Girl Scout troops and similar civic, outdoor and bicycling organizations.

To give you an idea of the kind of hike you can take on a bicycle, let's look at some of the bikeways now being maintained, beginning on the East Coast of the United States and traveling westward. In the Catskill Mountains around Fallsburg, New York, Sundays are set aside for bike hikes during late autumn when the foliage has taken on every color of the rainbow and every shade of every color. On those days, no automobile traffic is permitted along the route, which takes in seven miles of private roads plus forty-five miles of town roads and some lengthy trails along abandoned railroad beds. The local park provides bike hikers with picnic, rowing, fishing and camping facilities.

Many little-used rural roads have been turned into cycling trails

Also in northern New York State, there's a fifteen-mile bikeway around Webster, and a whole system of bikeways around Rochester. The routes were surveyed by the Rochester Bike Club, and maps are distributed by this club as well as by the local chambers of commerce, the Girl and Boy Scouts and a bank, the Marine Midland Trust.

Down South, near Kingsport, Tennessee, bike trails wind through the mountain country where wildlife abounds and there are many beautiful spots to camp. In Florida, bike trails are laid out along the edge of the Everglades and past many historic sites such as old Spanish missions and forts. One of these bike paths, around Coral Gables, is twenty miles long, and there's a sixty-miler through Dade County, from Homestead to Coral Gables to Miami to North Miami Beach.

The Midwest has a vast network of roads for bike hikers. Ohio has a Northern Tour, Southern Tour and Eastern Tour that practically blanket the state. From the city of Dayton to the local Scout camp, thirty-nine miles out in the country, there's a bikes-only trail, and nearby is the fifty-mile Historic Trail for cyclists. Ohio also has a Covered Bridge Bikeway, and there's a beautiful bicycle tour of covered bridges through Parke County, Indiana. These picturesque and historic old bridges are reason enough to follow the bikeways, but there's an added attraction: some of the covered bridges (as well as some uncovered ones) cross streams that are ideal for picnicking and fishing. Be sure to bring along a "take-down" fishing rod —the kind that can be pulled apart into short lengths and conveniently tied on your bike frame or over a rear fender.

At Mackinac Island, Michigan, and at Wild Horse Island in Polson, Montana, there are wildlife areas where no automobiles or motorcycles are allowed, but bikes are welcome. In fact, wildlife refuges in a number of places across the United States are open to hikers, with or without bikes, as long as the local regulations are obeyed and care is taken not to harm the animals or the plant life.

Bikeways differ in layout from one locality to another, but they all have similar basic advantages. Around Sheboygan, Wisconsin, for example, you can find a sixty-mile-long "children's safety route." No child is expected to ride that far in a day, but it is possible to ride just a short stretch of the route or to stop overnight along the way. Another sixty-mile route has been laid out through the parks of Omaha, Nebraska; this bikeway system employs special paved roads that are wide enough for bikes but do not permit car traffic.

In and around Medford, Oregon, a whole system of bikeways was built with the help of local Boy Scouts, who contributed their labor as well as some paving materials where necessary. There are many other bikeways, some of them outside of the continental United States. If you would like to ride a bike through the forests of an exotic place that lies even farther west, Hawaii Volcanoes National Park has long, beautiful bike trails.

A first bike hike should be no longer than fifteen or at most twenty miles, and that distance should be covered in easy stages, with a stop for lunch, and at least a couple of stops to rest,

Bikeways are clearly marked, and often lead to good camping sites

Favorite bikes for hiking are these "roadster" or tourist models

stretch and walk through places of special interest. American Youth Hostels, an organization which provides low-cost overnight shelters throughout the country (and which is affiliated with the International Youth Hostel Federation) furnishes detailed information, guidebooks and other aids for bike hiking in the United States and abroad. AYH advises cyclists to condition themselves for hiking by riding their bikes only five miles a day for about a week. Toward the end of the week, you should try to cover this distance in half an hour, and then try it with a ten-pound load in your bike's baskets or bags. Next you try to go ten miles in ninety minutes, resting at the halfway mark, and after that you gradually work your way up to longer distances. Following a month of this kind of practice, a healthy adult should be able to ride fifty miles in a day—and with a full pack. However, my advice is to make most one-day bike hikes no more than twenty-five or thirty miles long. This gives you enough time for stops to rest, explore, go fishing, eat lunch, take pictures or engage in other activities, and if you stop once in a while you won't become too tired.

To avoid discomfort and fatigue, it's also important to assume a correct riding position, and to adjust the saddle and handlebar properly. Actually, you should not make a long trip on a brand-new bicycle because the saddle ought to be used a few times beforehand and thus broken in. You can adjust the saddle correctly for your build by raising or lowering it, moving it forward or backward and tipping it upward or downward. Sit squarely on the saddle, and place one leg straight down, with the pedal on that side at its lowest point. Adjust the saddle so that, with your leg straight, you can rest your heel on the pedal. The front tip of the saddle should be directly over the crankshaft (the round part from which the pedal arms extend) or not more than two inches behind it. And the top of the saddle should be horizontal or tipped very slightly forward—never backward.

Adjust the handlebar so that the top of the center post is at about the same height as the saddle. Then tilt the handlebar up or down until you can grasp the handgrips without bending your wrists more than a little bit. Handlebars come in two basic shapes—the "dropped" type which curves downward and the raised type which curves upward. Racing bicycles employ the dropped type because the lower your hands and back are, the more power you can put into your pedaling. For hiking, however, either design is fine.

You can put your hands in any of three positions, and it is relaxing on a long ride to shift from one to another occasionally. The basic position is the obvious one—with your hands right on the grips at the ends of the handlebar. The second position is with your hands on the curves of the bar, and the third is with your hands on the level part just in toward the center from the curve. You will find that a low position gives you the most power and control, and the least wind resistance, but you will have to straighten up a good deal of the time to avoid back fatigue.

Seated firmly on the saddle, you should have the ball of each foot on the pedal. You can buy toe clips which are helpful in maintaining a good position for long trips, though they were originally designed for racing. Try to develop a smooth, continuous rhythm of pedaling. If you make the mistake of "saving your strength" by attempting to pedal and coast, pedal and coast, pedal and coast, you'll have slower going and will become tired. The only time to stop pedaling is when you're going downhill. Some people enjoy timing themselves; someone who hasn't done much long-distance bicycling can usually pedal comfortably at a rate of one revolution per second—sixty a minute. A good cyclist can move the pedals around at least eighty times a minute, but an average of seventy is right for flat travel without any interference from strong breezes. Let your ankles bend a little with each stroke, giving a slight extra push beyond the low point of the pedals.

For short rides, just about any bicycle will do. However, for real hikes the balloon-tire bikes are not recommended, even though they seem to remain popular among children. They are too heavy, the tires tend to go flat too easily, they usually have only one gear, or "speed," and the brake mechanism—worked by the pedals—prevents getting full power from the chain drive.

The best all-around bike is the "roadster" type, also called the tourist bike, the lightweight or the English model. It weighs about thirty to forty pounds, has relatively thin tires with inner tubes, employs two hand brakes—one for the front and one for the rear rims—and usually has a slightly upturned handlebar and a three-speed gear which you can control with a finger. For level going, you leave the gear level at its high position, but flick it down to second or low for medium or steep uphill going; this will force you to pedal more slowly but will put extra power into each stroke, or revolution of the pedals.

There is also a type called the club bicycle which is pretty much the same as the roadster but has dropped handlebars and lighter construction. It's a bit more expensive. Racing bikes are still more costly, and they're built for

Bikes were perfect transportation for these girls on a trip to the Cape Cod seashore

speed at a sacrifice of comfort, so they are not recommended for general use or hiking.

Whatever kind of bike you get, you will find that both boys' and girls' models are available in several frame sizes. If you are less than five feet six inches tall, you should get one with a twenty-one to twenty-two-inch frame; the frame should be one inch bigger if you are from five feet six to five feet eight inches tall, another inch bigger if you are over five feet eight inches tall—and still another inch bigger if you're a towering six-footer-plus.

One excellent accessory for a bike hiker is a pair of pack bags or baskets which can be attached so that they hang down on each side of the rear wheel. I prefer the bags to the baskets, because they are flexible and therefore hold more clothing, food and hiking equipment. They are made of canvas, plastic or leather; the material doesn't matter much, as long as it's light and durable. There's usually a flap, with a buckle and strap for closing it. In loading these bags, the important thing is to balance them. If you have much more weight on one side than the other, the whole bike will be off balance. This can slow you down, tire you out and sometimes even cause a fall. You'll rarely need more than thirty pounds of gear, and fifteen pounds to a side is about the most you should ever try to haul on a hike. Half of that is usually enough to include food, a camera, a first-aid kit, sleeping gear and accessories.

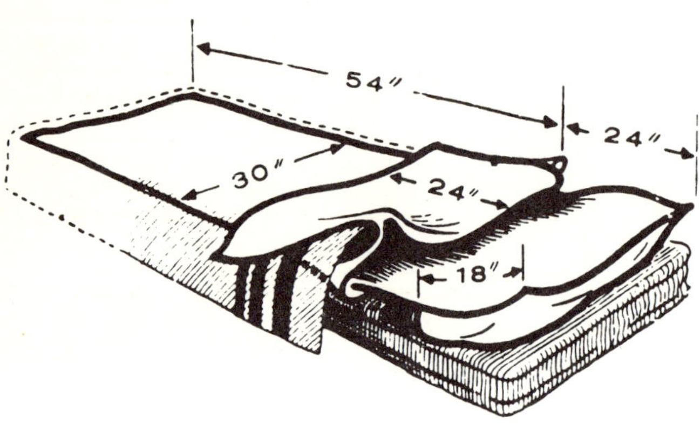

Many bike hostels require you to have your own "sheet sleeping sack"—a top and bottom sheet sewn together at the edges, with a built-in pillow case at one end

You won't need a sleeping bag if you take advantage of a roadside or trailside hostel for overnight shelter, but many of these hostels require you to have a "sheet sleeping sack" which you place on a cot that is provided for you. Mattresses and blankets are also provided, and also a kitchen where you can cook your meals. A sleeping sack can be bought through local councils of the American Youth Hostels, or you can make your own. It's really nothing but a top and bottom sheet, sewn together around the edges and with a built-in pillow case at the top end. The sack should be about seventy-eight inches long and thirty inches wide, and the top sheet should have a loose twenty-four-inch flap that can be turned down to protect the blanket.

Many hikers take advantage only of a hostel's kitchen facilities; instead of using the dormitories for an overnight stay, they sleep out in sleeping bags and tents. This is more fun, though it involves loading the bike with extra weight.

Hostel associations publish annual handbooks which are printed in the language of the country where they are issued. Many use symbols with a key in several languages to help foreign bike hikers. These books list all the hostels, with their locations and facilities. Many of the European handbooks contain maps, and they can be bought for fifty cents each from AYH. At the same price, American Youth Hostels can also furnish large topographical maps of England and Scotland. In the United States and Canada, maps are available (many of them free) from bike clubs, local Youth Hostel councils and the tourist bureaus of states and provinces. To get a state map, just mail your request to the State Tourist Bureau at the capital city of the state that interests you; no other address is needed.

* * *

INFORMATION SOURCES

Here are the addresses of organizations that can send you guidebooks, maps, tips on hiking and hosteling and other information:

American Youth Hostels, Inc., 20 West 17th Street, New York, New York 10011. Bicycle Touring League of America, 260 West 26th Street, New York, New York 10001.

International Bicycle Touring Society, 846 Prospect Street, La Jolla, California 92037.

League of American Wheelmen, 5118 Foster Avenue, Chicago, Illinois 60630. Canadian Wheelmen's Association, 4000 Beaubien Street East, Montreal, Province of Quebec, Canada.

For a price list of equipment and accessories designed for hosteling hikes, write to American Youth Hostels, New York Metropolitan Council, 14 West Eighth Street, New York, New York 10011. And for literature on how to plan a bike-hiking vacation, write to Mr. Robert Cleckner, Field Director, Bicycle Institute of America, 3812 North Lowell Avenue, Chicago, Illinois 60641.

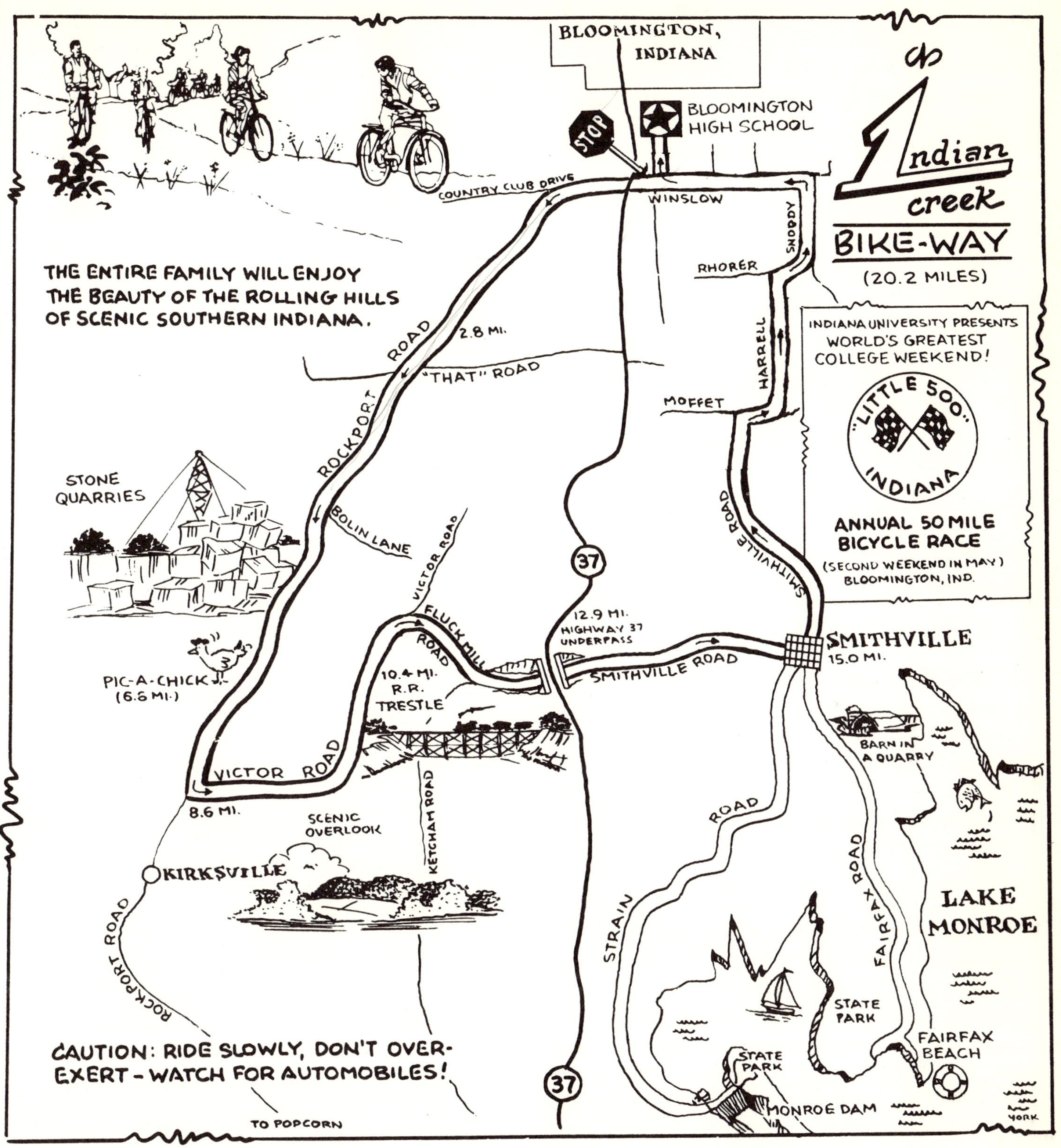

Maps of bike routes are available from bike clubs, Youth Hostel councils, tourist bureaus and civic groups. Here's a typical one, showing 50 miles of safe and beautiful country roads around Bloomington, Indiana

A camp stove, eating utensils and an ice chest, or cooler, are among the things that can add to your comfort and pleasure during a long camp-out

WHAT TO TAKE CAMPING

There are many ways to go camping: with a station wagon, a hard-top trailer, a truck camping vehicle, a trailer-tent—or on horseback, by canoe, on a bike or afoot. Some of these methods require more equipment than others, and a couple of them also demand special preparations.

Horseback camping trips are usually made with a pack train, and the riders should be led by a guide who knows the region, knows horsemanship and can teach you tricks and techniques that result in a safe, happy journey. Like the captain of a ship at sea, the guide is "chief" of the expedition; his instructions must be obeyed. Furthermore, before going on a horseback trip a camper should have at least several weeks of riding experience. If you haven't been around horses much, you should take lessons at the nearest riding academy, dude ranch or horse-rental stable.

A canoe or boat trip also demands a leader, someone who knows the waters, knows how to handle the craft and can teach skills along the way. Again, his instructions should be obeyed. And before taking a trip by water, a camper must know how to swim even though he or she will be wearing a life jacket while afloat. If you're not a good swimmer, you can arrange to take lessons at a Girl or Boy Scout facility, Red Cross, "Y" or some other agency that offers a swimming program.

Once a campsite is chosen, one of your first jobs is to put up your tent

Special skills are required for canoe trips. You should master swimming and boat-handling, and you should have an experienced leader

Special skills such as horsemanship or swimming may be important only on certain kinds of camping trips, but there are many more basic skills that are necessary, no matter how or where you camp. After you've hiked into the wilderness on foot a few times and camped outdoors, with or without a tent, you will know the most important techniques for any kind of outdoor living. You'll be used to selecting and handling your equipment properly, and you may even begin to feel that the use of a camping vehicle or commercial campground is a bit tame for you.

The first thing to do, of course, is to gather your equipment. Clothing and sleeping bags have already been discussed, so the next item to consider is a tent. Its selection must depend partly on the number of people who will sleep in it, but a large tent—designed for use by several people in a family or group—is recommended only if it is to be set up and left at one camping site for a fairly long period. A big tent is invariably heavy, and is never really compact even when folded or rolled very carefully according to the directions that come with it. If a campsite is to be occupied for less than two weeks, it makes more sense for a group to carry several two-man tents than to lug sections of a single larger one.

On the other hand, even when I'm camping alone, I rarely use one of the tiny models known as "pup tents" which must have been designed for one very small person. You can't move around comfortably inside such a tent and, sometimes more important, you may want some additional dry space for stowing your gear. For most purposes, therefore, a two-man tent is ideal; it will usually measure about five by seven feet, which is ample space for two sleeping bags and packs.

Many materials are used for making tents. In my opinion, waterproof ones are unsatisfactory because when waterproof material is used for anything but the floor it tends to make the interior clammy, hot and uncomfortable. Read the descriptive tag that is attached to most new tents, or question a sporting-goods salesman, bearing in mind that you want your shelter to be fairly water-repellent (with a waterproof floor cloth), very tough and light in weight. It should also have some ventilation; I like models that feature a rear "window" with bug-proof netting and a zip-down flap.

Most modern tents have zipped netting at the front entrance, plus closable front flaps for windy or rainy weather and a built-in floor coated with rubber or plastic. If your tent lacks a floor, you should spread a plastic or rubberized tarp, poncho or similar rainwear as a ground cloth to keep dampness away from you and your sleeping bag. (If you ever need an emergency shelter, incidentally, a large tarp can also be draped over a leaning pole, with its sides pegged down, or can be draped between two trees like a lean-to.)

Tents come in a variety of shapes as well as many sizes. Among the small ones, simple triangular models—the "pup tent" shape—used to be most popular, while the most common larger ones were cabin-shaped or "umbrella" types. All of these tents had interior poles to hold them up, and they're still made that way. In recent years campers have begun to favor tents of more modern design, which sometimes have strange shapes because they rely on *outside* supports so that all of the interior space can be employed for sleeping and for stowing gear.

Probably the most common type comes with light metal rods which have sockets so that they can be put together to form an exterior frame. The tent roof and corners can be attached to this outside frame with loops of elastic cord. This type has light metal tent pegs, also called stakes, that can be driven into the ground at the corners and along the sides, but the structure is so sturdy that you don't even need the pegs unless there's a high wind. Regardless of

Horseback camping trips are usually made with a pack train, and should be led by a guide who knows the region. Riding practice is necessary before making such a trip

your tent's design, always remember that metal stakes work very well in firm ground, while homemade wooden ones hold better in soft dirt or sand. Wooden stakes should be a foot or a foot and a half long, with a long four-sided point, and they should be driven in at about a forty-five-degree angle.

Frequently, a store that sells tents will rent them as well, and will also rent other camping equipment. Many campers rent the gear for their first few excursions so that they can decide which type they like best; tents and other equipment can then be bought. The extra rental expense doesn't seem very important when you consider that an American or Canadian camping tour costs only about a third as much as a vacation of the same length with stops at motels and restaurants. In Europe, too, camping expenses are comparably low.

Some sporting-goods stores provide checklists of personal items that should be carried by campers, but you can easily make up your own. Before starting on a trip, you should go over the list carefully to make sure you haven't forgotten anything.

You will want to add items to suit yourself, but here is a list I use: underwear, socks, extra boots, swim trunks, shirts, sweater, hat, sunglasses, poncho, light jacket, gloves, first-aid kit, compass, maps, soap, small metal mirror, razor, shaving cream, toothbrush and toothpaste, towel, box of facial tissues, roll of toilet tissue, handkerchiefs, canteen, collapsible metal cup, water-purifying tablets, rucksack, sleeping bag, tent with frame rods and stakes, hatchet, pocketknife, sheath knife, sewing kit, waterproof matches, candle, magnifying glass, take-down fishing rod with line, nylon leader, reel, lures,

This is a hunter's "base camp," set up to be used for a two-week stretch. A special indoor camp stove is in use, and its pipe extends out of the right side of the tent

extra hooks embedded in cork and kept in metal container, flashlight or lantern, binoculars, camera and film, field guides, coil of rope, insect repellent, roll of aluminum foil, cooking and eating utensils.

In case you're wondering, the magnifying glass is another fire-starting gadget, like the metal match that was mentioned earlier. If you lose your matches, run out of them or get them wet, gather a little pile of dry tinder, hold the magnifying glass over it so that the sun is concentrated and makes a hot, bright spot under the lens—and in a couple of minutes the heat will become so intense that a little flame will start. Aside from starting fires, a magnifying glass is useful for examining rocks, leaves, insects and other natural specimens.

Still another item that you ought to consider is a collapsible camp stove. There are many foldable, compact models with one, two or three burners. Except for the little single-burner models, a good one usually has sides and a back that pop up to serve as reflectors. These reflectors not only help in cooking food quickly and thoroughly, but can also direct welcome warmth toward a tent, a sleeping bag or a lean-to shelter. There are special chimney stoves for use inside large tents, but no fire or ordinary portable stove should ever be used inside a shelter, for this can be very dangerous. However, a device called the Coleman space heater is safe to use inside a tent, and it provides welcome warmth.

If there's no wind, a small fire can be built about five feet from the shelter entrance, but it should be farther away if there's even a slight breeze. Be sure there are no branches or leaves hanging low over your fire or stove. A campfire, cooking fire or stove should always be on cleared ground, with no leaves, twigs or even dry grass for five feet around it. This means that the first thing to do in building a fire is to clear a ten-foot circle of ground so that the fire can be located at the center of the cleared spot.

Generally, I like to build a small stone fireplace, line it with aluminum foil to act as a reflector, and then build a wood fire—and I will

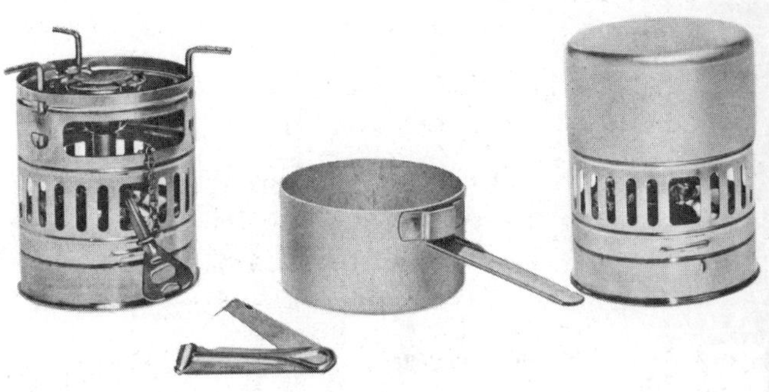

Three common portable camp stoves: above, a two-burner Coleman gas model with built-in reflectors; a single-burner Primus with a tiny reservoir of gasoline and a top that becomes a cooking pot; below, a single-burner Primus Grasshopper model, which attaches to a disposable cylinder of propane fuel

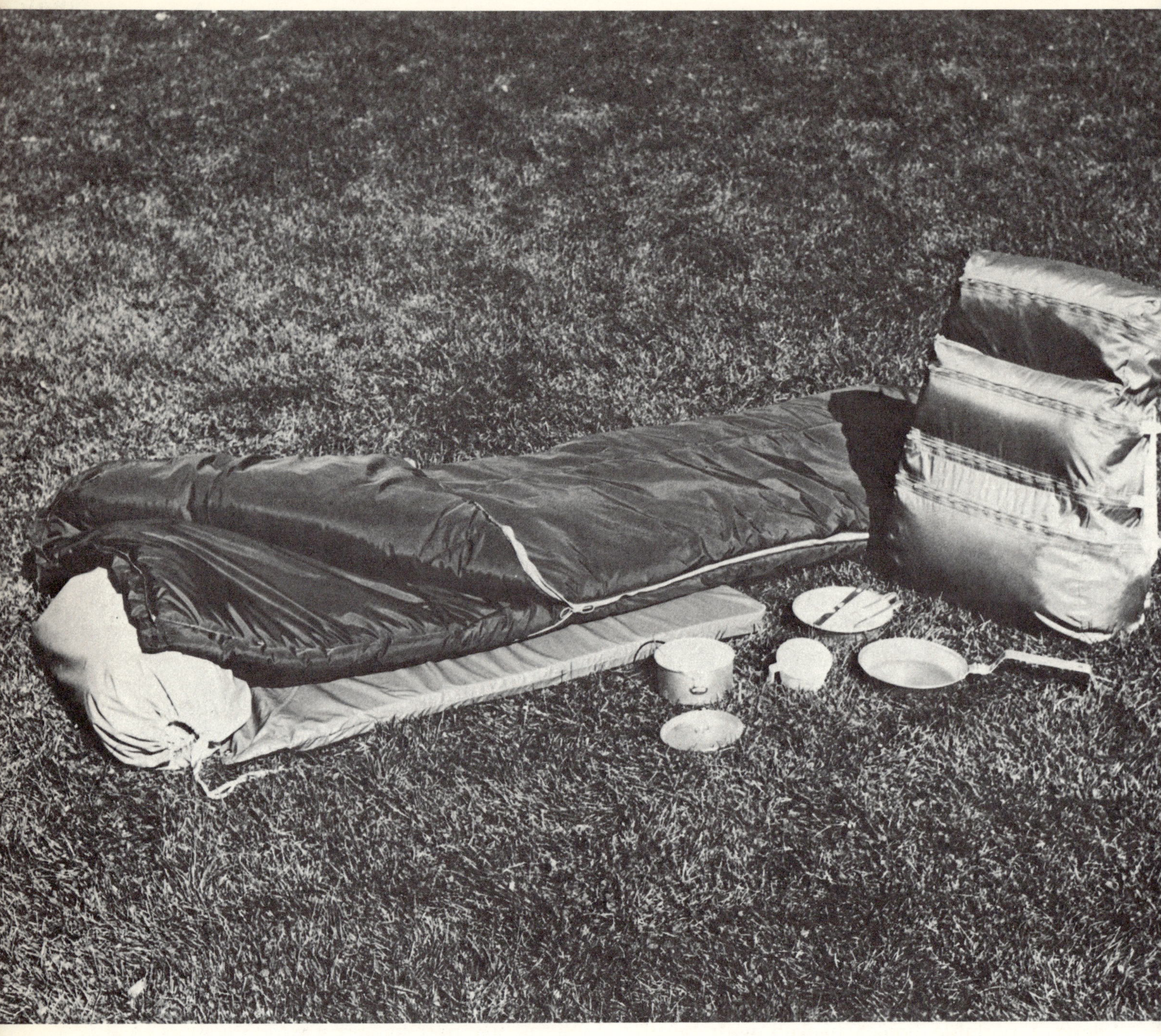

teach you how to do this in the next chapter. I do, however, use a small camp stove to heat up quick snacks or to cook meals for more than two people. There are three basic kinds of portable stoves. One burns gasoline (slowly and economically) from a little tank; the second type burns kerosene in the same manner, and the third burns compressed propane gas from a cylinder. Gas is slightly more expensive than the other fuels, but the compact cylinders do away with the need to carry or pour gasoline. The tank or cylinder can be shut airtight, and the flame is adjustable with either type. All three kinds of stoves are light, compact, easy to cook with and completely safe if you handle them with normal care and follow the instructions that come with them. One of the least expensive and most efficient stoves to operate is the Primus kerosene model.

It is possible to enjoy a meal in the wilds even if you don't have a single cooking or eating utensil aside from a knife. I have often folded heavy-duty aluminum foil into cooking pots and drinking cups, and I have wrapped it around potatoes and ears of corn for roasting. I have also used a forked stick to hold food over a fire—and to hold it to my mouth once it cooled sufficiently. "Roughing it" that way can be fun, but for an extended trip you should have at least some basic metal utensils: dishes, cups, knife, fork and spoon, frying pan, cooking pot, ladle and coffee pot. Before you go camping, you can find everything you might need in your own kitchen. If you plan to be in the wilds for some time, however, it's better to buy a camp cooking kit, because this will be much lighter and more compact than ordinary kitchenware, and will provide you with extra utensils. Sporting-goods stores sell such kits, usually with each utensil nesting inside a slightly larger one so that the whole collection can be packed into very little space.

Careful planning is the key to eating well in camp. Use up the perishable foods first, and then go on to dried and canned foods, with occasional treats such as fresh-killed fish or game and fresh-picked fruits and vegetables. (Extreme care must be used in gathering wild fruits and vegetables; the safe and good-tasting ones will be discussed in Chapter Sixteen.) If you're going to be in camp for some time, take along a portable cooler packed with perishables; when you're hungry, a camp cooler is worth more than its weight and space.

Menus should be planned in advance, and a camp cook should be elected or the members of the party should agree on how to rotate the job. The cook must figure out how much food one person might eat per day (campers have big appetites) and then multiply it by the number of people in the group. A typical first-day menu, including perishables that ought to be used up quickly, might include a breakfast of orange juice, bacon and eggs, toast and milk or coffee; a lunch of sliced tomatoes and cucumbers, cold cuts, potato chips or sticks, cookies, milk or tea; and a dinner of chicken, green beans, fresh potatoes, fresh cake or fruit and milk or coffee. But by the third day, your meals might be a breakfast of canned fruit, ham, pancakes or French toast and coffee; a lunch of cheese and canned luncheon meat or canned tuna with tea, coffee or powdered milk in water; and a dinner of stew, roasted corn, salad or canned fruit, candy and coffee, milk or tea.

Although experience will show you which camp foods work out best, I want to mention several camp treats that my children, my wife and I have enjoyed. For example, French toast made with stale bread and powdered eggs is delicious; pancake, biscuit and muffin mixes are wonderful. Dehydrated potatoes are excellent mashed and are fairly good scalloped, fried or "hash-browned." Rice, noodles and spaghetti are fine. All sorts of freeze-dried foods (which are frozen and dried in a vacuum and retain their natural color, shape and texture) taste just about as good as fresh meats and vegetables. Freeze-dried foods are a great boon to campers because they keep "fresh" for years at almost any temperature. Concentrated-food kits are sold in some sporting-goods stores. They offer variety and make fine lunch packs.

Of course, nothing in the world—including grilled trout—tastes as good in the morning as a fresh-caught perch, coated in cornmeal and flour, sprinkled with just a little salt and pepper, and deep-fried in bacon fat. It may even be true that nothing in the world tastes as good in the evening, either.

* * *

After a long hike and the work of pitching camp, it's great to sit by a fire in the evening. This is a time for telling stories and singing songs

12

PITCHING CAMP

Now let's suppose you've obtained your trail maps, packed your gear and hiked to the general area where you want to spend your time. Where and how do you pitch camp?

The first thing to do is find the very best site. You may notice a beautiful view from the top of a high hill, but such a spot will probably be too windy; on the other hand, along a valley floor there may be a pretty little stream that looks inviting, but it may become a torrent in a heavy rain. A flat space halfway between the valley and the crest of the hill would be much better.

Try to pick a site near water but not right at its edge. And if you camp where you aren't absolutely certain there is safe drinking water from a well, spring or brook, purify it by boiling it at least five minutes—or, better yet, fifteen. Purifying tablets should be used as an added precaution or emergency measure only.

Look for a level spot but one with good drainage. A flat, clear space with gravelly soil covered by tough grasses is about perfect because it will usually drain well. You may have to clear away some brush or rocks, but the effort is worth the resulting comfort. An ideal camp site also has a supply of fallen wood nearby. It will be needed to build your fire and keep it going—and it will also be useful for making tent pegs, or holders to hang a pot over a fire,

These hikers have made camp on a level spot near a hill that blocks the wind

Three people can work together in putting up a tent. While one person is busy clearing away brush, debris and stones from the area, the others spread the tent flat on the ground, put up the frame, attach the tent material to the frame and drive in the tent stakes

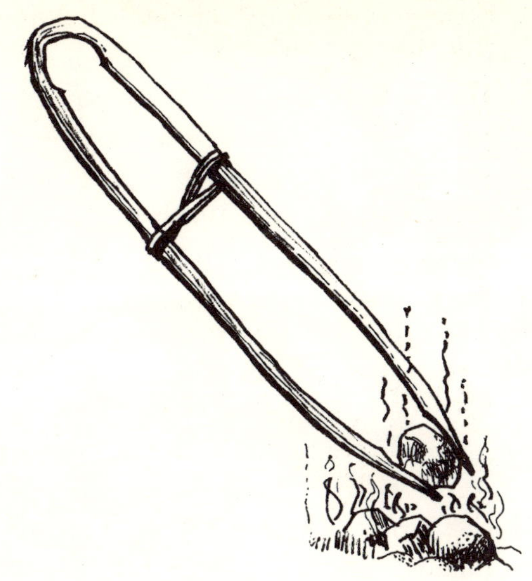

*Fire tongs can be made by bending a green branch
into a U shape and tying it with leather bands*

or all sorts of other things. Dry wood is best for
the fire, but a fallen branch that's still green
and springy is perfect for making fire tongs for
handling hot coals. Bend the branch into a thin
U, tie it in that shape with leather bands, then
thin it slightly at the bend for flexibility and at
the tips to create flat gripping surfaces. Wood
is essential for many purposes, and a clearing
surrounded by woods that give shade is a comfortable and lovely site.

In cold weather, your tent should face away
from prevailing winds, and it will be best to
place it with its rear to a hill or some protective
woods. In hot weather, place it where it will
catch the breeze and be in the shade most of
the time. As a general rule, a tent should face
to the southeast; that way, it gets the morning
sun but is apt to be in the shade during the
warm afternoon, and it will also shield you
from strong winds.

The easiest way to pitch a tent is for two or
three people to work together—and it might be
a good idea to practice in a backyard before
trying it for the first time in the woods. Every
new tent comes with a sheet of instructions
which are fairly easy to follow. The first time
you put one up, it may take you fifteen or

twenty minutes, but after that a two-man tent
should require no more than six or eight minutes. One person clears away brush, debris and
stones, and does any ground-leveling that may
be needed. The other two spread out the tent,
put the frame together and erect the shelter.

Begin by spreading the tent flat on the
ground, facing in the direction you've decided
on. Then put up the frame and attach the material. If you use homemade wooden stakes, cut
notches in them for the rope; the notches must
be small or the pegs may split. If you have an
old tent that needs some rope replaced, bear
this rule in mind: sash cord is best for small
tents, quarter-inch rope for larger ones.

You will remember that good tent material
is water-repellent, not waterproof. But you can
make it rainproof. As soon as it's up, sprinkle
it with water. This is especially important with
a new tent. When the material dries it will
tighten slightly, which will keep it from sagging, catching water in the sagging spots and
leaking. If it rains (or looks like it will rain),
loosen all your tent ropes just a tiny bit to
allow for shrinkage; otherwise, everything
should be taut. If you use a short length of
inner tube as part of your tent line, it will have
enough spring so that you can always keep it
taut. To avoid tripping over ropes and pegs,
you might tie some or all of the ropes to handy
trees, strong bushes or exposed roots. This is a
particularly good idea in front of the tent,
where there is the most traffic.

In very dry areas or where the drainage is
good, that's all there is to putting up your shelter. Certainly, if your tent has a built-in floor
you will be ready to unroll your sleeping bag
and start a fire. But there is an added precaution that's sensible in case of rain, particularly
if you're not certain about the ground's drainage. This precaution is a drainage ditch, sometimes called a rain trench. It should be about
six inches wide and six inches deep, and it can
be dug with a shovel, the blunt edge of your
hatchet, a stick or any other handy tool. I often
take along a wide garden trowel for the purpose; this same tool is very good for all kinds of

digging chores—burying fish bones, making a pit fire for roasting, or even digging a latrine ditch.

Some camping manuals advise digging a rain trench only on the uphill side of a tent. I dig one all the way around the tent and extending in front just beyond the pegs, and then I dig a little drain-off ditch leading away several feet from the main trench. This will drain the earth so nicely that the ground inside your tent will stay dry even in a heavy rain.

As soon as all tents are set up, a camp council should be held, and another council should be held each evening. Although the camp cook may have been chosen before starting out, there are other matters to be decided. A routine ought to be set up so that someone different will serve as dishwasher for every meal—no one likes to do that chore all the time. Someone else should gather firewood and start the fire or tend the stove, while another person should scout the area and dig a latrine trench.

This trench should be located in a secluded spot, downhill and a good distance away from both your camp site and water supply. It should be at least two feet deep, and narrow enough to straddle. A small shovel, entrenching tool or garden trowel will do the job with fair speed. Leave the dirt piled along one side so that some of it can be scraped back in to cover human wastes after each use of the latrine. (Some campers pack chlorinated lime and sprinkle it in after each use, as this disinfects and helps to deodorize.) Next to the trench, hang a roll of toilet tissue on a forked stick, and cover it with an empty can or plastic bag so that rain won't ruin it.

If extra privacy is desired, you can hang up tarps or old blankets around the trench, or build a screen pretty much as you would build a frame-and-brush lean-to shelter. You can even fashion a small sign and hang it near the entrance to let people know when the latrine is in use or vacant.

For a more sophisticated—and comfortable—latrine you can make a sapling-pole bench over the ditch. A little way past each end of the trench, drive two long sharpened stakes into the ground, angling them in toward each other at a forty-five-degree angle so that they cross and can be lashed together very securely. One of the stakes at each end should be long enough (at least four feet) so that a back rest can be lashed across. Once the sets of stakes are dug in

To keep the ground dry inside the tent, you can dig a six-inch-deep drainage ditch, using an ordinary garden trowel

Chores should be shared by all the campers. These four companions have been elected to scour the pots after a big lunch

and lashed at each end, lay a long log or strong, thick sapling pole across them to form a bench-like seat above the trench for its entire length. Lash it securely in place and then lash on another pole higher up as a back rest.

Since building a latrine is enough digging for one camper or even two, another member of the party should dig a garbage pit—also downhill and at a good distance from the camp, the water supply and the latrine. It, too, should be at least two feet deep. It should be in a cleared spot, where fire will present no danger. This is where trash will be dumped—and it should be burned out each morning. After the burning is done, make sure the fire is completely out. Before breaking camp, the pit should be filled in with earth so that you leave the woods as you found them—clean and beautiful.

Since washing can be done in a stream or with heated water next to the fire, only one more major job is left in setting up and maintaining your camp—making your fire. Although it isn't necessary to build a fireplace, I prefer to, whenever I can find large, flat stones. There are three reasons: First, stone retains warmth, so the fire stays hotter longer and cooks things with a good, even heat; second, stone acts as fireproofing insulation, so there is no danger of flame or hot bits of firewood tumbling out and spreading flames along the ground; and third, a flat stone back and side structure can be lined with aluminum foil to make a fine reflector oven and to direct warmth toward the tent or tents. Just be sure to make the fire far enough from the tents so that there's no danger from sparks or flames. Also be sure to use dry stones, as heat can make damp ones crack or even explode.

Clear all leaves, twigs and brush from the fireplace area—a space ten feet across. Then lay several flat stones on the ground to form a bed measuring a foot and a half across or more. Prop up additional flat stones to form the sides and back, digging them into the ground a little so that they won't topple. Line the bottom, back and sides with foil. Now make a loose pile of kindling on the floor of the fireplace. The best materials are dry leaves, grass, wood shavings and twigs with a few larger twigs dropped on top to keep the flame going once it's started.

A few "fuzz sticks" will help, especially if it's hard to find enough dry tinder. A fuzz stick is a small dry branch along which you've cut a series of loose curls, like peelings, with your knife. It works particularly well if it has some loose, dry bark to help it get started.

Get your lit match in underneath the loose kindling—if you drop it on top, it will burn for a moment and go out. It's best to light the kindling in two or three places. Then start piling on larger twigs and small, dry branches. At first there should be more air space than wood, because a fire needs oxygen or it will go out. To get it well started, you may have to put your face down near the ground and blow at the bottom of the fire, thus creating an upward draft that ignites the slightly larger pieces of wood.

Incidentally, if you're alert you may find the very best kind of kindling pile ready-made in the form of an abandoned bird or squirrel or mouse nest, or a heap of dry, shredded bark. And don't forget that a metal match or a candle can help start a fire under difficult conditions.

This is a small criss-cross fire, built in a stone fireplace lined with aluminum foil, which serves as a reflector. The author is blowing on the kindling to get a good flame started

There are three basic ways to build a good fire once it's started: the tepee or V structure, the criss-cross fire and the hunter-trapper fire. The tepee fire is easiest to make and is best for just getting warm or for making a quick, easy meal. You simply pile sticks loosely over the burning tinder in a tepee shape, starting with pieces about six inches long and working up to branches a foot or so in length and perhaps three inches thick. The center of the fire will burn hottest and fastest; as the ends of the sticks burn away, you carefully push them in toward the center, and pile on more as needed. The V fire is based on the same idea but with less than half of the tepee used so that the fire has a V shape, usually held together by two side sticks that are slightly larger than the others. This kind of fire is easiest to make if it's propped against the back of a fireplace. It's smaller than a tepee fire but burns more slowly and lasts a little longer with less work.

Aside from the fact that it burns up quickly, the big trouble with a tepee fire is the difficulty of holding cooking utensils on top of it unless you put up a spit (two forked green sticks with a third one going across and the pots hung from this) or prop a griddle over it on a pair of green logs or some rocks. And a griddle may get in the way when you try to feed the fire.

To make a fast, easy fire with a fairly level top for cooking, the criss-cross structure works well. You start by making a small tepee fire. Then, around its outer rims, you build up criss-crossed side walls of sticks—the way the sides of a log cabin are built up with two logs on opposite sides and then two more crossing them on the two other sides, and so on. Each pair of sticks you lay on should be a little closer to the center of the fire than those underneath; otherwise they may roll off the blaze. The criss-cross structure also has one drawback, for it's rarely big enough for more than a single pot or pan, and you have to work to keep its top reasonably level.

A hunter-trapper fire combines the first two fire structures in a different way, and is best for cooking a large meal or staying warm for a long time. This kind of fire is laid between two "fire dogs"—big rocks or large, green logs that will hardly burn. The fire dogs should not be exactly parallel to each other but slightly closer together at the rear end. This will allow you to

Here is a tepee fire, being used to cook dinner. Notice how the camper has wedged a branch between two heavy logs to form a crane that holds the pot over the fire

This is a hunter-trapper fire, with two thick logs serving as "fire dogs" to hold the grill over the glowing embers

get at the front end easily and will provide room to put big pots and pans on top, but it will also give you a narrower rack at the rear where you can cook with smaller pots and pans.

Between the two fire dogs you simply build a tepee or V fire. If you want to have it last a little longer, make it an inward-sloping criss-cross fire. It will last still longer, and burn slower, if you lay most of the firewood facing in one direction, lengthwise between the fire dogs.

Whatever structure you use, keep your fire small. Big fires create a hazard, take a lot of work and generally burn the food. As a matter of fact, it's best to make your fire before you prepare any food and then let it burn down a bit, although soft woods will burn up very quickly. Cooking can be done better—more evenly—over hot coals and embers than over leaping flames. If you want your fire to last a while and continue to give off warmth after the meal is over, put on a couple of larger logs, but don't go to sleep while they're actively flaming.

An untended fire is always dangerous. The fire will last longer, but will also be a little smoky, if you use slightly green logs. If, like most campers, you enjoy the smell of a campfire, a bit of smoke won't bother you. And if the fire is built in a sturdy, safe fireplace and has burned down to glowing embers, you can then go to sleep in its warmth.

The next morning, after breakfast is over and the cooking fire has burned down to smoking embers, it's fun to send smoke signals. You can work out your own code for the puffs of smoke. To send up signals, the campers simply hold a blanket a couple of feet above the embers and flap it to release smoke puffs. Be careful not to get the blanket too near the fire.

For fast roasting of corn or wieners or for toasting marshmallows, cut a few forked or pointed sticks. Use fairly hard or green wood because you don't want the sticks to catch fire and drop your food into the flames. For hanging stew, soup, cereal, water or coffee pots over

A frame can be built to hold pots over a fire. The wood for the frame should be green, and it should be built high enough to prevent burning. Notched branches can be used as hooks for the pot handles

When the fire has burned down to smoking embers, you can send up smoke signals — but be careful not to get the blanket too near the fire

a fire, drive two long forked sticks into the ground on either side of the fire; they should be at least three feet high to prevent burning. Then lay a green pole across them. Find two or three green sticks with branches growing out at an angle to form a hook that can go over this pole. To hold the pot handles, simply cut notches low down on these sticks. Similar hooked sticks can be used to lift utensils away from the fire by their handles without burning yourself.

When getting ready to leave camp, burn and bury all garbage. Then make sure the fires themselves are completely drowned and buried. And then do your best to erase all signs of human use, because the beauty of the outdoors is greatest when it is just as nature made it.

The United States Forest Service maintains more than 14,500,000 acres of government-controlled Wilderness Areas where the land is kept in the same primitive condition as when men first wandered on it. To camp in a U.S. Wilderness Area, you must first check with the nearest Ranger, get a fire permit and take along a shovel, axe and bucket to control fires. This is just as it should be, for it helps to guarantee that the land will continue to be left the way nature made it.

* * *

INFORMATION SOURCES

For information on Wilderness Areas and other fine camping sites, write to the American Forestry Association, 919 Seventeenth Street N.W., Washington, D.C. 20006.

For information on such areas specifically in the West, and also for literature on western dude ranches, horseback trips and canoe trips, write to the Dude Ranchers Association, Billings, Montana 59103.

For further information on Wilderness Areas and addresses of regional offices of the Forest Service, write to the Wilderness Society, 1244 P Street N.W., Washington, D.C. 20007, or Box 1229, Santa Fe, New Mexico 87501.

For a directory of organizations providing recreational aid, literature and facilities, send thirty cents to the Superintendent of Documents, U.S. Government Printing Office, Washington, D.C. 20402. Ask for the directory by name; it is entitled "Private Assistance in Outdoor Recreation."

13
IS THERE A DOCTOR IN THE CAMP?

Here are two essential pieces of equipment for campers: a first-aid kit and a manual on administering first aid

According to statistics gathered by such agencies as the National Safety Council, outdoor activities are safer than staying at home, crossing the street in a city or riding in a car. Even if you do become ill or suffer an injury while away from home, most physicians advise keeping treatment to a minimum until you can see a doctor, because improper treatment can make matters worse. But you should, nevertheless, know what to do in case of an emergency. I recommend studying the American Red Cross First Aid Manual and keeping a copy with your gear for fast reference if the need should arise. In fact, it's a good idea to take a course in first aid at your local Red Cross Chapter.

The contents for a basic first-aid kit were listed in Chapter Five, and you should know how to use this equipment to treat common injuries and illnesses until you can get to a doctor. After reading this chapter you may want to add a few items to your basic first-aid kit, but before doing so you should consult your physician. Some people are allergic to antibiotic ointments, and others are sensitive to antihistamines or even strong soaps; in a case like that, the doctor will recommend substitutes. Still other people are allergic to insect stings, and before going camping they should get a desensitizing treatment from a doctor.

Having mentioned insect stings, let's begin with what to do about them. The stinger of a bee, wasp or hornet, has a tiny poison sac which causes most of the pain and swelling. Unlike most stinging insects, the worker honey-

Like the pilot black snake (above), most reptiles are harmless; in fact, they are helpful to man. A few, however, like the well-hidden rattler (below), are poisonous. When you learn to recognize these you can avoid them

bee leaves its barbed stinger in the wound, sac and all. With a pair of tweezers or a knife blade, pull out the stinger, being careful not to squeeze the little sac. Once a stinger is removed, treat the sting as you would that of a hornet, wasp or other insect, by sucking out the poison and then applying an ice pack or soaking the injury in water as cold as possible. Even an application of plain cool mud will ease the discomfort slightly. It will also help to take antihistamine tablets, following the directions on the bottle or package. You can soothe a sting somewhat with calamine lotion, Caladryl (a preparation combining calamine and an antihistamine) or an anesthetic ointment such as Nupercainal. The best advice is to avoid getting stung in the first place by using insect repellent and by not frightening or disturbing stinging insects.

You can get a headache in the woods as well as anywhere else, and the treatment is to take aspirin as directed on the label of the bottle or tin. Five grains of aspirin every four hours is also recommended if you catch a cold. When you have a cold, eat lightly, drink lots of fluids and, if necessary, use a nasal spray.

If you're subject to motion sickness or nausea, try to prevent it by taking Dramamine or Bonine as directed on the package. For an upset stomach, take milk of magnesia or another antacid over ice. In a one-to-four mixture with water, milk of magnesia is also good as a rinse for mouth irritations, and if you eat a poisonous plant (though there's no excuse for doing so), two to four tablespoons of the same stuff will help you eliminate the poison from your body. The same dose, as frequently as recommended on the label, will cure ordinary constipation. However, if constipation is accompanied by severe abdominal pain, there is a possibility of appendicitis and you must get to a doctor as soon as possible.

For diarrhea, or for dysentery caused by spoiled food (there's no excuse for that, either), take paregoric as directed on the label. Stay on a bland diet, drink plenty of liquids, and if you suspect dysentery, see a doctor.

Poisonous plants can be dangerous externally as well as internally, of course. Poison ivy, oak and sumac were discussed in Chapter Six, but they're worth a reminder: if you know you've touched one of these plants, immediately wash with strong soap to prevent infection, and rinse thoroughly to remove all of the plant oils; if a rash develops, treat it with calamine lotion—and again an antihistamine helps.

In addition to calamine and antihistamine, you might want to pack some oil of cloves or toothache wax. In case of toothache, you can apply oil of cloves directly to the painful spot and take some aspirin. If you lose a filling and have an air-sensitive cavity, you will ease the pain by filling the cavity with toothache wax.

For an earache, gently squirt a solution of boric acid and warm salt water into the ear. An experienced adult should do this, for the ear is a delicate, easily injured mechanism. In ointment form, boric acid helps irritated eyes as well. If you get a foreign object in your eye, rinse the eye with clear water, and if there is discomfort for some time take aspirin and apply boric acid or mercuric oxide ointment. If it still bothers you, tape a soft pad firmly in place to keep the lid from moving. Get to a doctor quickly, if you think the foreign object has remained in your eye.

Abrasions and minor burns can be treated by washing them and then applying an antiseptic-antibiotic ointment and covering with a loose, soft dressing and bandage. More severe burns can be soothed with a coating of petroleum jelly, cold cream, cooking oil or shortening, and they should be dressed loosely with fluffed-up facial tissue or a soft pad. Sunburn can be treated with the same soothing oils, but commercial suntan lotion is better.

Severe cuts should be washed and coated with an antiseptic-antibiotic ointment. The edges of the wound should be held together with a bandage so that the cut stays closed. Profuse bleeding can usually be stopped by applying pressure directly over the wound, and a tourniquet should be used only as a last resort; it should be applied as directed for the particular wound in the First Aid Manual and should be loosened every fifteen minutes.

In the case of a puncture wound, clean it, suck it to get out any infective matter, apply antibiotic ointment and then employ hot soaks for two days. For a "through-wound" (as when a fish hook is jabbed through a finger) coat the hook with an antiseptic and then push it the rest of the way through, cut off the hook's barb and then pull it back out. Then treat the injury like any other puncture wound.

Painful bruises can be relieved by a frequent application of cold water or an ice pack for the first twelve to twenty-four hours to reduce the swelling, followed by hot packs or soaks for the next twenty-four hours. Sprains get the same treatment, and the limb can be kept raised to reduce swelling. It should then be wrapped with an elastic bandage or a tightly applied triangular bandage.

As mentioned previously, foot powder and proper shoes and socks usually prevent blisters, but if you do get one, heat a sewing needle in a flame to sterilize it, prick and drain the blister, apply an antiseptic ointment and cover it with a soft padded bandage.

In the woods, the smallest danger is from animal bites, but there's no sense in taking chances by not knowing how to treat such wounds. Let's begin by reviewing the procedure for poisonous snake bites. The patient should be kept very quiet because any activity speeds up circulation and thereby spreads the venom. A tourniquet should be applied above the wound for the same reason—to retard the flow of poison. The snake's fangs leave two small punctures in the skin. With a sharp, sterile blade, cut an incision a quarter of an inch deep across each of these punctures. Then squeeze or suck as much blood as possible from the wound, spitting it out very frequently; this will remove most of the venom, which isn't harmful when small amounts are taken into the system orally rather than injected into the bloodstream by a bite. Obtain medical help as soon as possible.

By the way, aside from snakes (the rattler,

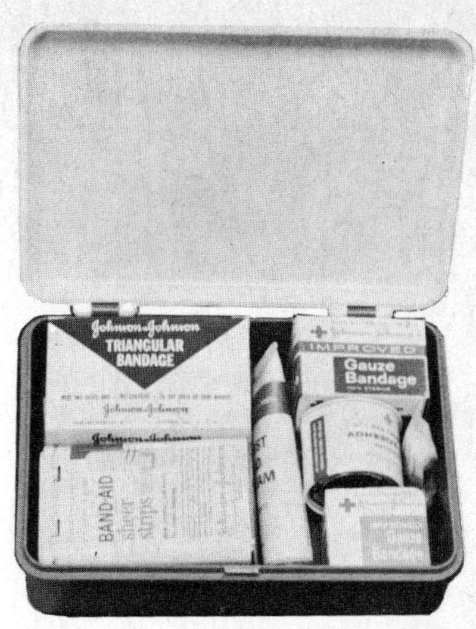

A first-aid kit should contain adhesive bandage strips, adhesive tape, squares or a roll of bandage, elastic bandage, antiseptic, tweezers, scissors, a tourniquet, aspirin and snake-bite equipment

cottonmouth, copperhead and coral snake), the only poisonous reptile in North America is the gila monster (pronounced *"heela"* monster and sometimes called the beaded lizard). This is a big lizard, up to two feet long, but it moves so slowly that bites from it are extremely rare. It is found only in the southwestern desert country, chiefly in Arizona. A gila monster's bite should be treated like that of a venomous snake, and so should the bite of a poisonous spider or the sting of a scorpion.

Other animals are even less likely to bite. If they do, the wound should be treated like a cut. However, it is possible for certain animals to get rabies, and this is particularly true of the dog, cat, fox and skunk. If you ever get bitten by one of these animals, go to a doctor immediately. If the animal is a domestic dog or cat, write down the information on its license tag, if possible, so that you can find its owner and learn whether the dog or cat has had rabies inoculations. If not, you will have to get shots yourself, and no time must be lost in treating this very dangerous disease.

* * *

INFORMATION SOURCES

For information on taking a first-aid course and obtaining the Red Cross First Aid Manual, write to the American Red Cross, 150 Amsterdam Avenue, New York, N.Y. 10023.

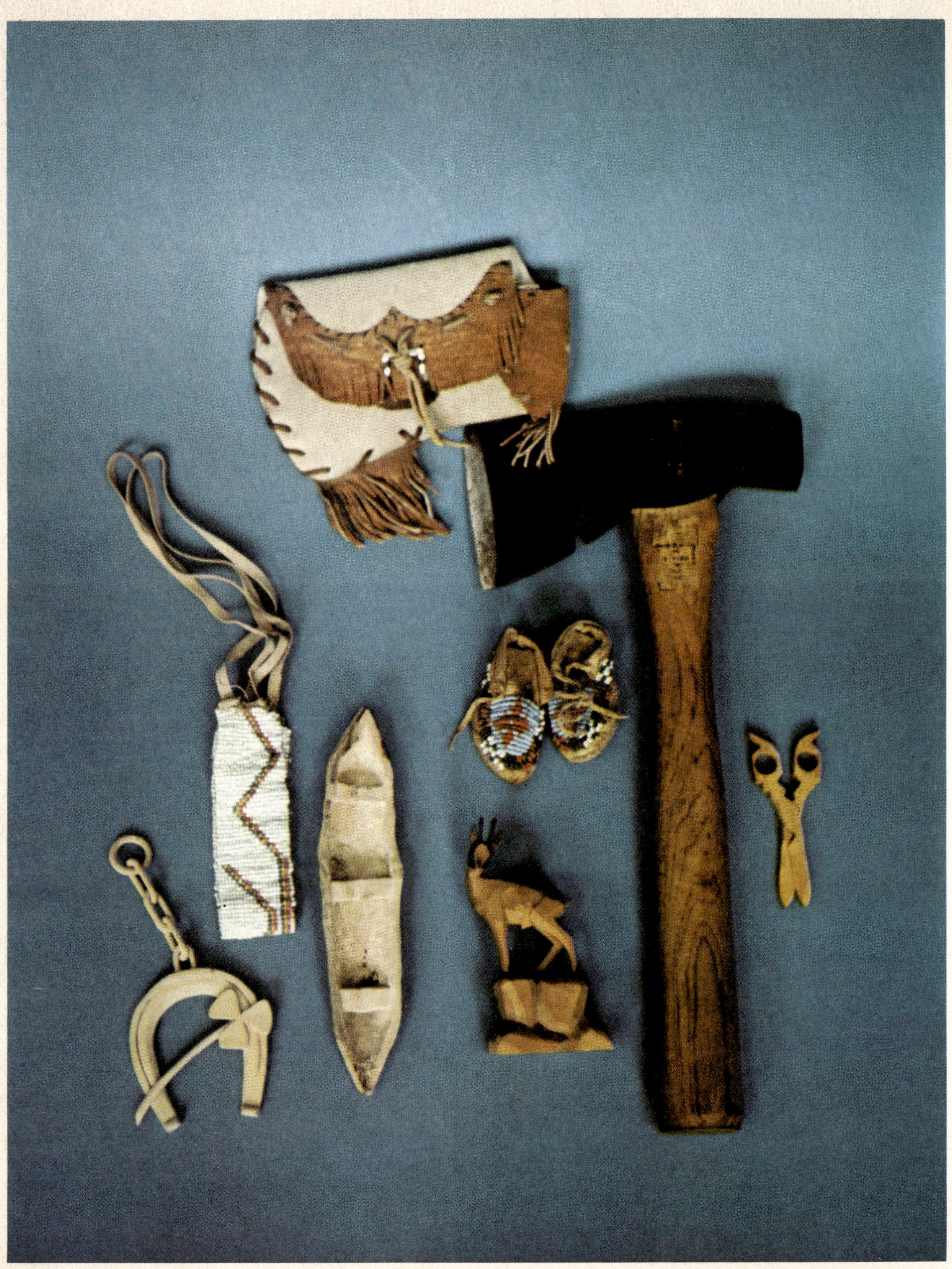

Here are some good examples of camp handicrafts. At top is a buckskin-and-cowhide hatchet scabbard. The beadwork includes an Indian headband and a pair of doll moccasins. The woodcarvings are (from left) a horseshoe, clover-and-chain made from one piece of wood; a canoe; a European mountain goat; and a pair of scissors (also made from one piece of wood and resembling an owl's head when closed)

14

HANDICRAFTS AROUND CAMP

There may never be time enough to get your fill of hiking, exploring and studying nature, but a cold or drizzly day will come when you don't feel like wandering far from your tent. Then you'll want something interesting to do around camp. You can complete literally hundreds of handicraft projects while at a camp site, and the more of them you try, the more dexterous you will become.

On the rare occasions when their packs aren't crammed full, the youngsters in my family like to take along wooden "model kits"— miniature airplanes, racing cars, boats and other things of that sort. In such kits, the parts usually come roughly shaped, but you must finish some of them, fit them together and sometimes paint them. One summer day in a Wyoming souvenir shop we found a couple of perfect model kits—miniature covered wagons of the kind called Conestoga wagons, which were used by the pioneers to cross the prairies. These miniatures, about a foot long and very realistic, were intended for use as lamp bases, but Thomas and Natalie decided they would rather use them to hold collections of rocks and seashells. Building each wagon was an excellent handicraft project, and the whole family helped with whittling a few of the parts for a better fit, nailing together the sides and bottom, attaching the wheels, yoke and brake, installing the frame for the cover and, finally, sewing on the cover itself. This gave all of us practice at several skills, and when we completed the project (at a Vermont camp thousands of miles from where we had bought the wagons), we were proud of the results.

During idle camp hours, this knife sheath was decorated with snakeskin and fringed leather trim

The author's children, shown with two covered wagons they made as a camp project

The woodcarving is a chamois (a European mountain goat). Next to it is a hardened piece of artist's fungus, on which are sketched animals seen in the woods

If you don't feel like working with a model kit, there are lots of handicraft projects waiting right in the woods. As an example, let's start with a whistle, which can be used to signal other campers. Find a small twig three or four inches long and about an inch thick, and split it lengthwise. Hollow out a small depression—not even a quarter of an inch deep—across the center of each of the two flat surfaces. Now place a fairly wide blade of grass lengthwise along the flat surface of one of the halves, centered over the depression. Put the other half on top and use string or thread to tie the two halves together in their original position. The blade of grass works like the vibrating reed in a musical reed instrument; blow hard into the depression and you'll find you have a good loud whistle.

You can get the same effect by holding a blade of grass tightly between your thumbs, holding them to your mouth and blowing between them just below the knuckles. It won't be quite as loud and the blade of grass will probably break every time you blow a long note.

A shriller and more durable signaling instrument is the so-called willow whistle, which isn't always made of willow since any hollow twig will do. Find one about six inches long and plug one end with something solid, such as a smaller twig. Beginning about three-quarters of an inch from the other end, cut the hollow twig at a forty-five-degree angle to give it a diagonal mouthpiece-shaped end. The diagonal surface is the bottom of the mouthpiece, where your lower lip goes. On the other side—the top of the whistle—cut a notch about an inch from the tip of the mouthpiece. This notch should go about a third of the way through the tubular twig. Next, whittle a wooden plug to fit snugly into the mouthpiece. It should almost fill the tube, but the top surface of the plug should be flat so that there's about an eighth of an inch of space between it and the top of the mouthpiece. Now just put the whistle to your lips and blow.

You can vary the pitch to get a musical sound, like that of a recorder, by using the awl-blade of a Scout knife to bore two or three little round holes along the top of the whistle. The note you blow will depend on how many of these holes you cover with your fingers.

With larger bits of wood you can make many more things. For instance, using some string and flat wood scraps you can make a puppet, and perhaps put on a campfire puppet show some evening. Like the holes in the whistle, holes for the puppet strings can be bored with the awl-blade of a Scout knife. Or you can make your own pack board by lashing, gluing and screwing together a bottom and two side slats, then lashing and nailing on three rungs evenly spaced from top to bottom. Holes for the lashings are made the same way as for the whistle or puppet.

Three sapling poles can be lashed together to form a tripod stand for a wash basin; if one of the three poles is long enough, you can also hang your mirror and towel on it. You can find branches of the right shape to be rough-finished into backwoods coat hangers, fire tongs or pot holders. And you can whittle clothing

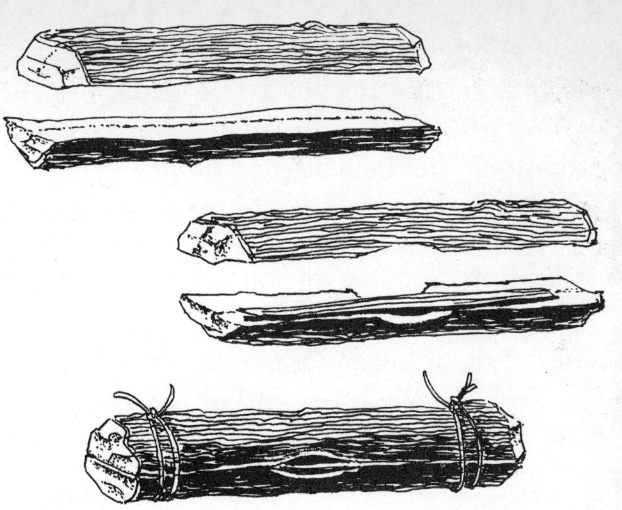

The drawings above show how to make a whistle by splitting a piece of wood, putting a blade of grass between the halves and binding the pieces together again. The little hollow in the center is the mouthpiece

This picture shows how to carve a willow whistle, or hollow whistle, with a diagonal mouthpiece, a plug filling most of this mouthpiece, and a notch cut a little way forward of the mouthpiece

From flat wood scraps and three round branches you can make a pack board. The flat pieces form the bottom and sides; the branches form the cross-pieces

hooks that can be tied to a tree trunk or tent pole. From fallen logs you can chop, saw and whittle stools and benches or a table.

A very useful camp-made item is a "coat tree." To make one, look for a fallen sapling with some branches still on it near one end. Cut these branches off fairly short, leaving just enough of them jutting out to serve as clothing hooks. Sharpen the other end of the sapling to a point and drive it into the ground upright next to your tent. There you have a convenient coat tree on which to hang jackets, ponchos and the like. Whittlers who are artistic sometimes make a coat tree from a fairly thick pole or log, and carve its lower part into a camp totem pole.

Another kind of whittling that's easy and fun is soap sculpture. However, it should be mentioned that some adult campers object to soap sculpture, because the artist almost never wants to let anyone wash with his masterpiece once it's finished. Still other interesting carvings can be made from fruit pits, nut shells and even large berry seeds or cherry stones. Large left-over soup bones can be sawed, sanded and polished into handsome neckerchief slides, while small ones can be made into finger rings or Indian necklaces.

In addition to whittling and building things out of wood, there are many other forest handicrafts. Ground-running vines as well as the inner bark of some fallen trees can be braided into Indian necklaces and bracelets, or woven into mats. Long, tough grasses are even better for weaving mats, and with a little ingenuity these grasses can also be fashioned into human-shaped and animal-shaped dolls.

To make a human-shaped doll, gather a good thick clump of dried grass about two feet long and bend it double so that the ends can form legs. At the other end, where you doubled the grass, shape a head and tie it off with extra strands of grass. Then break off some of the grass body far enough down so that you can form a pair of arms of a natural length. Wrap strands of grass around them to hold their shape. Separate the lower part of the doll into two legs, again wrapping grass around them.

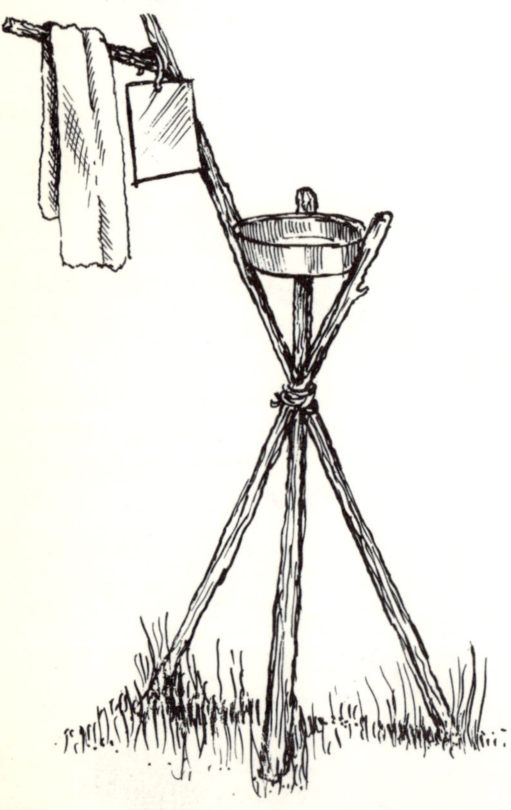

A simple tripod of sapling poles or branches can be lashed together to form a wash stand, towel rack and mirror hanger

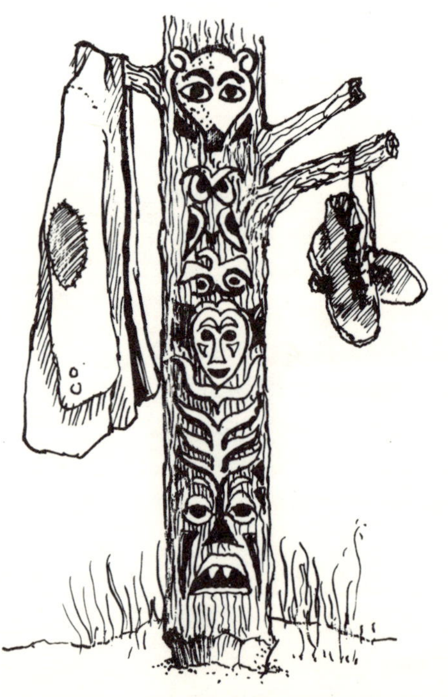

A dead tree or a log, sharpened at one end and driven into the ground, can be carved into a totem pole. Leave the stubs of some branches on it and you will also have a coat-and-shoe tree

Long strands of dry grass can be twisted together, bent into shape, tied with other strands — and molded into an Indian doll

You can make the body or head thicker or rounder by wrapping more grass around it, and you can even weave grass "hair" onto the head. As for the clothing, that, too, can be made from grass, or it can be sewn together from rags.

If you prefer, you can give the doll an Indian apple head. Just carve the features of a face into a peeled apple and set it in the sun to dry for several days. It will shrivel slightly and turn red-brown. When it's all dried out, it looks like the face of a little old Indian.

A far different skill that sometimes provides humor around an evening campfire is shadow-craft. Place the fire reflector, or a flashlight or lantern, so that light shines on a tent wall. Then put your hands up near the wall, holding them in various positions to throw shadows that look like all sorts of animals, birds, monsters and people. It takes a bit of experimenting to make a realistic shadow picture, and the results are occasionally strange, horrible or downright funny. The campers can take turns trying it.

One of my favorite woodland pastimes is to hunt for and make things out of artist's fungus —which also goes by such names as shelf fungus, bracket fungus, shelf bracket, sketcher's notebook and mahogany polypore, and is scientifically known as *Ganoderma applanatum*. This is a big, harmless, fairly hard, leathery fungus that looks like a shelf growing out of a live tree trunk, stump or fallen log. It is found often on beech and oak trunks. The top of this shelf (looking at the fungus alive, as it grows outward from a tree trunk) is brown, hard, smooth and divided into semicircular ridges, or zones. The bottom is white or light tan and not as hard. The top is nearly undamageable, but any scratch on the bottom surface will turn dark brown.

If you grasp the fungus along the edges near its base, being careful not to touch the underside because even a finger mark will turn dark brown, you can break it away from the tree. You can then use a sharpened stick to write an account of your camping trip on the white surface. The writing will turn a rich brown. Put the fungus away in a safe, dry place where it won't be touched, scratched or bumped for sev-eral days. At the end of that time it will have "cured" and hardened, and new scratches will no longer turn brown or even show on the light surface.

Once dried, this plant lasts just about forever, giving you a permanent record of your camping experience. Do not try to lacquer or varnish the fungus, as there is no need to, and doing so will merely turn the entire light surface dark brown so the writing won't show.

Some artists draw pictures on the light surface, which is why the plant is frequently called artist's fungus or artist's sketchbook. I think it's more fun to draw on the plant than to write on it, and a sample of one of my fungus drawings is shown in a photograph accompanying this chapter. Such a drawing makes a nice display for a shelf or mantlepiece when you get home, especially if you group it with one or two woodcarvings. (After you've done some whittling, you'll find that you can carve lifelike animal sculptures without much trouble.)

With a knife or saw, you can easily smooth off the wood-like base of the fungus so that it will stand upright. Another handsome way to show off your artist's fungus is in a display box made from an old picture frame and hung on the wall.

Pictures and writing tablets aren't the only things that can be made from this unusual plant; remember that it's also called shelf fungus. It is often glued and nailed to a wall, with the flat, light side up, as an attractive rustic shelf or plant holder.

To make it into a plant holder, all you have to do is scoop out a depression in the middle with a knife—the fungus is woody inside—then fill this hollow with earth and plant flowers or ivy in it. One final trick with shelf fungus is to make a candle holder of a fairly small specimen. Glue and nail on a wooden handle, and bore out a hole in the middle for the candlestick. To prevent a low-burning candle from charring it, insert a metal catsup bottle cap in the hole upside down to serve as the actual candle socket. As you can see, nature provides a wide array of serviceable materials for many handicrafts.

Imagine tracking a bobcat close enough to take a picture like this! It can be done if you know what to look and listen for

15

ANIMAL SOUNDS AND TRACKS

The forest is almost never really silent; to those who listen carefully it whispers secrets, disclosing the presence of a partridge, telling of a lynx pouncing on a rabbit, murmuring that a brook is meandering through a thicket of spruce and hemlock or a breeze is ruffling broadleafed shade trees just over the next hill. When you depart from your camp site to go exploring, listen for the voices of the woods and watch for the tracks of its inhabitants. These sounds and sights will reveal interesting stories to the observant and will make it possible to stalk animals in order to hunt or take pictures.

I recall once seeing the tracks of a large bobcat, or lynx, in a snowblanketed Minnesota forest. It was easy to tell what had made the tracks; they were larger than those of a domestic cat, and they looked like the footprints of a dog except that there were no claw marks —for cats retract their claws when walking. I followed the trail a little way and saw where it crossed the tracks of a rabbit. The prints of a sitting rabbit consist of two little round dents, the front feet, ahead of two longer, outward-pointing marks, the rear feet, and sometimes the powder-puff tail will leave a little depression between the hind feet and slightly to the rear. But the tracks of a *running* rabbit are different. This animal gets speed by pushing off with its powerful hind legs and, on each leap,

Chipmunks thrive on nuts and berries

the front legs come down first and then the rear legs come down *ahead* of the front ones as the rabbit hunches for the next leap. Therefore the hind foot prints are in front of the forefoot prints. The hind feet come down evenly, but one forefoot is usually slightly ahead of the other.

The rabbit tracks followed by the lynx were running, and they led through the brush in a zigzag escape pattern. I followed a little way, listening, and finally I heard what sounded like the distant squeal of a baby. Most of the time rabbits are nearly silent, but that shrill cry is made when one is injured or attacked. Now I knew the whole story told by the tracks and the forest sounds: a bobcat had caught a rabbit and would soon be having dinner. Since I had a camera with me, I kept on the trail, approaching silently, and I was able to snap a picture before the cat saw me and bounded off into the timber. My friend Lennie Rue has used the same stalking techniques to photograph bobcats and countless other wild animals.

Like the rabbit's cry, most of the sounds of the forest can be identified. If you sit quietly listening in the woods a number of times and then investigate any sounds, you will begin to recognize the voices of the wilderness. A barking fox, for instance, sounds like a young dog yapping. The male fox goes *yap-yap-yap-yurrrr*. A female has a similar bark, but it isn't as loud or coarse; it sounds as if she is constricting her throat and inhaling while she barks, and the result almost resembles the squawk of a blue heron—*hyip-hyip-hyap-hyurrr*.

The song of a wolf is far different, a smooth, spine-tingling howl or a mixture of short barks and howls—*harr, har howoooooooooo, hooooooooo*. A great horned owl makes a hooting sound reminiscent of a wolf howl, deep and throaty but shorter—*whoo, whoo, whoo*. The cry of a loon also has some similarity to this sound, but long, drawn out and rippling—*h-h-o-o-o-o-o, h-h-o-o-o-o-o*. The loon is a large, beautiful black-and-white water bird that looks almost like an oversized duck but has a pointed

A female red fox brings dinner — a ground squirrel — to her kits. She makes a squawking, yapping bark and leaves small, dog-like tracks

bill which is very efficient when it dives for fish. On the northern waters, you can often see a loon swim a short distance, then dive smoothly beneath the surface and appear again far away with a fish in its beak. The people of the North Country often say that the eerie *h-h-o-o-o-o-o, h-h-o-o-o-o-o* cry of a loon is like the laugh of a lunatic.

One of the most interesting sounds in the wilds is that made by the ruffed grouse, or partridge. It sounds like a drum and is produced in a most unusual way. I remember vividly the first time I heard it. Quite early one morning I stood by a cooking fire I had just made, stretching and yawning and warming myself, thinking about breakfast as I watched the thin ghosts of smoke rise lazily and disappear. It was May, and the camp was deep in the Adirondack Forest Preserve of New York State. I was the first one up that morning, the sun was not yet above the trees and the air was almost the same grey as the smoke wisps. The timber that rimmed the clearing was dew-fragrant, hemlock-dark, mysterious.

Except for the crackle of the tiny flames, all was silent. I felt wonderfully alone and free, on my own but sure of myself. As I gazed at the fire I was startled by an abrupt rustling at the edge of the woods, close to the ground. I stood motionless, looking in the direction of the sound. In a moment I saw a small red squirrel scamper up a tree. Then, as I grinned at how startled I had been, I was startled once again, this time by a more distant and far more mysterious sound.

It was like the beating of an Indian tom-tom deep in the woods. *Drum . . . drum . . . drum . . . drum-drum-drum-drum-drum-drum . . . drum . . . drum . . . drum . . . drum . . .* The beats, slow and hollow, then faster and faster, then slowing down again, faded away in less than half a minute. There was a pause, and the beating began once more. I've heard the same tom-tom many times since that morning in May, and it no longer startles me, for I know what causes the sound; but it remains mysterious enough to be exciting whenever I hear it.

The strange wilderness rhythm is the drumming of a male ruffed grouse, standing on a log and beating his wings to attract a mate. Without rising, he beats his wings against the air so powerfully that he produces a sonic boom, a miniature version of the boom that a jet plane makes when it passes overhead. The tom-tom of the ruffed grouse can be heard every spring in the northern half of the United States, in southern Canada and even in eastern Alaska.

If you know what the drumming is, it becomes not only exciting but beautiful—a signal for warm weather and new life to come to the wilds. Yet it isn't heard by everyone who walks the woodland trails. Even though it's a clear, determined thumping, I once had to call it to the attention of a companion strolling with me. To discover the surprises hidden among the trees and brush, you must realize that they are there, you must watch and listen, knowing that in the woods you are never alone. For every creature you see, there are dozens more, watching you and remaining hidden.

The ruffed grouse can make a loud drumming noise by rapidly beating its wings

When you do hear the drumming, walk toward it quietly. It will stop after a moment. The grouse has heard you, too, and does not know whether you are a friend or enemy. Keep walking. Suddenly you will hear an even louder, faster drumming and a *whoosh*—and you'll see an exploding blur of wings as Old Ruff takes off. He will zigzag away among the trees with astounding speed. Then you will understand why the grouse is sometimes called Thunderwings.

Mention has already been made of other woodland sounds: the chirping of a bandy-legged cricket as he saws away with his wings, the booming, the croaking and the shrill piping of pop-eyed, bubble-toed, green-backed mump-mouthed spring peeper frogs as they inflate and deflate their throat sacs. Some drumming birds, such as the western sage grouse, make a popping noise by using their throats rather than their wings. The male sage grouse has many tiny air sacs in a pouch on his chest and throat. To attract the attention of a female he wishes to court, while also warning other males to keep their distance, he makes short trotting runs back and forth, inflating and deflating the sacs with a *pop, pop, pop*. The male woodcock uses still another approach to show off for his lady: he whistles with both his throat and wings as he spirals high up into the air in a corkscrew flight, then plummets back to earth. On the ground, he whistles a sound like *peeent*.

And there are many, many other sounds in the wilds. The bull elk makes a high-pitched bugling sound with his throat, while the females of these species bawl somewhat like a domestic cow. The bull moose grunts and coughs and sometimes moos. The mourning dove coos, the crow caws, the sparrow whistles, the buck deer rattles his antlers against trees as a challenge to other bucks, and the caribou grunts, rumbles and snorts.

Frequently you will hear a sound in the forest but will not be able to follow it to its source. However, even without seeing the source you may sometimes recognize it—from the descriptions given here, from calls described by experienced campers, and by learning to recognize tracks. After all, if you hear a yapping and then spot delicate little dog-like tracks you can be pretty sure a fox is nearby. The pad marks of a fox are small, as are the claw marks, and sometimes they are dimly outlined with a rim left by the long fur of the animal's feet.

A bull elk makes a high-pitched bugling sound with his throat, and leaves much larger, rounder tracks than those of deer

In identifying tracks, the first rule is to know what animals are in the region. The second, of course, is to know what the prints look like. You will recall that deer prints look like split hearts with the points at the front. Moose and elk tracks are much larger and rounder, with a wider split between the halves. In mud or soft ground, moose and caribou tracks also have two smaller half-moon indentations at the rear. These round marks are left by the dewclaw, a small protuberance that hangs down behind the hoofs of some animals.

Wolf prints look like they were made by a large dog. Skunk tracks look almost like miniature human hand prints (the front feet) and footprints (the rear) with very long claws, and instead of going straight ahead they veer off to one side or another as the animal waddles along.

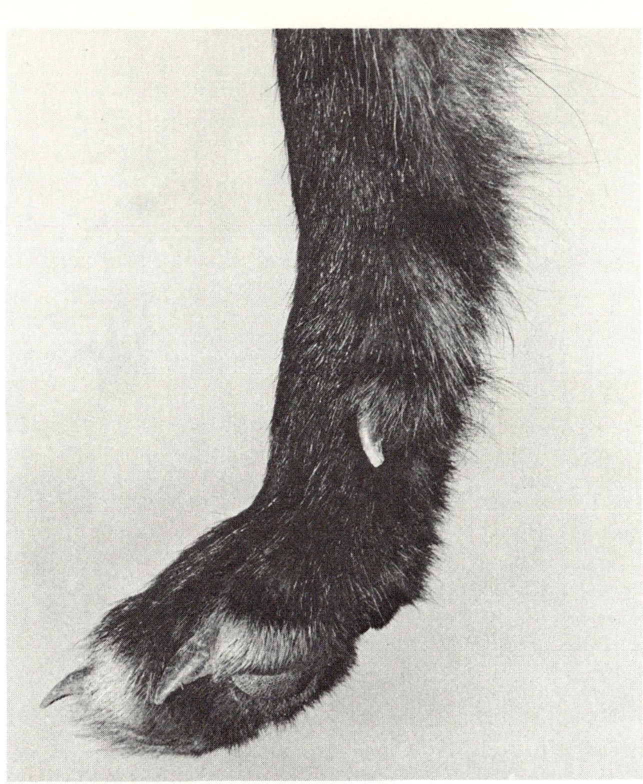

Above is the right front foot of a red fox. The long fur sometimes leaves a rim around the footprints in snow

Above right, dog-like tracks of a fox in deep snow; below right, triangular sets of cottontail rabbit tracks

Beaver tracks also look like fat little human footprints, but they are webbed and toe in at a sharp angle. Sometimes they are blurred by a wide swath raked by the flat tail that trails along behind. Muskrat tracks are much thinner, and the tail (which is flattened vertically on a muskrat rather than horizontally, as on a beaver) leaves a dim, snaking, curving trail between the footprints.

Squirrel tracks look rather like rabbit tracks but smaller and with the forefeet placed evenly instead of one in front of the other. The tail sometimes leaves a long wispy indentation. Chipmunk tracks are smaller, with all four about even in size, and the individual pads and claws are sometimes delicately visible. Mouse tracks are thinner, the claws are longer and the prints of the rear feet are longer than those of the front feet.

The opossum's hind feet leave prints almost exactly like miniature human hands, spread out and with the thumb extended way out to the side. The raccoon leaves a miniature human footprint, and so does the porcupine, but the porcupine's is much fatter—almost oval.

Like the pigeon-footed beaver, the bear toes in. The rear print of a bear looks pretty much like a fat human footprint—this time not in miniature—while the front print looks like it was made only by the ball and toes of the foot.

Bird tracks are easy to spot, though it is sometimes difficult to tell one species from another. Almost all bird tracks have three long, spread-out points facing forward and diagonally to the sides, plus one short one pointing to the rear. With a goose or duck, you can see the dim depression left by the webbing between the claws. With a ruffed grouse, there may be a ragged, furry-looking outline because the downy feathers reach all the way to the feet. With a heron, the points are long, thin, and of almost equal lengths. Because of the way a pheasant crooks its feet in walking, the long, thin, spread-out points sometimes look like they were made up of segments. Turkey tracks are big and fat, and they appear to toe in as a beaver's prints do; frequently a turkey's huge wing feathers hang all the way to the ground and leave wispy lines.

The tracks of small birds such as robins and sparrows are the most difficult to tell apart. All of them are thin and narrow. The robin's, of course, are slightly larger than the sparrow's, but if both kinds aren't present for a comparison, it's hard to guess which bird left the prints — at least, it's hard for me. But birds will frequently answer a whistle or call, even if it doesn't sound much like their own. You may attract them by hissing, or by kissing the back of your hand. And birds tend to gather with other birds of their own kind. These traits often make it easy to look up and see for yourself what made the tracks at your feet. Practice identifying and following tracks. Sooner or later, the effort will be repaid with wonderful photographs or a full game bag.

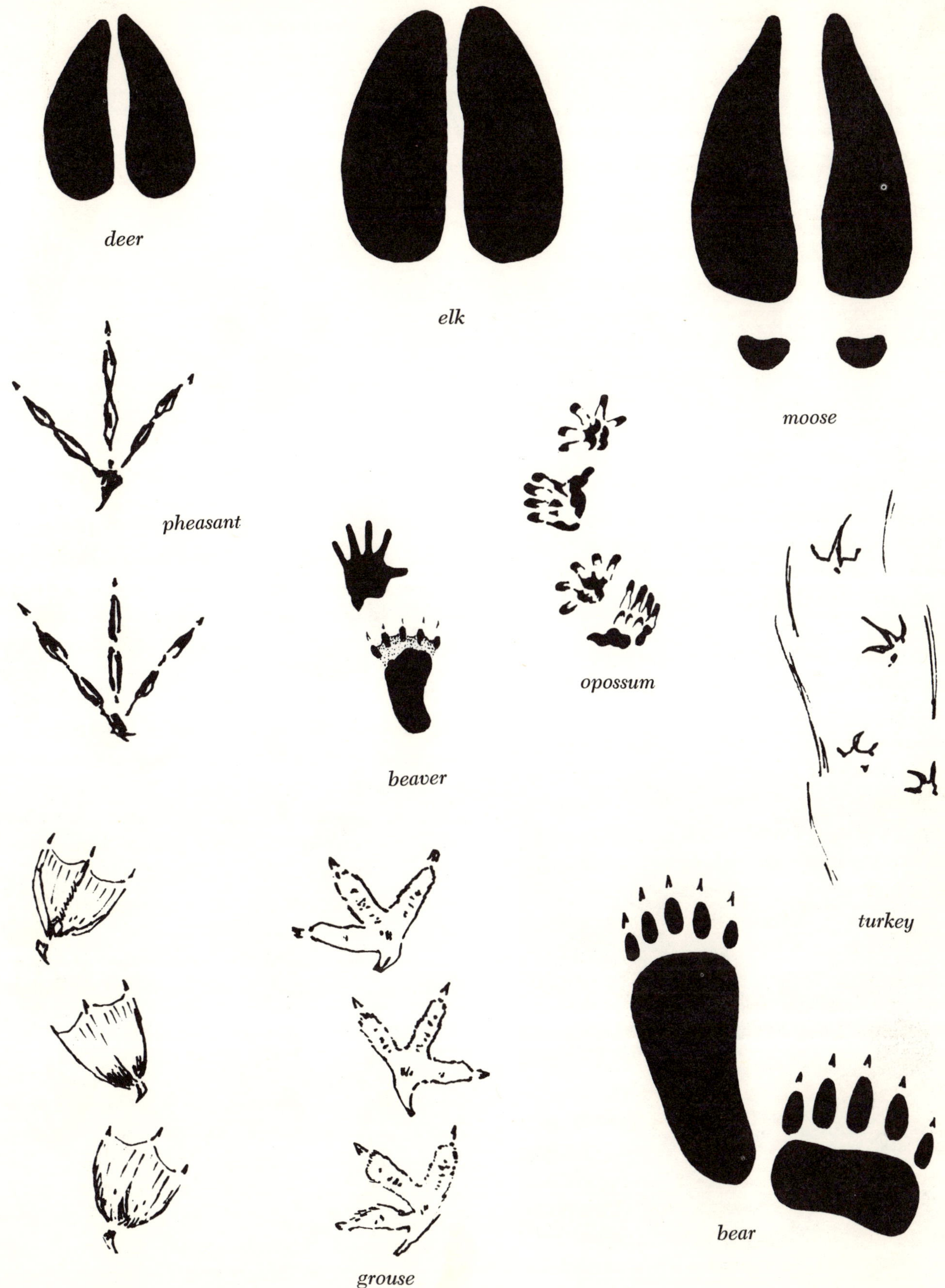

deer
elk
moose
pheasant
beaver
opossum
turkey
goose
grouse
bear

16
GETTING ALONG WITH PLANT LIFE

The Iroquois Indians used to make chewing gum by mixing the pitch from dead pines with beeswax. Personally, I prefer spruce gum, and I don't mix it with anything. Next time you walk through spruce woods, notice the crisp, fresh odor; the same flavor that's in the odor is in the sap which will ooze from a spruce trunk or limb if it has been bruised. Upon exposure to air, the sap begins to harden, and the trick is to find a blob of gum that is medium-hard. If it's very soft it will stick to your teeth annoyingly and if it's too hard it will break into little particles. But when you find some that has the right consistency, it makes fine chewing gum. In the Southwest, a shrub called rabbit brush, or chamisa, has a soft inner bark that also makes good chewing gum. Wild plants can provide candy, syrups, foods, seasonings, beverages, even medicines and soap and rope and clothing.

In a wonderful old book called *Wildwood Wisdom,* an outdoorsman called Ellsworth Jaeger observes that the Bible, in the Book of Genesis, declares God has given us "every herb bearing seed . . . and every tree, in which is the fruit . . . yielding seed . . . for meat." There are so many useful plants growing around any camp site that it would be impossible to describe them all in a single volume. Instead, I will tell you about some of the most common and valuable plants, and will warn you about those which can be harmful rather than beneficial.

The sap from coniferous trees provides antiseptics, soothing poultices and even chewing gum

Above, wild raspberries provide sweet and nutritious food. Below, a wild apple tree is wonderful for climbing, and it not only bears fruit but furnishes blossoms that can be candied

Plants sometimes reveal secrets about animal life; leaves and twigs nibbled off above eye level mean deer have probably been searching for winter-browse

You already know about poison ivy, oak and sumac, and you should add stinging nettle to the list. Unless you are abnormally sensitive to it, nettle won't produce a lasting rash, but it does cause a burning sensation for a little while. Nettle is a single-stalk plant that grows from two to four feet high, and has little hanging blossoms, saw-edged leaves and small needle-like hairs; these hairs do the stinging. For any skin irritations of this kind, the best medicines are calamine lotion and antihistamines, but nature provides two other remedies in case you rub against poison ivy or one of the other poisonous plants and have no store-bought medicines with you. One of these soothing remedies is a solution of hemlock twigs and needles that have been boiled for half an hour in a pan of water. The other is a beautiful wild plant called the jewelweed, also known as touch-me-not because the ripe seed pods explode when touched.

Jewelweed grows from one to five feet high and bears orange or yellow flowers, often speckled with red, drooping from slender branchlets. These blossoms are cone- or trumpet-shaped and curving, with a spur at the rear and an opening at the front; about an inch long, they look a bit like orchids. The leaves and stems are smooth and waxy, and the leaves have a serrated edge. To relieve skin irritations, crush these leaves and stems and apply the juice, which neutralizes the poisons, or make a poultice of the crushed leaves. This also soothes bee stings.

Any plant that severely irritates the skin is apt to be far more poisonous—occasionally lethal—if eaten. There are also some plants which are harmless to touch but still deadly poisonous if eaten. Perhaps the most famous are amanita mushrooms, which grow in many varieties but usually have several traits in common: a shape more or less like an umbrella, a ring or collar partway down around the stem and a cup-shaped envelope at the base. A "toadstool" is actually any umbrella-shaped mushroom, but the name is most often used for poisonous types. My advice is *never* to pick and eat wild mushrooms except under the supervision of a mushroom expert, and even an expert should carry a very detailed field guide.

As mentioned before, the common yellow buttercup is somewhat poisonous. There are also plants which are partly poisonous. The young shoots of the pokeweed are edible when cooked (though why anyone should want to eat them I do not know) but, raw or cooked, the roots and pokeberries are poisonous. This plant grows from four to twelve feet tall and has a reddish stem and smooth green leaves. The small whitish flowers are sometimes tinged with purple; the berries ripen from green to dark purple. Birds at times eat these berries and become ill or intoxicated; people who make the same mistake are endangering their lives.

Pokeweed has a wide distribution, but jimson weed (sometimes called thorn apple) grows only in warm regions such as the South and Southwest—which is just as well. The seeds and the plant itself contain a dangerous narcotic poison. It has large, beautiful, funnel-shaped white or whitish-violet flowers, prickly seed pods and leaves that look a little like those of a thistle.

Locoweeds grow in several varieties in the West, and the name comes from the Spanish word for "crazy." The plants were so named because eating them will make a human or animal drunk as well as extremely sick. These very poisonous weeds have small leaves and clusters of small flowers, usually lavender or purple, that resemble sweet peas.

The camas, or wild hyacinth, is a harmless plant of the lily family that grows in many areas, is closely related to the onion and has an onion-like bulb that was relished by the early settlers. But there is another variety of the plant, called the death camas, which is very dangerous to eat. Luckily, the death camas grows only along the Pacific Coast and is easy to tell from its harmless relative. The long-petaled flowers of the edible species are blue, while those of the death camas are white.

You must never judge a plant's effect by its smell. Skunk cabbage is aptly named, yet it makes a passable survival food if you boil the young shoots or roast the roots as the Iroquois Indians did. On the other hand, cowbane—or water hemlock—is dangerous even though it is a member of the parsley family and has tuberous roots that give off a pleasant aromatic flavor. Cowbane is found in marshy ground from the Atlantic to the Rockies, grows from three to six feet high and has erect stems streaked with purple. It has numerous small white flowers which are pretty but are as poisonous as the rest of the plant.

There are far more edible plants than poisonous ones, though it would obviously be a mistake to eat anything of which you weren't absolutely sure. Many wild vegetables, fruits and nuts are delicious. Wild asparagus, as an example, looks and tastes like domestic asparagus, except that it should be eaten when the spears are no more than a few inches high or it will be tough and woody. Originally from Europe, wild asparagus is now found throughout most of the United States as well. It grows into a tall, lacy plant with berries—by which time it is too old to eat—but you can locate the young sprouts by looking for the tall, dried plants that bloomed the previous year.

Day lilies, which grow in fields and along roadsides, have typical orange lily blossoms that are edible. You can also pick the unopened buds, boil them and serve them with butter and salt, or dip them in a thin batter and fry them, or add them to soups.

Delicious and nourishing—loaded with vitamin C—are several kinds of wild onions which are found just about everywhere. Chives, garlic and leek are members of the onion family. Their leaves are flat or tube-shaped and are hollow, and all of them have a sharp onion smell. If a bulbous plant does not have this smell it is not an onion; don't eat it unless you're sure what it is. The most common type of wild onion has long, thin tubular leaves and a small bulb; it looks like a skinny scallion and it sometimes has little pale lavender blossoms. It tastes best before it is ready to bud. The larger leaves are sometimes a bit strong, but the smaller ones are tender and delicious.

Mint, spearmint and peppermint are short plants usually found along streams or in wet ground. They are fine for making sauces or brewing tea—and, personally, I like to chew on them just as they are. Their square stems, rough leaves and mint smell make them easy to identify.

Watercress grows in large patches or clumps in cold streams. The young shoots and leaves make a wonderful salad. And with a pork bone, a pot of water and a mess of watercress you can make an excellent soup. Violet leaves and blossoms, either raw or cooked, are also very good.

The long, rough leaves of dandelions, which grow virtually everywhere, are good, slightly bitter salad greens if picked before the buds produce their yellow flowers. When boiled, dandelion leaves taste more or less like spinach, but better.

Like dandelions, purslane can be found just about everywhere. Creeping along the ground, it grows no higher than a couple of inches. It has fleshy little succulent leaves and yellow flowers which open on sunny mornings. All of the plant is edible. You can use it as a salad, in soup or stew, or boil it for about twelve minutes and eat it with butter and salt. If you pick only the young leaves they will grow back and the plant won't be harmed.

Among other plants whose leaves and shoots may be eaten—and as nourishing pleasure, not punishment—are chicory, milkweed, clover, great burdock, fiddlehead ferns (better than asparagus when boiled!), marsh marigold, wild grapevine (the young shoots as well as the ripe grapes themselves), evening primrose and plantain. You can eat rose hips, the juicy sweet pulp of the mesquite pod or the closely related screw bean, or the inner stalk of the yucca. Jack-in-the-pulpit is sometimes called Indian turnip, but it will burn your tongue if you eat it raw, for it's hotter than horseradish; bake or boil it and it loses its heat, becoming quite good. Raw cattail roots are not quite as hot as horseradish, but they should be boiled or roasted for a better, gentler taste. Heart of cattail, on the other hand, is delicious for munching raw or for adding a new taste to a salad.

Jerusalem artichoke, Indian cucumber, wild carrots and radishes—the list could go on and on, though my favorites—wild nuts and fruits —have not yet been discussed.

There is no trick to recognizing wild raspberries, strawberries, blueberries and blackberries, for they look just like domestic raspberries, strawberries, blueberries and blackberries. I've spent many happy hours picking wild blueberries on the rocky islands of Georgian Bay in Canada, but my favorite fruit will always be wild raspberries. I've picked so many of them in the woods and fields of Vermont that I thought surely I would pick the state clean of raspberries. Yet I have never arrived back in camp with even one raspberry left. I suppose it might be a good game to see how many you could pick and save without eating them on the spot, but I would rather eat than play games.

Nuts are very good, too. Growing wild, profuse and delicious, you will find hazelnuts, walnuts, butternuts, pine nuts, hickory nuts and pecans. It you aren't sure how they look, carry a field guide; every outdoorsman should learn to recognize the most common trees.

Sassafras and wintergreen are used to make tea; chicory to make coffee. The Seneca Indians also roasted and pounded the shells of sunflower seeds to make a kind of coffee. It isn't bad, though I prefer to peel and eat the seeds themselves. In the dry deserts of the Southwest, the barrel cactus is sometimes cut open by thirsty hikers because this plant holds clear water in its pulpy interior. Several varieties of maple, as well as hickory and sugar pine, yield sap that can be simmered over a slow fire to make syrup and boiled a little longer to make sugar. Delicious snow candy can be made by dribbling the syrup onto clean snow; it tastes like a cross between hard caramel and sweet molasses.

Seasonings are made from the wild spice bush, wild mustard, chili, mint, fermented maple or birch sap (Indian vinegar), sweet

Learn to recognize different kinds of trees and shrubs. In a forest like this, the evergreens alone can furnish nuts, medicine, even twine

The blossoms of fruit trees can be jellied...

... but fungus plants are a different matter; unless you're a mushroom expert, look but don't touch

Growing along the edge of a little brook, this thick foliage conceals sprigs of mint, clusters of wild onions and patches of watercress — all good to eat

Raspberries like these grow well in the wild, and so do blueberries and strawberries

bay, ginger and other plants. As for medicinal plants, jewelweed and hemlock have already been mentioned, and there are other plants that can be used for various medicinal purposes. The gum from spruce, hemlock, balsam, pine and other conifer trees is antiseptic and healing, so it is sometimes applied to small cuts. For inflammations, a slippery-elm poultice is made by boiling the inner bark and then mashing it. Witch hazel bark is boiled into a strong tea, cooled and applied to sprains and bruises as a soothing lotion. The oil of pennyroyal (a low, pungent plant with tiny blue flowers) is used for stomach disorders. Boneset (a stout, hairy plant with large clusters of white flower heads and with narrow, wrinkled leaves growing from opposite sides of the stem) is used in small doses of tea as a tonic, in large doses as a laxative; taken hot, it also soothes a sore throat.

The inner bark of fallen basswood trees can be twisted into twine, braided into rope or woven into rough clothing. The inner bark of slippery elm can be split into fine, strong threads. You can actually use it for sewing or weaving as well as for cord. Other "cord" trees include the leatherwood, hickory, white oak, Osage orange, buckeye and red cedar. Mulberry has a fine fiber that was used as thread by the Indians, and swamp milkweed has strong fibers that can be used as twine. For lacing canoes and making baskets, the Indians split the roots of white spruce, which they called *watar*.

Many campers enjoy spending one day and night away from camp with only a sleeping bag and a "survival kit," playing the survival game and living off the land. Before doing so, scout the area carefully to make sure you can find enough natural food.

Besides edible wild plants, there are many animals and fish that can be eaten. Even the lowly crawfish is good when boiled like a shrimp—which it resembles. Crawfish can often be scooped with the hands from sheltered rocky spots along the edges of streams, though you must be fast with your hands. It isn't as difficult as it sounds, however. I arrived at camp after dark one night with my son, and he asked if he could explore the shore of a pond with a flashlight. I went with him and watched as he stalked a scurrying crawfish, cornering it in a sandy hollow and quickly scooping it up. Alive, a crawfish is greyish and not very tasty-looking, though it has a very interesting appearance. But the same thing can be said of its larger relative, the shrimp, and both are good when boiled. It takes quite a few crawfish to make a meal, however, so probably the best thing to do with any you catch is use them for bait. Fish love them—which means you can turn a captured crawfish into a fish dinner.

The vegetables being boiled with this game dinner include wild carrots and chives

A survival kit should include your basic first-aid kit, a couple of bouillon cubes (in case you're unlucky and don't find much else to eat), a twenty-foot fishing line and two hooks, wooden matches, facial tissues, a candle stub, needle and thread, water-purifying tablets, a magnifying glass, a mirror for signaling, and your compass. With those items plus your sleeping bag and all the edible plants that nature offers, there's no reason why you can't spend an adventurous day and a well-fed, comfortable night in the woods, without your tent or usual pack.

Cleanliness is important for good health, but you won't need soap in your survival kit if you can find some Southern buckeye, soapwort, yucca root, Missouri gourd, California soap plant or wild lilac. To use a yucca root, just break off a piece, crush it with a stone and rub it with your hands in water until a good thick lather develops. It even makes a fine shampoo.

Soapwort is much more widely distributed than yucca, and is also known as European pink and bouncing bet. Growing from one to two feet high, it thrives along embankments. It has long, narrow, thick, oval leaves and profuse clusters of pink or white flowers with scalloped petals and a spicy odor. Just pick some leaves and crush them; the juices form a soapy lather that really works.

Buckeye soap is in the root, Missouri gourd soap is in the pulp of the gourds as well as the root, California soap plant soap is in the inner part of the root under a coarse outer fiber, and wild lilac soap is in the blossoms which can be crushed to make a fragrant and efficient lather.

Now perhaps one more use for a plant should be mentioned. When you're ready to break camp, you can give the ground a good sweeping with an Indian hickory broom. Take a long hickory stick and soak one end in water; then beat that end with a rock, a log or the blunt edge of your hatchet head. The wood will splinter into a brush-like broom and you're ready to sweep up.

Most ducks and geese like shallow water. These Canada geese are typical of the abundant wildlife to be found at the water's edge

AT THE WATER'S EDGE

Scientists believe that all of the earth's life—both plant and animal life—originated in the waters of the globe many eons ago. As the earth aged, the waters receded and more land appeared in many regions. And as the plants and animals evolved, adapting themselves to their surroundings, many of them sought the shallows and then many of those in the shallows began to creep out onto the shore. Today the waters of the world still teem with life, and this is especially true of the shallows and edges where the ripples lap the banks.

A great deal of adventure is to be had on and in the water, and dangers are present only for those who don't know how to treat the water with respect. If you haven't been brought up near a large body of water, the best way to get acquainted with aquatic adventure is to begin by exploring the edges of ponds, lakes, streams or the seashore. Along these edges some extraordinary discoveries await you.

The plant life alone is often astounding in wet places. In the bogs or swamps near some bodies of water, you may find meat-eating plants that live by trapping and digesting insects. The insects provide them with life-sustaining nitrogen, which is often scarce in very watery soil. The tiny sundew plant has pretty little white flowers; it also has hairy leaves, and at the end of each hair is a drop of liquid—which explains the plant's name. But

Walking along a shoreline can be an adventure if you're alert for small animals, plants and strange shells

unlike dew, this liquid is sticky and does not dry up when the sun shines. Any little insect that lands on a sundew leaf gets stuck there. The hairs then bend over and hold the insect tightly. It is killed and the fleshy parts absorbed. Afterward, the hairs open and the insect's shell or hard parts are blown away.

The Venus's-flytrap, a white-flowered plant found in North Carolina, has two-part leaves edged with little spikes and dotted near the ends with stiff hairs. When an insect touches a hair, the leaf is triggered. It snaps shut, with the spikes interlocking, to trap a meal.

The pitcher plant has a round red flower that may help to attract insects. The leaves are actually shaped like pitchers; these leaves are themselves flowerlike and veined with red, which may also help. The pitchers are usually partly filled with water. Insects frequently crawl into the leaves, only to find that downward-pointing hairs prevent them from climbing up again. Eventually they fall into the water, drown and are digested.

In this tiny stream there is a plant called bladderwort,
which actually eats insects, and there are also
fresh-water snails and mussels

In the shallows of lakes, ponds and streams, you will sometimes see the yellow-orange flowers of the bladderwort rising from the surface. The lower part of this water plant looks like a cross between roots and seaweed, and it has little bubbles, or bladders, on the submerged stems. These little hollow balls have one-way swinging gates. Water insects swim in but cannot get out again. Trapped, they are soon digested.

Other marsh and water plants, such as cattails, water hyacinths, duckweeds and water lilies, do not eat insects because they are specially constructed to absorb all the nutrition they need from water, air and in some cases the mud of water beds. Hyacinths and lilies are particularly beautiful, and water lilies are always a welcome sight to fishermen because large bass and sometimes pike and pickerel love to forage in the waters under the pads. Bass are generally present in the morning and evening, pickerel and pike at any time. When you're fishing and see a mass of water lilies, cast your bait or lure to the edge of the profusion of broad leaves and you're likely to find some action.

Cattails were mentioned before as food; they are also useful as candles if their tops are soaked in paraffin or kerosene. Duckweeds and water hyacinths are interesting because their roots don't reach down through the water to the mud. These plants simply float, soaking up nutrition from the water and air.

Incidentally, you may enjoy collecting leaf prints of both land and water plants. You can collect the leaves themselves and press them between the pages of a book to preserve them, but sooner or later they usually disintegrate. Their prints can be made in either of two ways. If you're interested only in duplicating the shape of the leaf, not its color, you can use carbon paper to make its print. Place the leaf on a newspaper with a piece of carbon paper on top; the carbon side should be against the leaf. Place another newspaper over it and then press it with a hot iron. Now remove the leaf and place it, with the carbon-coated side down, on a sheet of white paper. Put a newspaper on top again and press it once more with a hot iron. The shape will be transferred to the white paper as a black print.

For colored prints, you need rubber-base paints, white absorbent paper and a small paint brush. Lightly coat one side of the leaf with paint, matching the leaf's color as closely as possible. When the paint is almost dry, place the leaf on the paper with the painted side down, put another sheet of paper over it and rub firmly with your fingers. When you remove the top sheet of paper and the leaf, you will have a print.

Mineral and fossil collecting can also be very rewarding at the water's edge, particularly on a pebbly beach where there is a fast stream or some surf. This is because fast-moving waters loosen stones from the banks and stream beds, carry them along and often wash them up where they are easily seen. It has been claimed that the best mineral-hunting grounds in North America may be along the Colorado River (especially at the Grand Canyon in Arizona), but you can find attractive, interesting minerals near any camp site. Here are some minerals that are found quite often:

Because fast-moving waters loosen stones from the banks and stream beds, the water's edge is a good place to look for minerals and fossils. These samples include a piece of meteorite (center), obsidian, a mineral called fluorite and rocks bearing traces of aquatic fossils

*Biotite, a black mica, occurs as tiny flakes in granite and gneiss rock; mica splits into thin sheets that you can see through.

*Calcite, usually white, occurs by itself or in limestone, marble and chalk. It tends to break into pieces with a *rhombus* shape; that is, the edges slope at angles, but each side is parallel to the opposite side.

*Flint, grey or black, occurs in chips and chunks. When struck against steel it produces sparks and is sometimes used to start campfires. The Indians preferred it over most rocks for arrowheads because it is hard and can be easily shaped and sharpened by chipping away at it. It contains the same chemicals as quartz.

*Limonite, yellow or brown, is an iron ore. The Indians used it to make yellow paint, and they used another iron ore, hematite, to make red war paint.

*Muscovite, white, is another variety of mica. It sometimes occurs as fairly large sheets, and the pioneers used it for window glass.

*Quartz, most often white, grey or translucent, occurs as pebbles, stones and sand. It breaks into beautiful crystal shapes with many angles and facets.

In addition to minerals, you can often find rocks with fossil imprints—the hardened outlines or skeletons of animals and plants that lived ages ago, preserved forever when the rock was formed from mud, earth or organic material and bits of minerals.

Mineral-collecting is especially exciting when you can combine it with Indian-relic hunting. I've gathered a collection of southwestern arrowheads, spearheads and hide-scrapers made of flint, red jasper and the beautiful streaky-black volcanic rock-glass called obsidian. I have a collection of white quartz, too, and every piece is an arrowhead.

The water's edge is also a good place for insect hunting. Here you will find dragonflies which catch small insects in flight. The dragonfly has been called the hawk of the insect world. In its immature, or nymph, stage, it lives in the water, breathes with gills like a fish,

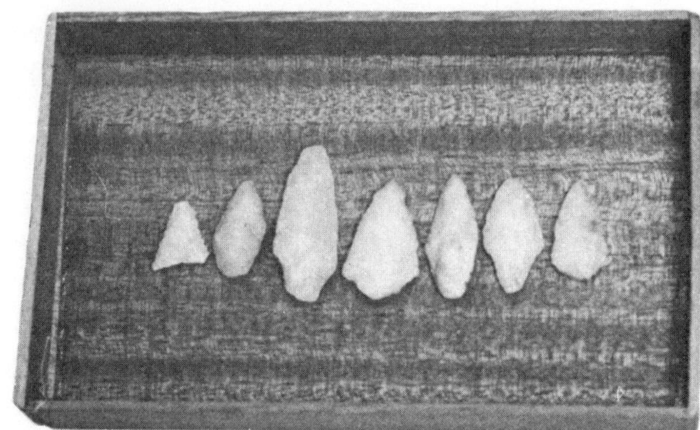

Mineral hunting can sometimes turn into Indian-relic hunting. The author's collection includes these arrowheads made of white quartz

has a long lower lip that can grab insects and tiny fish, and can suck water into the rear of its body and squirt it out again to propel itself along in a stream or lake.

The nymphs of caddis flies also have gills. Some of them build protective cases, or underwater cocoons, out of sand grains and twigs to protect themselves until they mature, at which time they grow wings and emerge from the water. At night they will come up to a light shone on the water.

The water scorpion is harmless despite its name, which it gets from the tail-like appearance of its two long rear legs. Hiding in underwater weeds to catch other insects, it sticks a long breathing tube up through the surface. Another species without gills is the diving beetle, which holds a bubble of air under its wings for breathing purposes.

There are water spiders which can walk on the surface, and there are also insects called water *striders* which do the same thing. They are so light that their legs do not break through the surface film; therefore, they can skate along on top. Then there are several species that are simply called water bugs. They look like long beetles with large folded wings. Be careful if you handle them, because they sometimes bite. Among some species, the female glues her eggs to the back of the male and the male then carries them until they hatch.

Seashells and freshwater shelled animals are another obvious treasure at the water's edge.

Along an ocean beach, there are literally thousands of species, but many people do not realize that shelled animals can be found in and near inland waters, too. There are freshwater mussels, and there are freshwater snails and land snails as well. Some land snails have large, beautifully curling shells that glow like mother-of-pearl. Animals with one- or two-piece shells and no interior skeleton are called mollusks. Most of them live in the water and will not survive long on the beach, but during and after storms fresh specimens are often washed up on shore. Although some species only appear at certain seasons, a good hunter is almost sure to find at least a few handsome shells in good condition.

Mollusks avoid bright sunlight, but if you wade along the shoreline at night you will often find lots of them. It's a good idea for two collectors to work together, so that one can search along with a flashlight while the other scoops up the shells and puts them into a container. A quiet bay is a fine place to do this.

These children are observing the slow progress of a slug (a kind of land snail that has no shell) as it inches along in a swampy area

Along the seashore, you'll have good results if you turn over rocks at low tide or dig in the sand. If you're a good swimmer, you'll have your greatest shell-collecting success by skin-diving. In addition to watching for the shells themselves when you dive, watch for underwater trails in the sand. Some mollusks can move about, and they leave a snaking trail behind.

Shrimp and crabs are, for the most part, animals of the sea, but certain species of these animals (as well as crawfish) inhabit fresh water. As mentioned before, crawfish make fine bait—and that brings us to the subject of fish.

A beach like this is a fine place to camp if you want to hunt for shells and aquatic animals. The samples shown here include a starfish and a seahorse, as well as some handsome and unusual mollusks

Many fish cruise through the shallows very near shore, hunting for insects, smaller fish and other food, especially in the early morning, at dusk and at night. And some of the fairly small ones seem to have little fear of human beings. When wading in knee-deep water, I have had perch brush against my leg. Sometimes you may see a baby catfish wandering along right next to a bank, and a carp will occasionally come all the way out of the water, with its jaw right on shore, in order to grab a morsel. You may get some of the smaller fish to crowd right around you by sprinkling stale bread on the water. Unfortunately, it makes poor bait even though the fish like it; the trouble is that it disintegrates instead of staying on a hook. Nevertheless, with bread you can attract chubs, dace, shiners and other minnows, carp, perch and various sunfish, including big fat bluegills.

Most of the water safety rules apply to swimming and boating and will be explained in the next chapter. However, the dangers of quicksand and bogs should be dealt with here, since these hazards can be encountered when wading or just walking in watery areas.

Actually, quicksand is not nearly as dangerous as fiction writers have led people to believe. It is not a *kind* of sand but merely an unusual condition involving sand. In brief, it is any sand whose grains have been pushed apart slightly by water pressure from below—for instance, by the water pressure of underground springs or seepage under dams. The water escapes upward, through the sand, preventing the grains from resting on and against each other. The sand is therefore in a loose, fluid state. It won't actually pull you down, but it will resist when you try to pull out of it. One danger lies in standing upright in it since you will not be able to tread water or swim out and may therefore sink. An even greater danger is

Camped almost at the water's edge, this family can beach the boat right next to the trailer-tent, and can also go fishing without leaving the campsite

Bass and many smaller fish can often be found in the weed beds that dot shallow areas like this one, just a few yards from land

in yielding to panic and violently fighting the quicksand; this will just get you in deeper.

If you are ever caught in quicksand, the first thing to do is flop on your back or stomach with your arms spread out. You will float better in quicksand than in water. Then, if there's no one near to help, wriggle one foot free at a time and one hand at a time. After that you'll be able to slide, swim or roll over and over until you reach solid ground. But be sure your movements are gentle and slow, not violent. If you thrash around you'll find that an arm or leg or your body has pushed itself deeper into the sand.

To rescue someone from quicksand, all you have to do is throw him a rope, plank, pole, branch, anything to pull him along and out. Quicksand sometimes forms underwater, and this type involves the one exception to the rule about violent motion. If you feel yourself caught in quicksand while wading, just fall over and swim fast to get away. The water will hold you up, and underwater quicksand loosens very quickly. If you know there's quicksand in the area, you can probe the ground ahead of you with a pole. On land, another way to detect it is by stamping; quicksand has a quaking feel which is noticeable from several feet away when you stamp hard on the ground.

Some tidal mud flats and very fluid bogs are more difficult to pull out of than quicksand. One way to get out is to lie down (slowly, not by flopping) and roll to safety. However, it's rare to get more than one foot caught in this kind of mud because you know you're stuck as soon as you make the first wrong step, and then you can simply pull your leg back.

I did this once, and the suction of the mud pulled off my boot. However, the experience was so frightening and I was so glad to get free that I didn't mind losing the boot at all. Probably if I had pulled backward instead of straight up I would have been able to keep the boot on my foot, but in some situations it's difficult to think of every little thing, including the price of boots.

18
SWIMMING, BOATING AND CANOEING

In my opinion, every boy and girl should be a good swimmer by the age of nine or ten. The older you get, the harder it is to learn new skills. Besides, swimming is so much fun and such good exercise that no one should be deprived of it. If you do not know how to swim, learn as soon as possible by taking one of the courses offered by youth organizations, health clubs and civic groups. No book can teach swimming properly, although some swimming coaches employ an instruction manual as a teaching aid. This chapter will help by discussing techniques and safety rules.

To begin with, never go into the water less than half an hour after a meal. Digestion is partly a muscular process, and it consumes energy. The combination of exertion and cool water after a meal can cause cramps that may on occasion be severe enough to prevent muscles from working temporarily—and this, obviously, is dangerous. A chill can also cause cramps, so don't swim when you feel uncomfortably cold. An expert swimmer can stay in the water for hours and travel long distances, but the average person should stay in no longer than half an hour—and should come out after just a few minutes when the water is cold. If the water is very choppy, it's better not to go in at all.

It's easy to rest on a small inflatable raft or float

Under the guidance of skilled coaches, these boys are learning to be good swimmers

Don't try to become an endurance swimmer overnight. To find out how far you can swim without getting overtired or winded, pick a starting point near shore and then swim along parallel to shore at a comfortable speed, not racing. When you begin to feel tired, stop and see how far you've gone. Then you'll know your limit.

Most swimming instructors and camp life-guards insist that swimmers use the "buddy system." Each swimmer is paired off with a friend, and must keep track of this friend to make sure no one gets into trouble. If there is an odd number of swimmers, they can be divided into pairs plus one trio. The important thing is not to swim alone. Even experienced swimmers generally avoid going into the water by themselves. There is nothing at all dangerous about swimming if it is done sensibly, and being sensible includes taking no chances.

When in deep water or swimming a fairly long distance, it is not a bad idea for an inexperienced swimmer to wear a life vest. However, a life vest should not be worn constantly because it interferes with learning to swim properly. It impedes movements slightly and it buoys you up unnaturally. If you get used to wearing one all the time and then try to swim without it you'll feel that you're sinking alarmingly low in the water and will be insecure. A life vest or flotation belt is a necessity for boating, because if you ever capsize you may be far from land or perhaps injured and unable to swim as well as you usually do. But for normal short-distance swimming, especially in fairly shallow water near shore, it is unnecessary.

If you feel yourself becoming a little tired, it is better to depend on your knowledge of how to rest than on an artificial aid such as a life preserver. You can rest by rolling over and floating on your back, breathing deeply and slowly, and with your arms spread out comfortably to provide some extra floating surface. You can also tread water for short periods, letting your body drop almost vertically in the water and paddling slowly with your arms and legs.

Marker ropes separate the shallow and deep portions of this swimming hole

Swimming coaches differ slightly in their methods of teaching, but most of them employ the same basic techniques. They start a swimmer at the edge of a pool, a dock or a float in shallow water. The swimmer gets into the water, holds onto the edge of the pool or dock and stretches out in a relaxed position on his stomach while he practices kicking gently and rhythmically. After a session or two of practice, he lets go of the edge and floats, with his head down in the water and his arms stretched out in front while he kicks. This will propel him through the water. At about this time, he should also practice floating on his back.

Next, in waist-deep water, the instructor usually supports the beginning swimmer at the waist, hips or abdomen, while the swimmer learns the basic crawl stroke and keeps up the kicking simultaneously. To do the crawl, you alternate strokes, first with one arm and then the other, bending your elbows slightly, cupping your hands slightly and comfortably, and bringing one hand up from your hip, out of the water and forward, fully extending it, and back down and rearward through the water. While one arm is forward, the other is at the rear, and your arms keep moving almost like a windmill. To breathe, you turn your head to one side (either side will do). For example, when your right hand comes forward you turn your head out of the water to the left; then when that hand starts back through the water, you turn your head straight forward into the water. Meanwhile, with your legs almost straight, you make short, rhythmic up-and-down kicks.

All of this should be done under the guidance of a coach or at least an experienced swimmer who can correct any mistakes you make and help you to learn good body position and movement. When you've mastered the basic crawl stroke, the coach will be able to teach you others such as the back stroke, side stroke, butterfly and breast stroke. They're all fun, and you may be surprised at how fast each method can propel you through the water. At the same time, you'll want to learn to dive and to swim underwater. The coach will help you with body and breathing exercises and with practice at holding your breath. He can also teach you aquatic games such as water polo, water volley ball, follow-the-leader, tag, water basketball and so on.

By the way, you can make your own temporary water wings and wash a pair of pants at the same time—but don't count on these water wings as a reliable life preserver. Though homemade water wings have been used by lifeguards in emergencies, I recommend the idea only for the fun of it. First dip the pants in the water to get them wet. Then tie the bottom of each pants leg into a knot. Next, get ready to jump into the water from a dock or boat, holding the pants above your head with both hands, grasping the waistband at the sides. As you jump, pull the pants forward and downward in front of you so that the waistband hits the water first. The pants will fill with air, each leg blowing up like a big balloon. The instant you hit the water, squeeze the top of the pants closed with your hands. If you hold the waistband bunched in one hand or tie it into a knot, the ballooned legs will stand up from the surface like giant water wings.

Once you've learned to swim, you will feel safe in any boat or canoe. However, any time you head into deep water or go a long distance in a boat or canoe, it's best to wear a life vest. The members of my family put them on almost every time we grab an oar, paddle or outboard motor; after all, we might intend to drift only a few feet from the dock and then change our minds and decide to cross a lake.

More comfortable and less bulky than a life vest — but just as effective — is a flotation jacket like the one this girl is wearing. Such jackets have become popular among boaters

This type of inflatable boat can be paddled, rowed or propelled with a double-blade, kayak-style paddle, and when deflated it can easily be transported in a car

Rowboats and canoes almost invariably used to be made of wood or canvas and wood or (in the case of homemade canoes) bark and wood. Such vessels were heavy and required fairly constant maintenance and repairs—calking, painting and varnishing, for instance—to keep them from leaking or even swamping. Aluminum boats and canoes were a great step forward, since they were a bit lighter and almost indestructible. Today, boats and canoes are often made of fiberglass, which is almost as light as aluminum, just about as durable and quite easy to patch. Some canoes are even made of light, tough plastic or a hardened rubber called Royalite. Modern materials make boat handling much easier than it once was, but an old rule still applies: to avoid scratching, tearing or denting the bottom of your craft when you beach it, try to lift the bow rather than dragging it.

That word "bow" brings up an interesting point. Some inexperienced boaters confuse the bow with the stern. The bow is the front of the boat or canoe, the stern is the rear. If you have trouble, remember that B is before S in the alphabet.

The most important thing to understand about a rowboat or canoe is very simple: you make it go forward or turn simply by pushing water the other way with an oar, a paddle or the propeller of a motor. Partly because a rowboat is usually heavier than a canoe and partly because its stern is square rather than pointed, outboard motors are used more often on boats than on canoes. But you can buy a special mounting board or brackets that will enable you to put a small outboard motor on a canoe for long trips or for trolling. Trolling means to move a boat or canoe slowly and smoothly along in the water, while you fish by trailing a

With an outboard motor, steering is easy. Pushing the rudder handle to the left or right simply makes the boat turn in the opposite direction

bait or lure behind. It's a good way to catch lake trout, pike, pickerel and sometimes bass and other fish.

An outboard motor has a rudder handle on it which you push to the left to go to the right, or push to the right to go left. It also has a throttle lever or handle to control speed or to stop. And you can put some models in reverse. Electric trolling motors, which are battery-operated, are very popular for trolling because they are nearly silent and vibrationless, and can be set to go very slowly without stalling. However, most outboard motors operate on gasoline. There is a starter rope that you pull or a starter button that you push to make the engine "turn over" and start.

A good rowboat has a metal oarlock (oar holder) near the center seat on each gunwale, or gunnel (the top edge of the boat's side). For the easiest, fastest rowing, you sit on the cen-

ter seat facing the stern, with a hand on the grip of each oar, and you pull the oar blades through the water from behind you forward to a forty-five-degree angle in front of you, leaning back as you do so. Then you lean forward as you bring the oars back through the air toward the bow and dip them into the water again. Good even strokes will keep the boat going fairly straight, but don't forget to keep glancing over your shoulder to watch where you're going. You may have heard the expression "to feather oars." This merely means to turn the oars and hold them in a nearly horizontal position between strokes; it reduces the effort and increases the speed as you lift the oars from the water, because it reduces water and air resistance.

To turn the boat, you must handle the oars as you would handle the rudder of an outboard motor. A pull on the left oar turns the

*When loading a canoe, most of the gear should be placed in the center, and the bow and stern should be kept light.
If three people are aboard they should sit or kneel in the bow, center and stern*

bow to the right and a pull on the right oar turns you left. For sharper turns, you can pull on one oar while you push on the other. And, of course, you can go backward by pushing on both oars instead of pulling.

A good canoe is as stable in the water as a flat-bottomed rowboat. It is also lighter, easier to handle, faster, capable of navigating rapids, shallows and tight spots where a rowboat can't go—and, in the opinion of most people, a canoe is a lot more fun. For most uses, the ideal canoe is a flat-bottomed model about seventeen feet long, three feet wide at the center and a little over a foot deep.

To paddle a canoe, you face the bow rather than the stern if two people are aboard, and that alone is an advantage since you can easily watch where you're going. When paddling alone, you will make better progress if you either sit at the center facing front or on the bow seat facing the stern. In the latter case, the stern becomes the bow and leads the way. When two people are paddling, one sits on the stern seat and one on the bow seat; the more experienced paddler should take the stern position, as this permits him to steer while watching the load and the bow paddler. Steering is always done from the stern position unless the stern paddler asks the bow paddler for help. The paddle acts like a rudder as well as a propeller, and a rudder is placed at the rear of a craft because it steers best from that location.

For good steering and ease of paddling, the stern paddle should be longer than the bow paddle. If you place a stern paddle upright with its blade on the ground in front of you, the top of the handle should be about level with your eyes. If so, it's the right length for your height. The bow paddle should reach to just below your chin. The best paddles are made of white ash, which has the right weight and a springiness that helps in paddling. Two other good woods are white spruce and hard maple. Handles and blades come in many shapes and there is no single best type. If it feels comfortable and paddles easily, it's fine.

Basic canoe instruction usually includes the

J stroke, which is the easiest paddling stroke to master but is inefficient because it makes the vessel turn slightly instead of going straight forward. To do the *J* stroke (or any other) you can place the paddle in the water on either side of the canoe; if it's on the left, your lower hand—grasping the paddle just above the blade—should be your left hand. Your upper hand—grasping the top of the handle—should be your right hand. If the paddle is in the water on the right side, your lower hand should be your right hand, and the upper one your left hand. Put the paddle into the water a little ahead of you, with your arms fairly straight, and keep the blade close to the canoe. Now bring the paddle back to the rear, and at the end of the stroke move it out and slightly forward again, feathering it up out of the water, so that the entire sweep takes the shape of a *J*. If you sweep the paddle straight back on the left side of the canoe, without putting the hook on the *J*, you will turn the craft to the right, and if you sweep it straight back on the right you will turn to the left. The hook of the *J* straightens the canoe out only slightly.

If you keep your arms fairly straight, relaxed but not bent much, your upper hand can push on the paddle while your lower one not only pulls but acts as a pivot to put extra sweep into the stroke. Moreover, with your arms in this position you can let your back do most of the work and will be able to paddle for quite a while without tiring. Another technique that may prevent you from tiring soon is to change paddling sides occasionally, although some expert paddlers never change sides. If two people are paddling, one paddles on one side and one on the other; after a while, they switch.

Once you master the *J* stroke, it will take only a little more practice to modify it into the pitch stroke, sometimes called the guide's stroke. This is a far more efficient way of propelling a vessel since it keeps you going straight instead of zigzagging. To do this, you move the blade straight back—and you do *not* hook the end of the sweep into a *J*—but as it goes back you turn the blade at a gradually increasing angle until you move it slightly out and feather it up out of the water at the end of the stroke.

There are only two other important strokes, the backwater and the sculling draw, though you will work out variations that produce the best results for you. The backwater is simply the pitch stroke reversed and is used to back up. The sculling draw is used to move the canoe sideways when you want to snuggle up to a dock, another boat or a beach. To do the basic draw stroke, you simply put the paddle in the water, out to the side with the blade facing the canoe, and draw it in toward you. A sculling draw is the same thing repeated several times without taking the paddle out of the water. Instead, you move it away from the canoe again and again in a criss-cross "figure eight" feathered pattern. On the first draw, the paddle should be slightly ahead of you; when you've drawn it in against the side of the canoe, feather it outward and rearward, and draw it in again, this time slightly to the rear, then feather it back out and slightly ahead and draw it in again.

There are a couple of games you can play with a canoe if you're a good swimmer. One is jousting, which involves two opponents in two canoes. Each player is armed with a staff, thickly and softly padded on both ends, and each player wears a life vest both for water safety and as extra padding. The two opponents paddle their canoes up fairly close, then stand up so that each player can try to push the other player out of the canoe with the staff. The winner is the one who doesn't get a dunking.

Another good game is a "gunnel-jumping" race. If you stand up in the stern—wearing nothing but a swimming suit and life vest because you're likely to lose your balance and fall in the water the first few times—you'll find you can stand first on the seat and then with a foot on each gunnel. Now if you bend your knees forcefully while leaning forward and then straighten up again with a shove, the canoe will move ahead a little. Practice flexing your legs this way and pretty soon you will be able to move the canoe with surprising speed, though

An outboard motor can be installed on a square-sterned canoe or one that's equipped with a special mounting board or brackets

Some modern canoes are made of aluminum, fiberglass or even plastic, but a few old-time craftsmen still prefer to make their own birch-bark canoes on wooden frames

A canoe trip may involve several canoes and a number of people, but one experienced leader should always head the group

the ride will be a good deal more erratic and bumpy than when you paddle. Several people can stand on their canoes and have a race. For still another good contest, several people can jump out of their canoes into the water at the sound of a whistle, and then see who can climb back in fastest. If you've ever fallen out of a canoe, you know that getting aboard in deep water is far from easy.

When you've become adept at canoeing, you can begin making canoe trips. It's exciting to explore remote waters, the truly wild rivers and streams, in a canoe. Paddling can be tiring, however, and portaging (carrying a canoe and the equipment you've loaded overland from one stretch of water to another) can be thoroughly exhausting. You should practice loading and portaging before you make your first long trip.

The secret of correct loading is merely a matter of balance. Place your packs and as much of your other gear as possible near the center. Keeping the bow and stern light makes paddling easier and keeps a canoe more stable. With the weight centered, you can even ride choppy waters without one end or the other plunging and perhaps going out of control.

Portaging across any piece of land usually requires at least two walks, one with the canoe and one with your pack. If you have a lot of equipment, you may even have to make a third walk. There are three main canoe "carries" for portaging. If you're alone, you have no choice but to make the one-man carry. Lash your paddles across the space from the bow seat to the center thwart, with enough space between them for your head. With the paddles lashed to the seats, you can carry the canoe upside-down overhead, with the paddles resting on your shoulders.

To keep a canoe moving straight in the water, the person in the stern paddles on one side and the person in the bow paddles on the other side

Shooting the rapids safely is an art. It should be attempted only by those who have become expert at canoeing

With two paddlers to do the work, short hauls can be made with a simple upright carry. The person in front lifts the bow up under his arm and holds the canoe with two hands, while the person at the stern lifts and holds the canoe hip-high with both hands. But a long portage requires a two-man shoulder carry in order to prevent exhaustion or a back strain. As with the one-man carry, the canoe is transported upside down. The front man holds the bow on one shoulder and steadies it with both hands. He should grasp the canoe very near the front so that it won't block his vision. The front man watches for obstacles, does the steering and calls instructions and warnings to the rear man. The rear man positions himself near the stern, with his head up inside the inverted canoe and the gunnels resting on his shoulders. He can see the legs of the front man, and he simply follows. A rolled-up towel makes a good shoulder pad to prevent discomfort with this carry.

Canoeing is like hiking in that you should work up to long trips gradually, getting into condition as you do so. Start with short voyages, heading for a goal only a couple of miles, or about an hour's paddle away. Then try longer trips and finally overnight excursions.

For long trips a repair kit is vital, and you can buy one at any boating-goods store. To repair a canvas canoe, you need Ambroid glue, unbleached muslin patches and a piece of sandpaper to roughen the edges and thus help the glue get a firm hold. For aluminum canoes all you need is a tube of liquid solder. And for fiberglass canoes you need epoxy-resin glue.

A common mistake among canoe campers is to leave a canoe right-side up at the water's edge overnight. This can lead to either of two mishaps. An upright canoe can be partly filled with water in a heavy rain, and if it's a wooden one this does the finish and the wood no good. And if left near the water, a canoe of any type can be lifted by a strong wind and carried away over a lake or down a river. This, obviously, is a far worse calamity than getting a little water in the craft. At night, haul your canoe well away from the water, turn it over and tie it down. Then you will still have a canoe in the morning and can resume your trip as a knowledgeable voyageur.

* * *

The boy shown above is putting live bait on his hook and the man shown below has used an artificial lure to catch a trout. Both methods work well if used properly

19

BASIC FISHING METHODS

The first fish I ever caught was a sunfish. It probably weighed about half a pound, but I was as thrilled as if I had hooked a battling fifteen-pound rainbow trout. There's something special about the first fish you land. Mine was caught at a Minnesota lake where my mother and father had taken me on vacation when I was six years old. My dad made an "Indian fishing pole" for me—a willow rod, a piece of string with a bent pin tied to the end and half a small worm as bait.

It may not sound like much of a fishing outfit, but such simple equipment is good to start with. When using fancy rods, reels and lures, inexperienced anglers tend to rely on their gear to do the work for them. That's how not to catch fish. When you have to depend on an Indian fishing pole, you know you can't cast or troll; it's entirely up to you to find your fish and put the bait almost in front of its nose without frightening it away. And you also realize that you must be patient. A fish is likely to be suspicious at the first sight of a worm on a bent pin that's tied with a big knot to a thick length of string. It isn't the same as a bait that conceals a hook carefully attached to an almost invisible leader which, in turn, is attached to a thin, almost equally hard-to-see line.

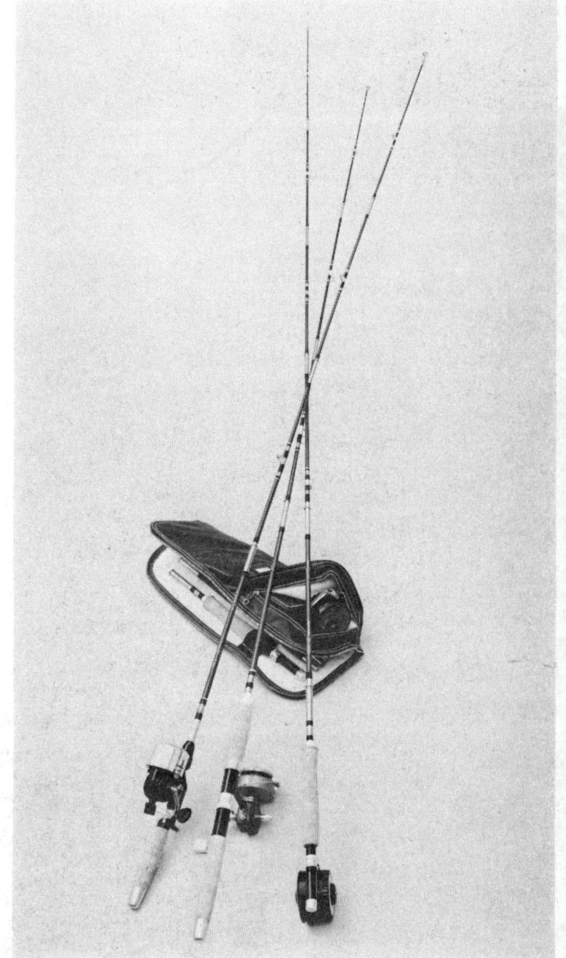

The rod at left has a closed-face spinning reel; the center one has an open-face spinning reel; the one at right is a fly rod

This huge bass is proof that an old-fashioned bamboo pole is excellent for certain kinds of fishing

Even after you graduate to more complicated equipment, there are certain kinds of fishing that can be done best with a simple cane or bamboo pole. For instance, there's a technique called "dapping" which is used in the South to catch panfish along the edges of lakes and ponds when the water is high. At such a time, many fish lurk almost next to the banks, under half-submerged logs, among rocks and below overhanging brush and earth. To go dapping, you use a long bamboo pole with a fairly short line attached to the front end. You tie a small hook to the line, with a light sinker (a lead weight) pinched onto the line a few inches above the hook, and a bobber (a cork or hollow plastic float) about six inches above that. The arrangement of hook, sinker and bobber will present the bait right where the fish are hiding—from nine inches to a foot beneath the surface.

You put several worms on the hook and then you walk the shoreline. Wherever you see a fallen log sticking into the water, or a jumble of rocks or a sheltered spot formed by the overhanging bank, you reach out with the pole and gently lower the bait into the water until the bobber rests on the surface. Jiggle it up and down a couple of times—still gently—to attract the attention of fish. Then just wait a few minutes.

In this situation a fish is likely to nibble at the bait cautiously rather than striking it hard. Then the fish will mouth it and start slowly away, so you may not even feel the bite. But you should be watching the bobber; when it suddenly ducks under the water, give your pole a little yank and with luck you've hooked your fish.

Most larger fish in deep water hit a bait or lure hard enough so that you won't be in any doubt when you have a strike. Give the fish a moment to grab the bait or lure firmly, and then set your hook by giving the rod a sharp rearward and upward tug. This rule does have some exceptions—fish that take a bait gently and must be waited out until they begin to run with it—but you'll find out how to handle individual species through experience and through the advice of other anglers who have caught the same kinds of fish before.

For both fresh water and salt water fishing, there are four basic types of rods and reels: bait (and plug) casting, spinning, spincasting and fly casting. However, there are many variations of each type. For instance, a surfcasting rod is a large rod that can be used with a spinning, spincasting or bait casting reel and is designed for long two-handed casts from the beach or surf into the sea; a popping rod is a long, light rod that can be used with the same kinds of reels and is designed for accurate casts of light lures or baits in either fresh water or salt water.

Most people, after fishing for a few years, begin to collect different types and sizes of rods and reels that work best for specific kinds of fishing, and I will describe how the basic types work. However, I want to say first that one rod-and-reel combination serves well for most kinds of fish in almost any body of water—large or small, shallow or deep—under all sorts of fishing conditions. That combination is a light fiberglass rod about six feet long with a medium-sized spinning reel.

The author's daughter caught one of her first fish— this pan-sized perch—with a worm suspended in the water under a plastic bobber

Now let's look at the different types of reels and how they work. For many years the most popular kind was the bait and plug casting reel, though spinning reels are now in greatest favor. A bait casting reel has a horizontal revolving spool on which the line is wound. It is attached on top of the rod, and has a winding handle on the right side. If it's a good model, it also has a "drag" button which can be adjusted like a brake for a certain amount of tension and can be flipped on to help fight a powerful fish. There is usually a little moving gate that keeps the line winding evenly. After some practice, you will find that with a revolving-spool reel you can make long, accurate casts using a large lure or heavy bait, and this type of reel has the power to help you haul in big trophies.

The idea of casting is to put the lure or bait close to where you think a fish may be, making it touch the water smoothly enough to avoid scaring that fish away, far enough out to reach the fish and accurately enough to be where the fish will notice it.

Before casting with a revolving-spool reel, turn the drag button to a fairly light setting. Then wrap your fingers around the butt of the rod—that is, the handle—so that your thumb touches the spool. Most anglers make the mistake of casting with the reel facing straight up so that the handle faces to the right. You will get better results if you turn your wrist so that the handle faces upward. Now you're ready to start the first stage of the cast, called the backcast.

Keeping your shoulder still and using more wrist action than elbow movement, bring the rod and reel straight up, while holding your thumb firmly down on the spool to prevent the weight of the lure or bait from unwinding the line. Without any further movement on your

These pictures show the correct way to cast with a revolving-spool reel. Pressing the thumb down (left) keeps the line from unwinding before you want it to. Turn your wrist so that the reel handle faces upward and then, with wrist action, bring the rod straight up (below). Again using wrist action, bring the rod forward smartly (right) while you lift your thumb. Press your thumb down again an instant before the lure hits the water

part, the tip of the rod will flex rearward, past the straight-up position. Then, again using wrist action, bring it forward smartly but smoothly while you lighten your thumb pressure. Press your thumb down again to stop the lure and line an instant before the lure hits the water.

The rod should not come down all the way to a horizontal position to complete a cast; it should stop just before it's level. If you think of your elbow as the center of a clock, and your arm and rod as a clock hand, the cast stops at about ten o'clock or two o'clock, depending on which direction you're facing. With a little practice, accuracy is fairly easy to achieve; it's just a matter of pointing the rod in the proper direction and judging how hard to cast in order to reach a desired distance.

A spincasting reel, also known as a closed-face spinning reel, has internal gears and a brake operated by a push button so that you don't have to control the line by thumbing it. The line comes out of a hole in the front of the housing. Aside from that, it works pretty much like a bait casting reel, is mounted on top in the same way and is handled in a similar manner. Most anglers find it easier to master a spincasting reel but (unless an expert is using it) a reel of this type will not cast as far or as accurately as other types.

A true spinning reel, also called an open-face spinning reel, is not completely enclosed in a housing and it requires finger control instead of thumb control. In fact, you cannot reach the line with your thumb because, for one thing, the rear of the reel mechanism is in the way and, for another, the reel is mounted *under* the rod rather than on top. The winding handle, or crank, is usually on the left side so that you can turn it with your left hand while holding and controlling the rod with your right hand at all times. However, some models have a handle that can be rolled over onto the right side for the convenience of left-handed casters.

The spool of a spinning reel is fixed rather than revolving. A special mechanism in the reel spins the line on or off the spool, and a gear arrangement permits this to be done with great ease and speed. At the front of the reel is a "bail"—a thin metal hoop that keeps the line from unwinding until you want it to. When you want to "open the bail" (release it) you merely swing it back. The moment you start to reel in line, it automatically closes again, guides the line onto the spool and acts as a light brake to help you play your fish. But it must be open while you cast, and during this operation you therefore need to control the line manually.

Before casting, place your right hand—your rod-holding hand—so that the line in front of the reel runs over the ball of your forefinger, taking care not to let the line catch in the crease of your finger's first joint. With your left hand, you can then open the bail and the line won't unwind.

Aim at your target, the point to which you plan to cast, with the rod in the ten o'clock position. This time you don't have to turn your wrist over; keep it positioned naturally, so that the reel is under the rod. Then flick your wrist to bring the rod straight up smartly to the twelve o'clock position. It will flex back a little past that point, which is desirable. Now, flick your wrist down again forcefully to bring the rod back to the ten o'clock position. As it gets there, release the line from your finger tip and the lure will be whipped out toward your target. Practice making your motions forceful but smooth.

A mistake that some inexperienced anglers make is to start the cast with the lure or bait reeled in all the way to the rod tip. You won't get any distance at all this way, and the lure may even snag in the line guide at the end of the rod. The lighter your lure is, the lower it should hang from the rod tip. With an average (medium-weight) rod and reel, for example, a lure weighing three-eighths of an ounce should hang a little less than a foot from the rod tip, while a one-eighth-ounce lure should hang down about two feet.

The spinning reel is a complicated little piece of machinery compared to older designs, yet it seldom needs repair and there is nothing complicated about using it. It is the best all-around reel because it will cast—accurately and far—anything from very light lures to very heavy ones and it can also handle every kind of bait.

The fly rod is, on the average, longer and lighter than other types, and the fly reel does little more than hold extra line that is not in use. Everything in fly casting has to be done manually. It is considered more difficult than other types of casting but, like any difficult art, it renders the greatest satisfaction when you master it.

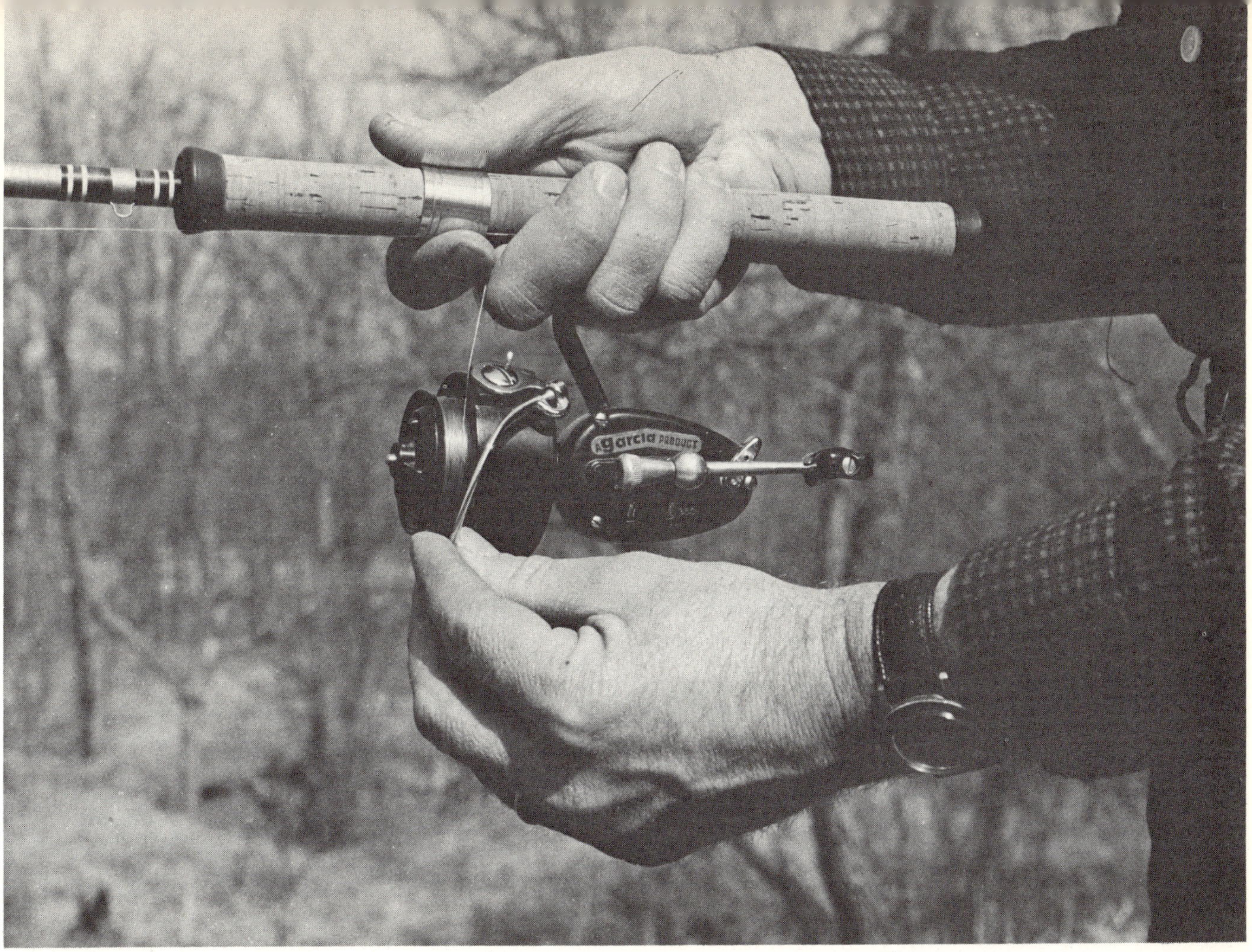
garcia PRODUCT

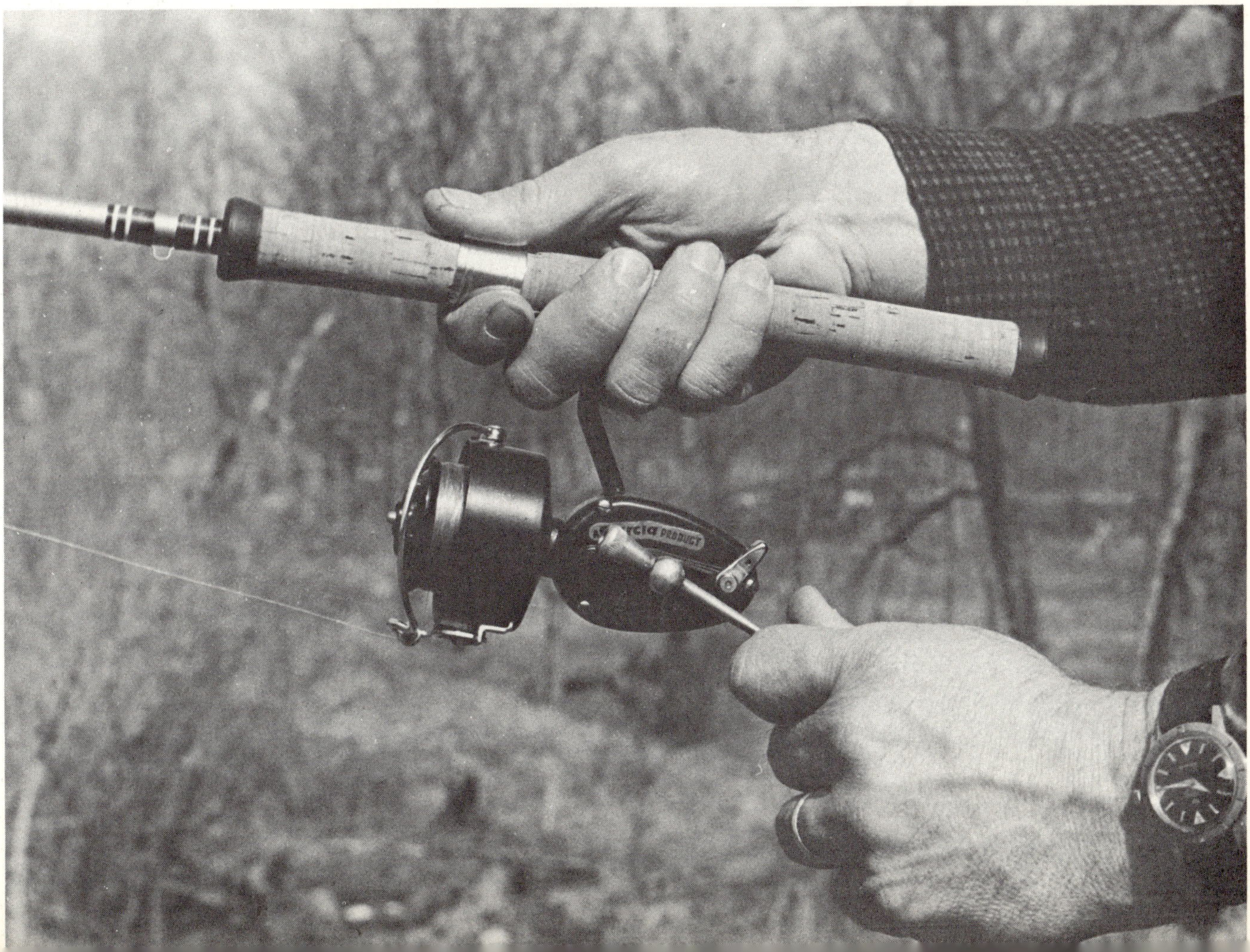
garcia PRODUCT

There are three basic difficulties in fly fishing. The first is manipulating the tackle without getting tangled in it or failing to cast your fly where you want it. The second is presenting a tiny artificial insect or artificial baitfish to the fish you want to catch in such a smooth way that you don't make your quarry suspicious. And the third is playing and netting a hardfighting fish on very light tackle that provides fewer mechanical aids for the angler. Achieving all this adds an extra thrill to fishing.

The fly reel is a very simple type with a comparatively large revolving spool and a short handle. (This applies to a "single-action" reel; there is also an automatic fly reel with a spring which rewinds line automatically when you press a lever instead of working the handle. However, the spring won't reel in a fish for you, so when you use an automatic fly reel you must pull line in with your fingers as you play the fish and then take up the slack by pressing the button. It's fine for small fish, but a single-action reel is best for most purposes because it permits you either to take in slack with your fingers or to reel in line by turning a handle, whether your fish is large or small.)

As I mentioned, the chief function of a fly reel is merely to hold line that is not in use. It is not employed at all during the cast. You hold the rod with your "rod hand"—the right one if you're right-handed—and use your other, or "line hand," to "strip" line from your reel. This simply means to unwind line by pulling it out.

Grasping the line between the reel and the first rod guide, strip off about thirty feet of line, coiling it into big loops and holding it with your fingers and thumb. You will make several "false casts"—whipping the rod back and forth several times to let out more and more line and get greater and greater distance, letting the line uncoil from your hand a loop or two at a time. Twenty feet of line is enough for a start; after you acquire skill you simply uncoil as much line as you think you'll need to send a fly the right distance. Since this is difficult and a book cannot answer every question that might come

up, it helps to have an experienced fly caster coach you.

Your rod hand should be grasping the cork handle firmly, with the fingers wrapped around, the thumb extended flat along the top and the reel underneath. With the line coiled in your line hand, use your rod hand to point the rod, holding it at about ten o'clock or a trifle lower. With a smart upward twitch of the rod, again using wrist action, snap the rod up past "midnight" to about one o'clock. Because a fly rod is very springy, its tip will flex well to the rear. As you bring the rod up, let out a couple of coils of line. Pause an instant with the rod at one o'clock, and the released line will stream out horizontally behind you.

During early practice sessions you should keep your eye on the end of the line to see where it is, but after a while you will be able to feel it and you can keep looking where you want to cast. When the line is straight out to the rear you'll feel a tiny tug, the signal to start the forward cast with a smooth but forceful forearm and wrist motion as if you were hammering a nail. At the same time, let out another

With a fly rod, you don't cast line directly from the reel. Instead, you unwind as much line as you want and coil it loosely in one hand, then let it go a coil or two at a time as you move the rod back and forth in the air

A sharp upward twitch of the rod will make its tip flex well backward — to your rear — and this movement will flick a good length of line into the air

To get your fly line out as far as you want it, you make several "false casts," without letting the fly touch the water. Note how far this angler has cast his line, and he still holds more coils in his left hand

coil. End the forward cast where you started, at about ten o'clock, but don't let the fly hit the water. Instead, pull back and repeat the process of false casting until you have let out all the line coiled in your hand or until the fly travels the desired distance in front of you. Try to do everything smoothly and rhythmically until, on the final cast, you let the fly touch the water.

Bear in mind that it isn't the weight of the fly that does the real work but the weight of the line itself. This is why lures as light as a fly can be cast. By substituting a tiny weight for a fly (whose hook might snag on something), you can practice on dry land, perhaps in a backyard or on a lawn. When you've become good at overhead casting, you will find you can easily cast to the rear or the side to reach any desired target, even when overhanging tree limbs rim a stream or pond.

To get extra distance into your casts, you can teach yourself to "double-haul" during both the back and forward false casts. This consists of pulling your line hand down away from the rod smartly and then bringing it up near the rod again before uncoiling line. The effect is to give the line extra tugs in the air, and this increases its momentum. It will be awkward at first, but it will eventually lengthen your casts.

A fly—to a fisherman, at any rate—means a small artificial insect or baitfish with a hook in it. There are six basic kinds: dry flies, wet flies, nymphs, streamers, bucktails and bass bugs. A dry fly floats on the surface and is used with a special floating fly line to keep it there. It looks like one of the many insects that either drop onto the water or hatch from a nymph stage that has been living underwater and then comes to the surface. Wet flies sink, and they are used with a sinking line and leader. They are usually winged, and look like insects that have fallen into the water. Nymphs are usually wingless. They are wet flies resembling insects that live underwater during the nymph, or pupal, stage before they have emerged and "hatched" into winged insects. An observant fisherman can watch hatches taking place, especially during the spring, and then he tries to pick a fly to "match the hatch" because fish love to feed on hatching insects. This works especially well with trout.

The other flies imitate small baitfish. A streamer is a long wet fly that, when in the water, resembles not a fly but one of various minnow species or other small fish on which larger fish often feed. A bucktail achieves the same effect but is fatter, with hair that streams out in a fish shape when submerged. Bucktails and streamers are often combined and are then aptly called bucktail-streamers.

Bass bugs are composed of a relatively large head made of wood or plastic with a trailing "skirt" of bucktail, some other hair or even rubber strips. To me, they look like a cross between a frog, a large insect and a small fish. I don't know what they look like to the fish they often catch, but they are very good for attracting bass and sometimes other species. (Fly fishing used to be restricted almost exclusively to trout and salmon, but it is now employed to catch all kinds of fish.) A bass bug is a surface lure, meaning that it rides along on the surface.

A closely related lure, generally used with bait casting or spinning tackle, is called a popper. It, too, has a relatively large wooden or plastic head with a trailing skirt, usually of rubber strips. As it rides along, it makes a tiny popping sound and plops about in the water. This action seems to trigger an attacking instinct, especially in bass, which are often caught on poppers.

Surf fishing may require long casts of a large bait or lure. With a special surf rod, you can make a two-handed cast

Wearing waders, this fisherman has gone out into the water with a spinning rod to catch a landlocked salmon

A lure can be so many different things that perhaps the word itself should be defined. A lure is simply a man-made gadget of any shape, color, size or type, designed to attract fish and with one or more hooks attached.

There is a thick type with a large three-dimensional body made of wood or plastic and usually painted to resemble a small fish. Called a plug and generally used with bait (and plug) casting tackle or spinning gear, it is probably the most popular type. But not all lures attract fish by imitating other fish or insects on which they feed. There are also lures which attract by flashing through the water. Fish seem to strike at them out of curiosity or annoyance.

This flashing classification includes spoons (spoon-shaped metal discs, shiny or painted bright colors, with hooks attached) and spinners (spoon- or propeller-shaped metal discs, also shiny or brightly painted and with hooks attached). Frequently, spoons or spinners are used with a strip of pork rind or colored plastic attached to the hook, which adds to their appeal for hungry fish. There are also combination lures such as spinner-flies. In addition, there are jigs, which look like the front end of a plug with the rear end composed of a hairy tail; the head is weighted, for "jigging" means to jiggle a lure or bait along the bottom of a lake, pond or ocean, where some fish prefer to feed. And there are also plastic imitations of eels, worms, frogs, squid, crickets and other morsels that delight a hungry fish.

Between the lure or bait and the main part of the line, a leader is sometimes attached with swivel snaps. It is usually a length of nylon, gut or some other strong but thin or transparent material. It should be strong enough so that it isn't likely to break while you are playing a fish, but it should also be hard to see in the water. Fish are easily "spooked," or alarmed, when they notice that a tempting morsel is attached to something that looks like an angler's line. For some sharp-toothed or sharp-gilled species, a thin wire leader is used to prevent having it frayed or cut off during the fight.

The line itself may be a braided synthetic material (dacron, nylon or similar plastic), or a single thick thread of such material, which is then called a monofilament line, or it may be braided linen or silk. For most purposes, monofilament is the most popular type of line, because it is light, strong and hard to see underwater. Lines come in many different "test weights." A test weight is a measure of strength —the limit of weight that, if applied very suddenly, will snap a line. It is considered sporting to use a test weight no heavier—and often lighter—than the probable weight of the fish you want to catch. The idea is to play the fish carefully to keep the line from breaking, rather than letting very heavy line do the work and simply "horsing the fish in."

Lures are sometimes called "artificials" since many of them are man-made imitations of living creatures. Baits are sometimes called "naturals" since they are the real thing. There are so many different baits that it might well take a thick book to list them all. The most popular —and effective—one in the entire world is the common earthworm. A huge variety of fish seems to consider the worm the most delicious of offerings. Moreover, worms are easy to dig up and to impale on a hook. Some of the other

Here are combination lures—beaded spinning spoons with bucktails. Those shown are designed for large fresh-water fish such as muskellunge

The lures in the top row are fresh-water plugs, used to catch bass, pike and many other species. Below them is a plastic salt-water squid for bluefish and striped bass. Next are three kinds of flies—a streamer, a bucktail with tandem hooks (two hooks, one behind the other) and a dry fly. Flies are used not only to catch trout but many other kinds of fish, and so are spoons like the two at bottom

most commonly used baits are minnows, craw-fish, nightcrawlers, small grass frogs, sand worms, hellgrammites, grubs, salamanders and other small lizards, crickets and grasshoppers. There are also cut baits, which can be just about anything from a small chunk of fish to a bit of pork rind or left-over lamb chop.

In the next chapter, I will have more to say about a few unusual baits and about the importance of using your imagination when you want fish to bite. For the present, however, I think it is more important to add that a good fisherman is one who asks questions of people in the area where he wants to go fishing. The proprietors of bait and tackle shops, as well as friendly local fishermen, will be glad to tell you which baits and lures get the best response from the fish species in the area. They will also give you advice about tackle and the right hook sizes for the local fish. As a general rule, a hook should be small enough so that you can completely conceal it in the bait, and you can usually do well with a slightly smaller hook than you think you need for a given species of fish. While you're asking local residents all those questions, you might also ask for directions to the best fishing spots; your fellow fishermen will be glad to tell you where the good waters are—except when they're saving those spots for themselves.

20

THE IMAGINATIVE ANGLER

You can eventually learn to fish well merely by doing it whenever and wherever you get the chance. However, it obviously helps to get some guidance from experts. You can do this at a fishing preserve—a privately owned lake, artificial pond or stream where you pay for the privilege of fishing. A typical fee would be fifty cents or so for a "permit" (an admission fee) plus a couple of dollars per pound of fish you catch. Among the preserves I know about are Fisherman's Dude Ranch at Des Plaines, Illinois; Eldred Preserve, in Eldred, New York; Paradise Creek Lodge, in the Pocono Mountains of Pennsylvania; and Whitewater Trout Ranch, near Los Angeles. Most preserves specialize in several species of trout, though a few offer bass. The preserve manager or one of his assistants will show you the techniques for handling your tackle and catching your fish.

Learning by doing is easier when you fish in salt water than when you go inland. Salt water ports from which fishing boats leave are usually dotted with bait and tackle shops whose proprietors are happy to give advice, and the advice is generally very good. Furthermore, you will probably pay to fish from a party boat (on which large groups of anglers go out for the day) or a charter boat (which you and your family or several friends can hire for a day).

Perch like shallow, sheltered, shady spots, so they can often be caught from a dock

To find fish, learn to "read the water." Trout pools like this, aerated by falls, are good spots to cast a fly

Learning to catch bluefish and other ocean species is easy because the skipper of the boat will help. These boys have an added advantage — the skipper is their dad

High mountain pools often hold large trout, and just hiking to such water is an outdoor adventure

The captains and mates of party and charter boats are almost always expert fishermen. They supply rods and other tackle as well as baits and lures, and they serve as coaches for any inexperienced anglers who may be aboard. Luckily, on some fresh water lakes and streams local fishermen make their living by working as guides, and these men, too, are happy to coach anyone who doesn't know the local fish species, the best tackle or the recommended techniques.

Many books have been written on the art of fishing, and it is worthwhile to read a few of them. Frequently, these books provide diagrams of useful line and leader knots, charts showing recommended test weights, pictures showing hook sizes for many different fish, lists of suggested areas for various kinds of fishing, and so on. Several universities now offer classes in how to fish, and fly-fishing schools are conducted in Vermont and Florida by the Orvis Company, a manufacturer of excellent tackle.

In addition, tackle and lure companies such as Eppinger, Heddon, Newton, Zebco, Weber and Scientific Anglers offer booklets of instruction and tips. These can be helpful in many ways. For example, they will give you an idea of what type of lure to use for a particular kind of fish under a particular set of fishing conditions. The best choice may depend on whether a lake is deep or shallow and what time of year it is when you go fishing. Lures are divided into three basic classifications: surface disturbers (which ripple along the surface to attract fish), sub-surface lures (which ride slightly beneath the surface when you move them by trolling or by reeling in) and divers, or bottom lures (which are weighted or have long "lips" that make them go deep). It helps a great deal to know which type most often produces fish under a particular set of conditions.

As you have probably gathered, it's wise to have a tackle box with a variety of lures as well as a supply of bait hooks of various sizes. You should also have an assortment of leaders, sinkers, bobbers, some extra line and a fishing knife. There are two popular types of fishing knives. One is shaped much like a hunting knife but its top edge is serrated and is used to scrape the scales from the skin of a fish, if you plan to roast or grill the fish with its skin on. The other has a narrow, curved blade that is excellent for filleting. (Illustrated instructions for filleting a fish accompany this chapter.) A good knife of either type has a cork, wooden or hollow plastic handle to keep it afloat if it is dropped overboard. I like both kinds of knives —each has its purpose—and I keep one of each in my tackle box. Another item I keep there is an old toothbrush. It's perfect for cleaning a reel if I accidentally drop one in the sand.

With all these bits of equipment, it is apparent that imagination as well as judgment will be needed to decide what to use and how to use it. A good angler must be both observant and imaginative. For example, when you look at a lake casually, you see a flat expanse of water. Now, bearing in mind a few fishing clues, try to imagine what is hidden beneath that flat surface. Here are the clues: steep cliffs usually indicate deep water near shore; a point of land jutting into the lake usually extends underwater as a bar; the mouth of an inlet has moving water; and weedy bays and coves are often inhabited by small baitfish.

*A red-and- white-striped spoon is a good lure;
in the water it looks like the kind of small fish
which the larger species like to eat*

Deep waters just below dams are good fishing spots, and so are rocky drop-offs. This boy has found both features in one small, easy-to-fish area

Between the dock and the float in this picture is a submerged weedbed. Such spots hold panfish

This little lizard is interesting in itself — and it would also make fine bass bait

A naked, gently sloping shoreline usually has poor fishing in the water near it, but all of the other places just mentioned would be likely spots to catch fish. They favor the deep, sheltered areas near cliffs and bars, and they hunt for smaller fish in the mouths of inlets and in weedy places. Another sign of good fishing is a buoy, which is often used to mark an underwater reef. A reef offers a sheltered spot for both large fish and the small ones on which they feed. Fish also like pools that are calm but are near fast-moving water, because such places are rich in oxygen content. A fish breathes with its gills, which take oxygen from the water.

If you're smart, you can look right into the water. Polaroid sunglasses permit you to see down to a considerable depth. You can see even further if you hold a diving mask on the surface and look down through it. Tricks like these are known as ways of "reading the water."

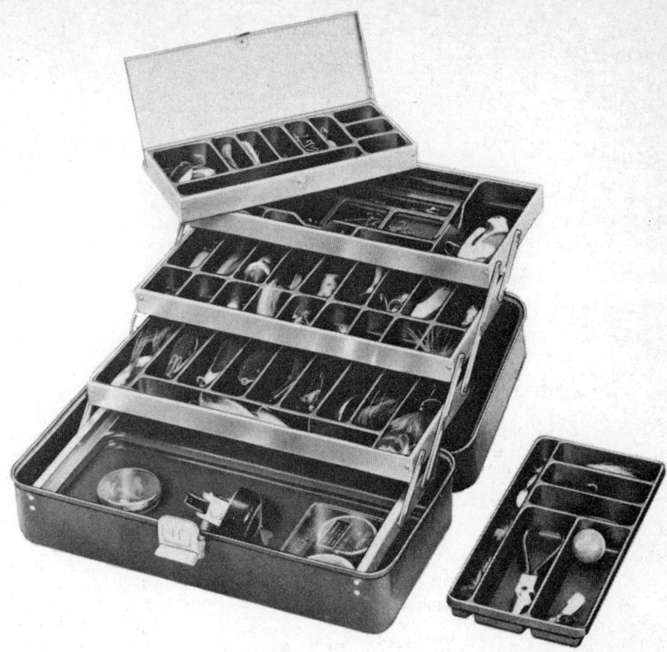

Your tackle box should contain a variety of lures, hooks, leaders, bobbers, sinkers, extra line, a knife, perhaps a pair of pliers — and anything else you think you might need while fishing

How to fillet a fish:

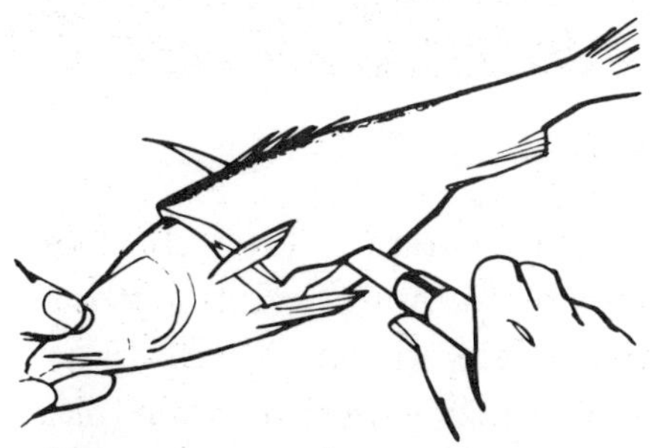

1. Make first cut just behind the gills. Slice down to the bone, then, without removing blade, turn it and slice straight along backbone...

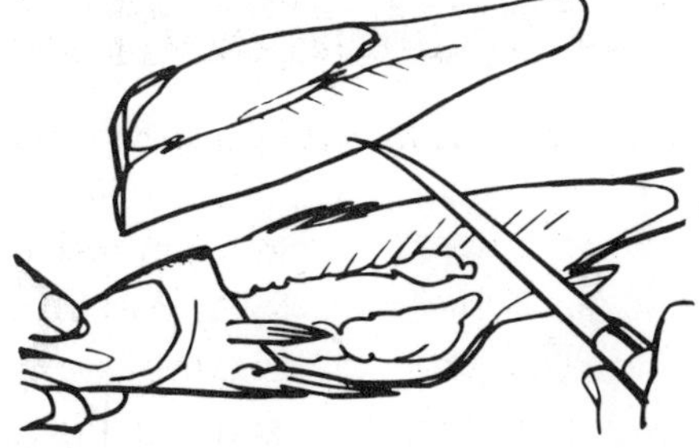

2. ...to the tail. Note that the fillet has been cut away from the rest of the fish. After slicing fillet off at tail, turn fish over and repeat procedure on the other side

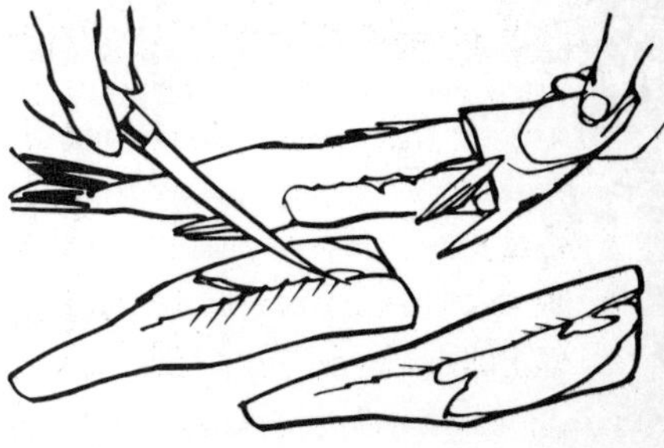

3. With both sides removed, you have cut away both fillets without disturbing fish's entrails. This is the neatest and fastest way to prepare fish. Now to finish the fillets...

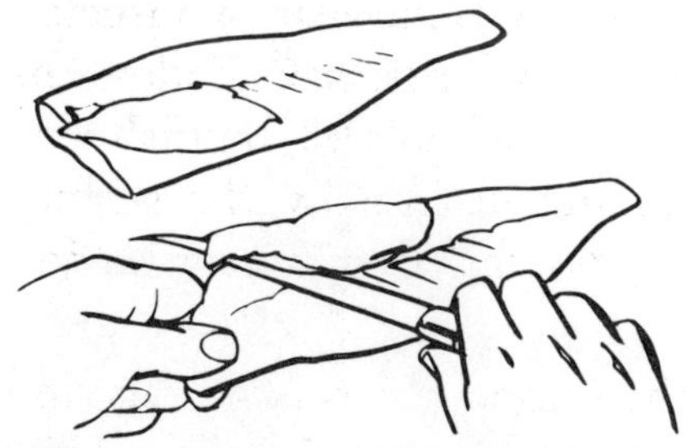

4. Next step is to remove the rib section. Again, a sharp, flexible knife is important to avoid wasting meat. Insert blade close to rib bones and slice entire section away. This should be done before skin is removed to keep waste to a minimum

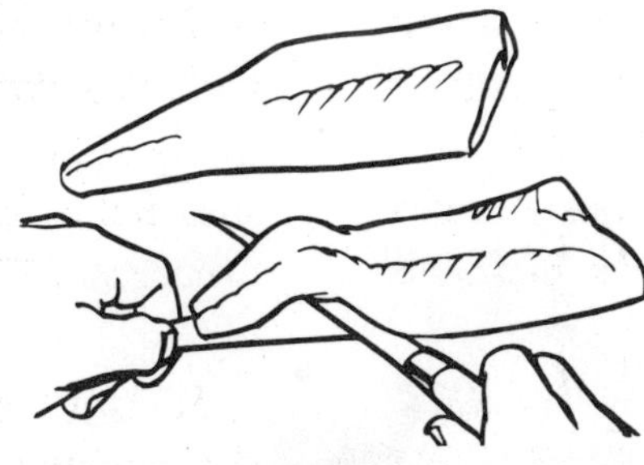

5. Removing the skin from each fillet is simply a matter of inserting knife at tail and "cutting" meat from the skin

6. Here is each fillet, ready for the pan, or freezer. Note there is no waste. Remember not to overwash fillets. This will preserve tasty juices and keep meat in its firm natural state

This trout was cruising over a gravel bar when he was fooled by a spinning spoon

You can often get a contour map of a lake from a conservation agency or from a local bait or tackle shop. It will have depth marks and lines indicating sunken islands, reefs, channels, steep shorelines and drop-offs. These are good spots. Also bear in mind that abrupt outcroppings, docks, logs, floats, breakwaters and jetties provide shade and concealment for fish; coarse rubble breeds insects and crustaceans (crawfish and the like) on which fish feed; the cool water of underground springs will attract fish; weeds are great places for pike, pickerel, panfish and largemouth bass, whereas a bare lake bottom is the kind of spot where fishing is just a waste of time.

In an earlier chapter, I explained that trolling is moving along slowly in a boat or canoe while trailing a lure or bait in the water. It is a good idea to troll lines from two rods at a time —one running shallow and one deep—to find out where the fish are lurking. By bumping a lure called a "weedless spoon" along the bottom, you can probe for hidden pockets without getting continually snagged on weeds. Vary your trolling speed until you find one that produces a strike. When you do get a strike, cast to the same place or troll through it again; where you find one fish you can usually find others.

If you see birds diving at the water, they are probably feeding on small baitfish or insects— the same things eaten by larger fish. Follow the birds. Also follow any schools of baitfish you see. Schools swimming just below the surface create a ripple, or "patch," that is easy to follow.

Be guided by the season, the time of day and the species. In general, most fish like cool water. It isn't the temperature that matters most to them but the amount of oxygen in the water. Cool water holds more oxygen than warm water. In the early spring you should fish close to shore, but the rising surface temperature drives fish to various depths as summer begins. Trout, landlocked salmon and walleyes will go down fifty feet or more. Bass drift into deep holes during the daytime, but at dusk they return to the shorelines to hunt baitfish, insects and frogs. Northern pike, pickerel and panfish remain in relatively shallow water—preferably weedy—even in warm weather.

Contour maps, available from tackle shops and conservation agencies, help you find the best fishing spots

If you find a likely looking spot, troll through it at least a couple of times, or cast and retrieve your lure or bait repeatedly. Never give up after just one cast. Imagine the reaction of the fish. On the first cast, the fish may notice something moving past but may not see it in time to attack it. On a second cast, the curiosity of the fish may be really aroused, but caution prevents a strike. On a third or fourth cast the fish, now alert and eager, may pounce.

Your imagination can be used in other ways, too, if you learn about the habits of various fish. Carp, for example, are semi-vegetarians, so they can often be caught with bits of half-boiled vegetables—especially carrots and parsnips—instead of bait impaled on your hook. A honey ball is another wonderful carp catcher. To make honey balls, simmer a teaspoonful of anise seed and half a cup of water in a saucepan for three or four minutes over medium heat. Then add five tablespoons of honey and go on simmering until a light syrup is formed. Next, add half a cup of flour, stir and remove the mixture from the flame. Add a cup of corn meal and knead it with a fork. Finally, cool the stuff slightly, pour it onto waxed paper and flatten

Having caught a pickerel in this spot, the author's son trolls over the same water again. He knows that other fish may lurk here

This 10-pound carp was caught by angler John Quick, who used a honey ball for bait

it. You will now have a clayish dough that can be put onto your hook a chunk at a time. Be sure to cover the hook completely, as carp are cautious creatures.

You will learn more and more of these secrets through experience and from other anglers, but I can't resist adding a few more tips here and now. Not only carp but several other species have a sweet tooth just as humans do. Trout, perch, bluegills, crappie and sunfish are fond of marshmallows. Take a small marshmallow or a piece of one and insert the hook in it with a full turn so that it is almost completely buried. Then pinch the marshmallow up around the eye of the hook, forming a pear-shaped ball that now completely conceals the hook. If you fail to pinch it, the marshmallow will quickly float off the hook, but if you put it on properly, it will stay there for a while, and a small sinker will pull it down underwater, where the fish will soon find it.

Another good homemade bait is a piece of sponge on an ordinary hook, well soaked in extract of vanilla. For some reason, artificial vanilla flavoring doesn't work (fish seem to be fussier than humans in some of their tastes) but genuine extract of vanilla has a flavor that will lure all sorts of panfish as well as trout.

"Chum" is a term for chopped up baitfish which is thrown into the water from a boat or let over the side in a perforated chum bucket. It is usually used in salt water, but it works in fresh water, too. Some stores sell dehydrated chum, which is far less messy to handle than the chopped-up kind. You may recall that I said fish like the taste of stale bread, but it won't stay on the hook. The fact is, they also like dog biscuit and the hard pellet type of cat food, which can be put into a homemade chum bucket. To make such a bucket, find any quart-size plastic container with a lid—an ice-cream container will do nicely—and punch lots of holes in its side and lid. Tie a stout cord through one of the holes so you can dangle it from the boat. For excellent results, try filling it with bits of dog biscuit mixed with boiled rice and oatmeal. Its odor will soon have fish prowling around your boat, and one of them is likely to grab whatever bait is on your hook.

The fact that fish can smell is a great aid to anglers. A combination of lure and homemade bait called a "bloodsicle" gives off an odor that particularly tempts northern pike and muskellunge. To make it, you wrap the rear end of a plug or spoon, or one of the hooks on such a lure, in cotton. Then you soak the cotton in pork, beef or chicken blood and put the lure with its cotton trailer in a freezer overnight. When you're ready to fish, just take it out and troll or cast with it. Because the "bloodsicle" is frozen, the blood remains in the cotton for quite some time, slowly melting into the water and attracting fish.

A musky can also be caught with an unadorned spoon, plug or spinner, or with a wide array of large live baits, including the small-mouthed stream fish called a sucker. The best size of sucker for this is between one and two pounds, but if you catch a big sucker you may want to save it for yourself; they're good to eat.

Skipper Don Bingler plays a bluefish. The circling gulls told him where to find them.

March is the best time for catching them. The best place is a medium-sized stream, and the best bait is a gob of garden worms on a small hook. Any kind of tackle, from a cane pole to a spinning outfit, is fine for catching suckers.

Any kind of tackle will also do for channel catfish, which put up a good fight and are delicious. There are many good baits, including elm-tree seeds, catalpa worms, shrimp, minnows and bits of liver. Since catfish like decaying matter, shrimp that have been aged to the spoiled stage are perfect. You'll have good fishing just after a rain, during a rise in a stream or where a river pours into a lake. Try fishing deep holes during daylight and then move into the shallows at night. As a matter of fact, night fishing in the shallows is a good way to catch many species. It's a lot of fun, but be sure to carry a flashlight and be even more careful than usual when handling hooks or casting in the dark. Nightfishing is generally best in July and August, when the heat makes fish sulk in the depths during the day.

If you're fishing for trout during May, June or July, be sure to note whether the inchworms have come out in your area yet; the farther north you go, the later in the season you'll see inchworms, or measuring worms if they're called that in your area. They are the little green worms that crawl by bringing their rear ends forward, humping up their middles and then advancing their front ends—"inching along." Actually, they are the larvae (baby stage) of the moth family called *Geometridae*.

Trout are absolutely delighted when the little creatures fall off leaves and branches into the water. You can make an imitation inchworm fly by wrapping a short length of green pipe cleaner around a small hook. If you can't buy colored pipe cleaners in your area, dip a white one in green vegetable dye.

In America, May is probably the best month of the year for catching the most fish of the most varieties in the most kinds of water. It's a good time to experiment with various baits or with lures of different patterns, colors, sizes and actions. And even though the shallows are usually full of fish during the spring, you should also experiment by trying your lures or baits in water of several depths. When you find the combination that hooks the greatest number of fish, keep using it until it no longer gets results. Then use your imagination and start experimenting again.

* * *

INFORMATION SOURCES

For information on how to attend a fishing school, write to The Orvis Company, Manchester, Vermont 05254. This company will also send you general information on fishing techniques and tackle.

Other sources for booklets of fishing tips include: Lou J. Eppinger Manufacturing, 6340 Schaefer, Dearborn, Michigan 48126; Daisy-Heddon, Inc., Rogers, Arkansas 72756; Newton Line Company, Homer, New York 13077; Scientific Anglers, Inc., Box 2001, Midland, Michigan 48640; Weber Tackle Company, Stevens Point, Wisconsin 54481; and Zebco Division, Brunswick Corporation, Box 270, Tulsa, Oklahoma 74101.

21
ON TARGET

Some outdoor writers recommend a .22 rifle as a first gun for a beginning shooter, but actually a single-shot BB gun is a better choice. This is not because a BB gun is any safer than a firearm that uses gunpowder and bullets. A BB is a round, hard pellet which is shot with sufficient force to inflict serious injury. A gun—no matter what kind it may be— is safe only if the person handling it treats it with the proper respect and good sense. I believe in starting with a BB gun because it is very light and easy to handle, has almost no recoil, or "kick," makes so little noise that it won't disturb neighbors when you practice in a populated area, and has sufficiently low power so that it can be used on a small range even indoors if you set up a proper backstop and observe the rules of safety.

Before proceeding any further, here are the common-sense safety rules that every shooter should learn:

*Treat every gun with the respect due a loaded gun. That way, you can't have an accident with a supposedly unloaded gun.

*Guns carried into camp or home, or guns not in use, must always be unloaded and must either be "taken down" (taken apart) or have their actions open. (The action is the part of the gun that does the firing; the loading port, or gate, is usually there.) Guns should remain in carrying cases when being transported to a shooting area.

Using a .22 rifle, this boy has scored well on a paper woodchuck target

Under the supervision of adult instructors at a firing range, these girls and boys are using Daisy BB guns to learn the art of shooting

Safety is the first consideration in learning to handle guns. These hunters know that you never carry a gun while climbing over a fence; one fellow will hold both guns while the other crosses

*Always be sure the barrel and action of a gun are clear of any obstructions and that you have only ammunition of the proper size (called caliber in a rifle, gauge in a shotgun) for the gun you are carrying; before firing, remove any oil or grease from the chamber (the rear of the barrel, where the cartridge or BB rests before it is fired).

*Always carry your gun so that you can control the direction of the muzzle even if you stumble, and keep the safety (a switch button or lever that prevents firing) on until you are ready to shoot.

*When you become a good enough marksman to go hunting, be sure of your target before you pull the trigger; know the identifying features of the game you're after.

*Never point a gun at anything you do not intend to shoot; avoid *all* horseplay while handling a gun.

*Never leave an unattended gun loaded. Store your guns and ammunition separately. It is best to keep guns locked up, with the key in the care of one responsible person, so that no one can handle them without permission; this prevents careless or irresponsible people from experimenting with guns.

*Never climb a tree or fence or jump a ditch with a loaded gun, and never pull a gun toward you by the muzzle.

*Never shoot a bullet at a flat, hard surface or the surface of water, because this can cause a dangerous ricochet (a bouncing or glancing off of the bullet in an unpredictable direction); before target practice, make sure your backstop is adequate.

BB guns, like all guns, are made both as repeaters and single-shot models. I prefer a single-shot as a first gun, simply because it takes time to load after every shot. For some reason, that tends to make a shooter aim extra-carefully; he wants every shot to count.

An instruction sheet is sometimes packed with a gun when it is shipped from the factory, but this is not enough to teach you everything about how the gun works. There are many types—single-shots, bolt-actions, lever-actions, pump-actions, double-barrels, autoloaders—and they do not all operate the same way. The first thing to do when buying a gun is have the dealer or an experienced shooter show you how it works, and this should be done several times without really putting ammunition into the gun. Even after that, a beginning shooter should handle a gun only under the guidance and supervision of an experienced shooter who can show him correct procedures, answer any questions and correct any mistakes in carrying, holding, shouldering, aiming or pulling the trigger.

If no one in your family is a shooter, you can still get proper supervision and coaching by joining a shooting club or participating in a shooting program given by a school, church, Scout troop, YMCA, summer camp, a chapter of the United States Jaycees (Junior Chambers of Commerce), 4-H Club, sportsmen's group or similar organization. Most such groups start shooters with .22 rifles, but some instructors use BB guns or similar air rifles at first.

The typical BB gun has an internal spring-operated plunger that compresses air in a small compartment when you cock the gun by moving a bolt-handle, lever or pump-handle. This type of arm is also called an air gun. Instead of a round BB, some of the more powerful models shoot a piece of lead that is elongated—shaped more like a bullet. Such a missile is called a pellet, though "pellet" is also a correct term for BB's and for the many little round balls fired from a shotgun.

Some BB and pellet guns do not utilize compressed air. Instead, they are powered by cartridges filled with compressed gas. You can fire many shots before the gas cartridge is empty and a new one must be inserted.

Guns that use gunpowder are called firearms. They are loaded with cartridges which hold a primer (an explosive chemical mixture), powder and a bullet. When you pull the trigger, an internal part of the gun called the firing pin strikes the rear of the cartridge. This ignites the primer, which in turn ignites the powder. The burning powder is trans-

Shooting .22 single-shot rifles, vacationers at a boys' camp learn how to get the proper sight picture

Loading a single-shot pellet rifle—which is an excellent gun for learning to shoot

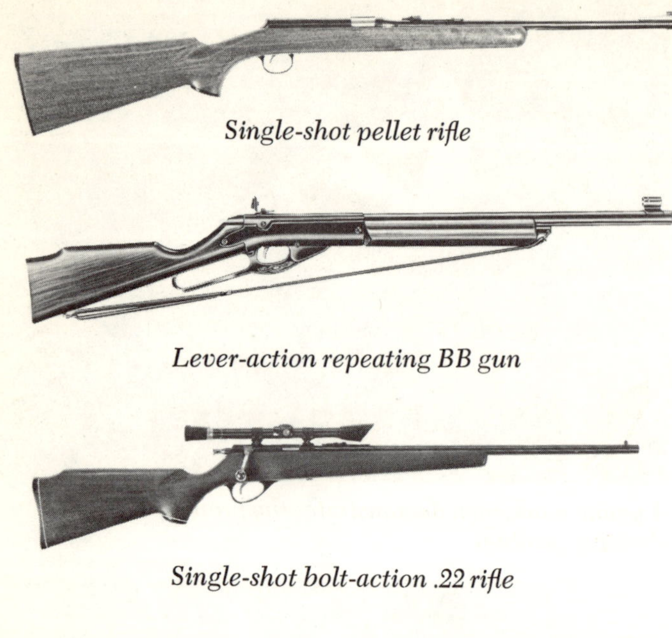

Single-shot pellet rifle

Lever-action repeating BB gun

Single-shot bolt-action .22 rifle

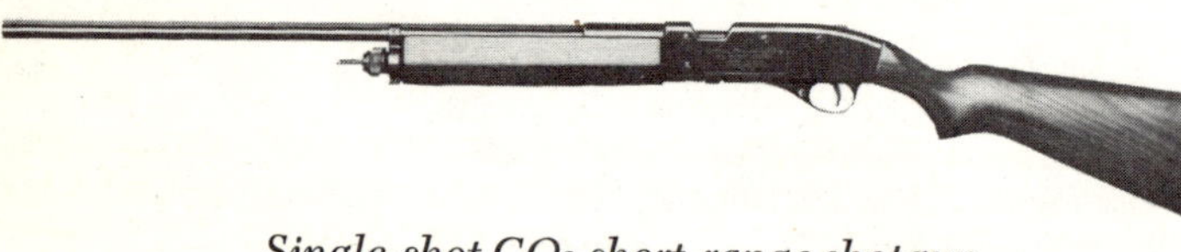

Single-shot CO₂ short-range shotgun

Single-shot conventional shotgun

formed into rapidly expanding gas, and this fires the bullet out of the cartridge and out of the barrel with amazing force.

After learning how a gun works, you should learn how to carry it safely. There are several safe carries—with the gun cradled over the crook of your arm and the muzzle pointing toward the ground; holding it in your hand ahead of the trigger guard with the muzzle pointing forward; cradling it over one arm with the other hand on the stock to steady it while the muzzle points upward and sideward; or carried on a shoulder sling with the muzzle pointing straight up and your hand on the sling or gunstock to control it. The main considerations are that you must be able to control the direction in which the muzzle points, and you must be sure it is never pointing at anyone —or at anything you don't intend to shoot.

Before jumping a ditch or climbing a fence, unload the gun and put it down, then reach back and get it after you are over; or unload it and let a friend hold it for you while you cross.

A practice range for a BB gun doesn't have to be any longer than twenty-five feet—a fifteen-foot range is sometimes used indoors—and you can use small commercial or homemade targets. (After a picnic lunch, I like to use the paper plates and cups as targets before burning them.) Right behind the targets should be a safe backstop. It can be an earth embankment, big cardboard cartons packed tightly full of newspapers or a pile of sandbags or logs. It should never be rocks or anything hard from which BB's or bullets can ricochet.

A father coaches his son as the boy learns to shoot a .22 from the standing, or offhand, position. The targets are tin cans and balloons

There are four basic rifle-shooting positions: prone (lying on your stomach), sitting, kneeling and standing (called the offhand position).

In the prone position, you lie flat on your stomach with your body about forty-five degrees off your line of sight (the direction in which you will fire). If you're right-handed, your body will be forty-five degrees to the left; if you're left-handed, it will be forty-five degrees to the right. Your legs should be spread comfortably and extended flat on the ground, with your toes pointing out and your feet resting on their inner sides to help keep you steady. Your elbows rest on the ground to make a tripod with your body and thus form a steady shooting platform. Your shoulders should be as level as possible, because this will also help to keep you steady and comfortable. Keep your left arm almost directly under the rifle so that bone, not muscle, supports the weight.

In the sitting position, you sit on the ground with your feet spread wide, your heels dug in slightly for steadiness and your elbows resting on your knees. This time, if you're right-handed, your feet and legs will extend to the right by about forty-five degrees, and to the left if you're left-handed. Bend forward with your back and shoulders. This will cup your shoulder into a "pocket" where you cushion the butt of the rifle.

There are several variations of the kneeling position. The one I prefer is to kneel on the right knee (if you're right-handed), rest your buttocks on your right foot, rest the elbow of your left hand on your left knee and lift your right elbow so that your right arm is horizontal. However, I almost never use *any* version of the kneel because this is the least steady of all positions. It used to be popular but no longer is because it lets you sway from side to side too easily.

In the offhand position, you stand with your body turned to the side as in the sitting position but turned more—about ninety degrees off the line of sight. Your feet should be parallel and about twelve inches apart. Your left elbow (if you're right-handed) should be directly

A young marksman demonstrates the proper prone shooting position

This is a fairly good sitting position, but the young lady will shoot better if she leans forward more and rests both arms on her knees

This boy holds his rifle well in a kneel, but the kneeling position is the least steady of all shooting stances

under the rifle and your right elbow and arm should be out at a ninety-degree angle to your body and therefore horizontal. This helps to lift and steady the rifle. If you're left-handed, just reverse the directions for all positions.

Your trigger hand (the right one for right-handed people) should be wrapped comfortably around the grip of the stock behind the trigger guard. The ball of the index finger presses the trigger, and this should be done with a smooth, steady, straight-back squeeze. Your other hand cradles the forward part of the stock (called the fore-end or forearm) under the barrel; it should be extended out far enough on the fore-end to be comfortable. The butt, or rear end of the stock, should be tucked in against your right shoulder (or left shoulder if you're left-handed). Don't tip your head to the side. Try to keep it as straight as possible, and bend it forward only slightly to get your lower cheek firmly against the stock. Also try to keep the rifle straight rather than "canted," or tilted.

Most BB guns and .22 rifles have a square-topped blade or a blade with a little bead on top as the front sight. The rear sight is usually a notch which may be shaped like a V, a U or a U with a squared-off bottom. Beginning shooters almost always look through the sights with only the right eye while squinting the left one shut. This is strange because most—though not all—of the best marksmen shoot with both eyes open. The front sight should be aligned in the center of the rear notch, and its top should be level with the top of the notch. The bottom of the bull's-eye or any other target should seem to rest on top of both sights and should be centered. This is called a correct sight picture, and it is also known as the six-o'clock hold.

On some rifles, the rear sight is a peep sight; instead of a notch, it is a small round hole. To aim with this arrangement, you simply center the bead or square top of the front sight in the hole, again with the bottom of the target centered on top of the front sight.

Once you've become proficient with open or peep sights, you'll want to have a telescopic sight on a rifle because a "scope" is much more precise and therefore better for both hunting and target shooting. When you look through a standard scope, you see crosshairs—two lines, one vertical and one horizontal, that cross in the middle. You simple center the target behind the lines where they cross.

I mentioned before that some shooting courses for beginners rely on BB guns. The biggest and most widely distributed classes of this type are held under the title of the Shooting Education Program, co-sponsored by the United States Jaycees and Daisy-Heddon, the manufacturer of Daisy BB guns. This program is open to all boys and girls from seven to fourteen years old. The Jaycee chapters cooperate with schools, businessmen and civic leaders to run the program, which involves a thirteen-week course of one-hour sessions with qualified instructors. The course is followed by local and state competitions. In over six-thousand communities where the Jaycees conduct this program, more than half a million youngsters per year learn to shoot, and each year the winners of the competitions—not only from the United States but also from Canada and Mexico—attend the International BB Gun Championships. This event is usually held during three days in July.

If you haven't learned to shoot, I strongly recommend this program, and it should be followed by a course with the .22 rifle, such as that given by the Boy Scouts or the Junior Clubs of the National Rifle Association. The National Rifle Association also conducts a father-and-youngster home-instruction course called the Ranger Program, and provides free targets, written shooting instructions and instructions for building safe indoor ranges and bullet stops.

The bullet stop, or backstop, for firearms must be bigger and thicker than for BB guns, even though firearms are shot on a longer range. When you first start practicing with a .22, twenty-five yards is a good distance. Later this should be increased to fifty and finally to a hundred yards or even farther.

When you have mastered the .22 rifle, my advice is to begin learning to shoot a 20-gauge shotgun with a comfortably short stock and a recoil pad. Like the .22 rifle, a 20-gauge shotgun has a relatively mild (though more forceful) recoil and a fairly low noise level. Such a shotgun is light and comfortable to carry; for hunting birds and small game, I use one more often than any other type of shotgun. Again, begin with a single-shot model. Such a gun can usually be bought inexpensively (as can a .22 single-shot), and after you learn to make every shot count you can graduate to a repeater. Shotgun ammunition is not as cheap as .22 ammunition, but it is not terribly expensive, either.

A few words should be said here about the single-shot Trapmaster Gas Shotgun made by Crosman Arms. This gun is in a special gauge, smaller than 20, and instead of using standard shells with gunpowder it is powered by cartridges of compressed CO_2 (carbon dioxide) gas. It works the same way as some BB guns except that, like all shotguns, it shoots a number of round pellets at one time instead of a single bullet or BB. Such a gun is used to hit fast-moving or flying targets. The CO_2 gun does not have the recoil, power or range of a gunpowder-operated shotgun and should not be exclusively used to learn shotgunning, but it's fine for inexpensive practice. The manufacturer also sells a target thrower and plastic aerial targets that fall apart when hit but can be put back together and used over and over. The pellets from a standard shotgun, fired by gunpowder, would damage these plastic targets but the less powerful CO_2 loads do not hurt them.

For conventional shotgun practice you can toss up clay targets (which cannot be put together after being hit). Such targets are sold in sporting-goods stores. For cheaper practice, you can also use beverage cans as targets. Either toss them by hand or use a can launcher, which is powered by .22 blank cartridges and actually shoots cans into the air. Launchers are sold at sporting-goods stores.

As mentioned, a shotgun fires an aerial pattern of pellets—hundreds at once—in order to hit speeding targets. This type of gun is used to hunt running game such as a rabbit, a squirrel (how good rabbit and squirrel stew is!) and occasionally a fox or other animal. It is used even more often to hunt flying game which is never shot with a rifle—such as a pheasant, quail, grouse, woodcock, duck, goose, and so on.

When you begin shooting at aerial targets, you must find a practice area at least 500 yards long, because a backstop won't do any good with pellets being fired up into the air. For safety, you must be certain there are no people, animals or buildings within 500 yards of where you shoot. A rifle bullet will go much farther, but shot pellets lose their velocity within 500 yards and are not dangerous beyond that distance. *Within* that distance, however, you must always remember that they can kill.

While there are four basic positions for shooting a rifle, a shotgun is always fired from the standing position, and even this is not done the same way as with a rifle. Since you will sometimes want to make fast shots at moving game, you must learn to bring the shotgun to your shoulder quickly in one fluid motion, called mounting. To do this, you push the gun slightly forward, already pointing it toward the target as you bring it up, at the same time releasing the safety button and seating the stock against your shoulder. It helps to lean slightly forward from the hips. With a shotgun, both arms are relaxed because you have to move with the target. Don't keep your right arm up high in a horizontal position as you did with a rifle, but simply crook it in a relaxed position so that your finger easily reaches the trigger. And don't worry about keeping your other arm directly under the barrel because it, too, has to move.

Cradle the fore-end in your left hand as you did with the rifle, but don't wrap your fingers and thumb around it; instead let them ride along it in a cupped position rather far out—that is, with your arm fairly straight—so that you can swing the barrel smoothly with the flight of the target.

A coach has just used a hand-trap to toss up a clay target, and the puff of dust in the air shows that the shotgunner has smashed it

Your right hand is held pretty much the same way as with a rifle, but your index finger curls around the trigger more because speed will sometimes be essential and you will really *pull* the trigger—almost slap it with your finger—instead of squeezing it.

Practice mounting your shotgun without tipping your head to one side, which is a common error. As the barrel comes up into line, move your cheek forward to meet the stock and try to keep your head straight, moving it down toward the stock rather than sideward. The shoulder line of your body should be about forty-five degrees off the line of fire rather than ninety degrees as with a rifle. This will be enough to cup your right shoulder, forming a

You can see an empty shell being ejected from an autoloading shotgun as the shooter continues to swing his gun past an aerial target

hollow for the butt of the stock, and it will also allow you to swing your body to either side from the waist up in order to follow the target. Good shotgunning requires complete freedom of movement, so you must be able to pivot from your hips. Also bear in mind that a slight forward lean from the hips helps you to absorb recoil without feeling an uncomfortable kick. As you follow the target, don't ever raise your head for a better view. If you don't keep your cheek firmly against the wood, the stock can slap your face unpleasantly during recoil.

As for your feet, forget about them. Foot position has some importance in the clay-target contests called trap and skeet, but in shooting for hunting purposes the main thing is to be able to stop walking in the middle of a step when you sight game and stand comfortably, ready to shoot. If, later on, you do go in for trap and skeet, a coach will help you with foot positions.

The pattern of pellets from a shotgun spreads out as it travels and is about thirty inches wide at a forty-yard distance. This is wide enough to hit flying game when you become adept, but it isn't as wide as it may sound and you will do a lot of missing at first. A trick that will help is to practice pointing your finger at moving targets and then think of pointing a shotgun as simply pointing an enormously long finger. If you keep that finger moving with the target even as you pull the trigger, you will quickly improve. It is more important with a shotgun than a rifle to keep both eyes open. Otherwise, you will see the target slightly to one side of where it really is, and you won't be able to follow it as well. Furthermore, you can judge distances better with both eyes open.

So far I've talked about following the target and moving with it, but most of the time you must also *lead* it—that is, shoot ahead of it. Moving your sight picture is fairly simple, because the sight on a shotgun is usually a single bead on top of the muzzle and you are pointing rather than trying to aim precisely. What you'll see, if the gun is correctly mounted, is a tiny bit of barrel, the bead and the target. In order to lead, simply swing the bead through the target and past it, pulling the trigger then without stopping the swing.

If you've ever ridden a bike to deliver newspapers, you probably rolled up the papers and threw them onto a porch from a moving bike. You know that to hit the porch you had to toss the papers where the porch wasn't. Now, in firing a shotgun, it's the target that's moving instead of you but the principle is the same.

Of course, if a target is moving straight away from you, you can hold dead on and hit it. But if it's moving away and rising, you must swing above it; if it's descending, you must swing below it. If it's coming toward you it may appear to be rising and then, again, you must swing above it. If it's moving to the left, swing past it from right to left; if it's moving to the right, swing past it from left to right. Sometimes it may be moving in a combination of directions—for example, rising and flying to the right. Then you swing diagonally, above it and out to the right. Just follow its line of flight, swing past it and fire without stopping the swing.

How *much* to lead it, unfortunately, is something you can only learn through practice, but here's a rule of thumb; if you miss consistently, you are probably leading too little, not too much. Try increasing your lead a little more on each shot until you're hitting consistently.

When you're first getting acquainted with a shotgun, you can become accustomed to its feel and also gain confidence in your hitting ability by firing at stationary targets. Set up several sticks at a twenty-yard distance and hang clay targets or cans on them. Mount the gun, find a target and pull the trigger all in one motion; then try it with the next target in line. Keep doing this until you no longer miss.

Then it's time to try flying targets. There is a spring-powered target thrower called a hand-trap, which is operated manually. Little more than a handle with a hinged front end that whips the targets out, it is inexpensive and, if you follow the instructions that come with it, you'll find it easy to work. Buy a hand-trap and have a companion use it to lob clay targets for

Upon seeing a bird rise from the ground, a hunter must bring his gun to his shoulder quickly and smoothly, while he leans slightly forward, toward his target

you, tossing them as straight away from you as possible. The target thrower should stand to one side of the shooter and on a line with him or slightly behind him, never out front. To save the expense of clay targets you may, of course, substitute a beverage-can launcher for the hand-trap.

For more fun, you and your companion can take turns shooting and throwing targets. After you've become pretty good at hitting targets that are going straight away, the target thrower should begin tossing them up at angles. It won't be long before you get the knack of leading and hitting them.

* * *

INFORMATION SOURCES

For further information on BB guns, write to Daisy-Heddon, Inc., Rogers, Arkansas 72756.

For further information on Jaycee Shooter Education Programs and BB competitions, write to Daisy-Heddon, or to the Promotion Manager, United States Jaycees, Box 7, Tulsa, Oklahoma 74102.

For information on NRA membership and shooter-training programs, write to the National Rifle Association, 1600 Rhode Island Avenue, Washington, D.C. 20036.

For information on other shooting programs, plus booklets on shooting, hunting and conservation, write to the National Shooting Sports Foundation, 1075 Post Road, Riverside, Connecticut 06878.

For descriptive literature on the Trapmaster CO_2 Gas Shotgun and accessories, write to Crosman Arms Company, Fairport, New York 14450.

For additional information on hunting, sportsmanship and conservation, write to the Hunt America Time Program, Izaak Walton League of America, 1326 Waukegan Road, Glenview, Illinois 60025.

* * *

22
THE IMAGINATIVE HUNTER

A woodchuck hunter uses his rifle scope to peer across a large pasture

Wildlife biologists say that there are more elk and whitetail deer in America today than there were when Columbus discovered the New World. During the nineteenth century the populations of many wild animals were depleted tragically—almost to the point of extinction. Factors that contributed to this loss included the spread of settlements and cities, carelessness that caused frequent forest and prairie fires, pollution of waters and the cutting down of vast stretches of woods by lumbermen who did not care enough to replant devastated areas. But the worst damage of all was probably done by "market hunters," who killed huge numbers of animals and birds in order to sell meat, fur and feathers.

There would probably be hardly any wildlife in America today if a great conservation effort had not begun at about the turn of the century. Many sportsmen—outdoorsmen who enjoyed hunting—joined this conservation movement, which is still being led by sportsmen.

The results have been wonderful. In 1900, only about half a million whitetails were left in all of North America, but by the early 1960's these deer numbered about twelve million in the United States alone. Half a century ago,

A waterfowl hunter rises from his blind when birds fly close enough for a shot. Decoys help to attract the birds within range

This deer hunter waited near a game trail until a fine buck came along, heading for a feeding area

A hunter flushes a pheasant in a corn field

A setter points a quail covey, hidden by vegetation

Crouched in a natural blind and accompanied by a retrieving dog, these hunters are bagging ducks and geese

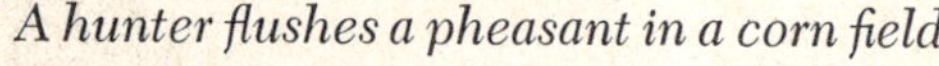

The author poses with a Texas mule deer. He found this fine buck in the heat of the afternoon, by searching for cool, protected bedding areas

pronghorn antelope were becoming rare, yet in Montana, Wyoming and several other Western states they are so plentiful now that some farmers and ranchers consider them pests. There are five times as many elk in the United States today as there were in 1910. Early in this century the wild turkey had almost disappeared except in the South, but this species has been restored in many states, and there are tremendous flocks in Pennsylvania, Wyoming and Oklahoma. Frequently, a few animals and birds have been transported from an area where they were abundant to an area where they were scarce or extinct; food was provided for them, damaged woodlands were reforested, the land was carefully managed so that the proper plants would grow in order to provide more food and cover, and hunting was forbidden until the game multiplied sufficiently. Hunters not only worked at these projects but contributed money to finance them through li-

cense fees and contributions, and today we have thriving game populations of most species.

Hunters have also introduced new forms of wildlife to America. The official state bird of South Dakota originally came from the Orient. It is the ring-necked pheasant. Sixteen of these birds were introduced in Oregon in 1882; larger numbers were later released in New Jersey, South Dakota, Nebraska and then in other states. The pheasant is now a common bird in many areas, as abundant as it is delicious to eat. The Barbary sheep has come to New Mexico, and the chukar partridge has traveled from India to California, Idaho and several other states where it has made itself at home. Even the red fox was originally unknown in America. Hunters brought some of these animals over from England a couple of hundred years ago.

As you can see, sportsmen have accepted

the responsibility of preserving wildlife. Any imaginative outdoorsman can visualize how barren the land would become if no one cared about preserving the plant and animal life. This is why good hunters abide by a creed such as this one:

I pledge myself to shoulder my responsibility toward the conservation of natural resources. I will use my share with gratitude, without greed or waste. I will respect the rights of others and abide by the law. I will support the sound management of resources, and the restoration of those that have been depleted. I will never forget that life and beauty depend on how wisely man uses the gifts of the soil, the water, the air, the minerals, the plants and the animals.

If you follow this creed, you will rarely hunt anything you do not plan to eat. Naturally, there are exceptions to the rule, as when crows or woodchucks become so numerous that they damage crops and some of them must be shot, or when bobcats or coyotes become too plentiful and begin to kill off the smaller wildlife. But there's no reason to waste even some of the so-called pest species that are shot. For instance, prairie dogs and woodchucks are rarely eaten, yet these clean little vegetarian animals feed on the same crops as domestic livestock, and they taste just as good pot-roasted or in a stew. Buy at least a couple of wild game cookbooks, and try to combine logic with imagination to decide which recipes will work nicely with several different species.

You must also combine the knowledge you've gained with observation and imagination if you are to be successful at hunting. Learn as much as you can about the habits of wildlife. Then try to imagine the logical actions and responses of animals in order to find game and get close enough for a shot at it.

Several good examples of how this works can be discovered in the way whitetail deer behave. Deer like to eat corn, but you won't often see a deer out in the middle of a cornfield during daylight because these animals have sense enough to hide from enemies. Along the edges of such fields, where woods begin, look for deer trails. Deer will feed in the fields at night and then go up onto high, wooded slopes and bed down in a concealed spot during the day. Think about this. It means that a good spot to hunt early in the morning would be about halfway up such a slope, where you might intercept a deer on its way home.

As you walk through the woods, glance frequently at the foliage in order to see whether deer are in the vicinity. Whitetails like to browse on cedar and red-maple sprouts, so notice whether these plants have bare twigs where the animals have been nibbling. Spots where such growth abounds are likely places to surprise a deer. Another good spot is a swampy lowland near a stream or lake; this offers deer a combination of high, weedy cover and plenty of edible plants. Still another good spot is an abandoned apple orchard, since deer love apples even when the fruit doesn't look fit to eat; and if the orchard is abandoned, the presence of human beings will not have frightened the game away. A grove of oaks, particularly white oaks, where there are lots of acorns will also attract hungry deer.

It's smart to scout a hunting area just before the season opens so that when the time comes you'll know where to look. In addition to the signs just described, look for tracks and deer beds—depressions where the brush and leaves have been crushed down by whitetails curling up for a rest. Also look for "buck rubbings"—saplings that have had bark rubbed off by deer antlers. A deer sheds its antlers each year and grows new ones during the summer. While they grow, they're covered with a membrane that looks like and is called velvet. When fall comes, the velvet dries and begins to peel and shred. A buck will rub against saplings to get the tatters off.

Some hunters wear black-and-grey-spotted red camouflage clothing which other hunters can see but whitetails cannot. Deer, like most mammals, are color-blind, so spotted red clothing looks to them like part of the foliage. However, it pays to know that birds can see colors. This is important when hunting ducks,

The top picture shows sprouts of red maple, heavily browsed by deer. The bottom picture shows a "buck rub" where a deer has rubbed his antlers against a sapling. Such signs can lead you to game

A dug-out spot in a snow trail like this shows where a deer has been feeding. If the trail looks fresh, it is worth following. While searching for food, the deer will not be moving very fast

geese, crows, pigeons and sometimes turkeys, because a red cap or jacket will scare them off.

Ducks and geese are most often hunted from a "blind"—a hiding place formed by putting up a structure of corn stalks, cattails, reeds, bushes or other tall plants. The blind is constructed at a spot where the birds have frequently been seen resting or feeding. The hunter hides inside the blind and tries to attract ducks or geese within good shotgunning range (no more than about forty-five yards or else you will merely miss or injure a bird without bringing it down). To attract the game, you can use decoys and a call.

Decoys are imitation birds made of wood, plastic, a composition something like papier-maché but sturdier, or sometimes rubber. Though you can buy decoys at sporting-goods stores, some hunters enjoy carving their own out of wood. An outline drawing of a mallard duck is shown with this chapter as a guide. You should make the carving life-sized or a little larger so that it can be easily seen from the air, and you should use waterproof paint to give it lifelike colors. Remember, birds can see colors and they are not easily fooled. To find the proper colors for any species of duck or goose, consult a field guide or "identification manual"—available in book and sporting-goods stores.

Carve the head and body of a decoy from two separate pieces of wood, because one-piece decoys tend to split at the neck. After carving the two pieces, drill a hole from the bottom of the body up through the spot where the head will fit, and a matching hole up into the bottom of the head. Through these holes you insert a reinforcing dowel—a cylindrical stick of hard wood—and cement all the parts together with waterproof glue. If your decoys are to be set out on land (geese are sometimes shot in corn, rice and other grain fields where they come to feed), you can drill a hole in the bottom for another dowel to serve as a "leg" and then stick your imitation birds into the ground with this leg. If the decoys are to be floated on the water—the most common procedure—you must attach a weight to the bottom to keep

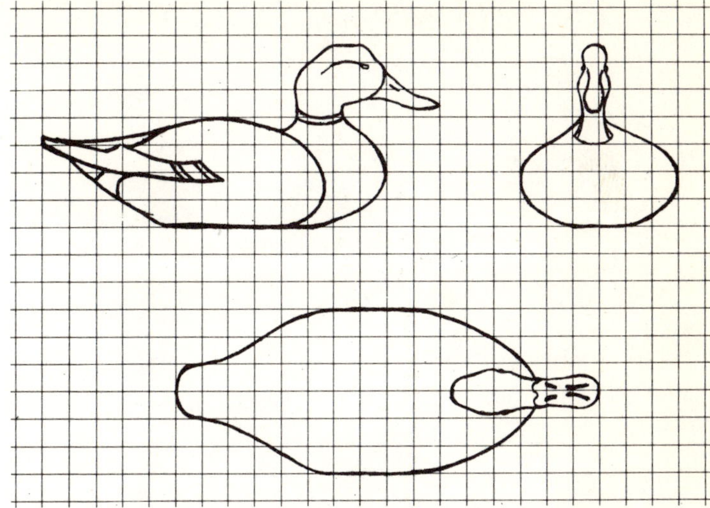

Here are three outline views of a mallard duck. Make a large copy of these drawings (each square equals about an inch, so your duck should be 15 to 16 inches long from tail tip to bill tip) and you'll have a good decoy pattern

With a friend who is wearing camouflage clothing, the author hunts ducks and geese from a decoy made of dead corn stalks

Duck decoys should be grouped naturally in the water near your blind, and they should be placed so that flying birds can see them at a distance

them riding upright on the surface, plus a rope and anchor to keep them from drifting away. There are many books on decoy-making, with patterns, colored pictures and detailed instructions for carving the birds and putting on the attachments.

In addition to decoys, a call is often used. A duck or goose call is simply a little horn made of wood or plastic, in which you can blow to imitate a duck's quacking or a goose's honking.

Calls are sold in sporting-goods stores. They work best if you cup a hand over the front end as you blow. You must listen to the birds and practice imitating them if the call is to sound realistic. You can buy phonograph records with calling instructions and the sounds of real birds so that you can practice at home.

A call is also used to imitate a crow, and crows and pigeons are often hunted from blinds of brush or small trees at the edges of fields. Once again you can buy commercial decoys or make your own. A crow decoy is much easier to make than a duck decoy. All you have to do is cut out a crow profile from a sheet of plywood, paint it black and prop it in a tree. As the crows come toward you, they will see the decoy more from the side than from above, so it needn't have a thick, three-dimensional body. However, you should really buy a composition or plastic owl decoy to go with your homemade crows. Owls and crows are deadly enemies. If crows see an owl surrounded by three of four crows, they think members of their own clan are attacking the owl and they will swoop in to join the fight.

Pigeons are fast, tricky fliers that are difficult

Hidden by tall swamp trees, this hunter uses a duck call. Calls are also employed to attract crows

to hit, but making decoys for them is easiest of all because pigeons don't seem to be very bright. Buy some thick, easily cut plastic such as styrofoam from a plastics-supply house and use shears, a saw or knife to cut out pigeon shapes. Then just paint them appropriate colors and set them in a feeding field. Or you can even cut pigeon dolls out of stiff cardboard, paint them and prop them up. Some hunters achieve the same results with bunches of rags.

After your gun has brought a couple of birds down, set out real pigeons as extra decoys. You can also use other birds you shoot as extra decoys to attract birds of the same species. Pigeons do not respond well to calling, but with decoys there will be no need for this.

Turkeys are sometimes shot at relatively long range with a rifle, and are sometimes lured near a blind and hunted with a shotgun. If you use a blind, you can once again employ a

Crows and owls are natural enemies. You can set up decoys to look as if an owl is being bullied by two or three crows. Then start calling to attract other crows; they'll fly close in order to gang up on the owl

call, though the favorite type is not a mouth call. It's a wooden box, and to imitate a turkey you do not blow into it but scrape the lid across it. This box call comes in two different versions. One employs a piece of chalked slate as the lid and the other employs a flat, chalked piece of wood as a sliding cover that achieves the same effect. These calls, too, can be bought in sporting-goods stores.

So far, this discussion has covered birds that can be hunted without a dog—although it's best to have a retriever with you when you shoot ducks or geese so that the dog can jump into the water and fetch the birds you bring down. Most of the species known as upland birds— that is, dry-land birds found at relatively high elevations and not in marshes or on the water —are best hunted with a dog.

There are two main classifications of upland bird dogs: flushing breeds, such as the springer

Wearing camouflage clothing and crouching in a natural blind, this Pennsylvania hunter used a call to lure a tom turkey into range of his shotgun

spaniel, and pointing breeds, such as the English setter and English pointer. Either type of dog runs out ahead of the hunter, sniffing the air for bird scent. When a flushing dog finds a bird he rushes toward it, flushing it out of hiding. The bird flies up into the air and the hunter can then shoot at it. When a pointing dog finds a bird, he stops short, stiffens and looks toward it. This is a signal for the hunter to approach—closer and closer, until he himself flushes the bird. Again it flies into the air and he can shoot at it. This is only a basic description, leaving out scores of details about how a dog works "in the field" and how the hunter trains him and works with him. To become properly acquainted with hunting dogs, you should read at least a couple of books entirely devoted to the subject, and you should go hunting with someone who owns a good pointer or flushing dog.

There are differences of opinion as to which type of dog, the pointer or the flusher, is best for hunting certain species of birds. Some species of birds "hold" for a dog. This means that when a dog approaches, the bird usually remains perfectly still, trying not to be seen. Such a situation is perfect for a pointer, for both dog and bird remain right where they are until the hunter's approach makes the bird panic and fly up. But some birds tend to run along the ground, hidden by underbrush, when a dog approaches. They don't "hold" well for a dog, but they don't fly up, either, unless they think they're being attacked. Such a bird can be hunted best with a flushing dog, because that type of dog virtually pushes the bird into the air.

Ring-necked pheasants tend to run rather than hold and then fly, so I find flushing dogs best for hunting them. Bobwhite quail, woodcock, chukar partridge and several other species hold well, so I prefer a pointing dog for hunting them. Ruffed grouse neither hold well nor run as a rule; they fly the instant a dog comes anywhere near them. For this reason, it has been said that there's no such thing as a good grouse dog. But this is not quite true. A

pointing dog with a very keen nose can scent a grouse from far away and will go on point before getting close enough to make the bird fly. The bird will take to the air like a winged streak of lightning when the hunter begins his approach, but you can generally get near enough for a shot before the grouse zigzags behind trees and completely disappears. Generally speaking, a pointing dog is useful for hunting more species of birds than a flushing dog.

Whatever breed you use, you must guide the dog to a likely area for finding birds. During the early fall, pheasants like to roost at night in dense, tangled woods and swamps and in weed patches. At dawn they move out into nearby fields to feed. Shortly before noon they seek shady spots and weed-grown gravel pits where they rest, digest their food and dust themselves. Late in the afternoon they return to the fields to eat again and then fly back to their roosts. Knowing these things, you can figure out where to hunt at various times of the day. To give yourself further help, look for droppings and tracks.

By late fall, pheasants begin a change in behavior. Frosts have thinned out the weedy patches of cover, and the birds spend the cold nights roosting in heavy brush and wooded areas. Since food is scarce and takes time to find, feeding periods are longer. The birds will now spend most of the day on the lee side (away from the wind) of heavy cover, in spots where they can find weed seeds or vegetables, fruit and corn left behind during the harvest. Patches of protective briars and brush will often hide a bird, but at midday try the sun-warmed slopes.

As autumn progresses, grouse look for higher and higher hills on which to eat and roost. These upland birds are found practically in the lowlands early in the season, but later on they will tend to stay on sun-warmed birch and poplar hillsides. But regardless of how far the season has progressed, they are also attracted to farm woodlots, juniper-grown hillsides, vine tangles, alder runs and pockets of birch and ev-

Springer spaniels — which do not point their game but flush it — are excellent for pheasant hunting. This photo shows Leonard Lee Rue with two of his springers and a cock pheasant they helped him bag

Among the good pointing breeds is the Brittany spaniel. This one is pointing quail

ergreen growth. They eat fruits, nuts, berries, plants and insects, so wherever you find a lot of one or more or these foods you've found a good place to hunt.

Bobwhite quail do not change their habits as autumn gets colder. These are covey birds— meaning that they band together in flocks of various sizes, from a few birds to as many as twenty. For safety, they roost together in a tight circle with their heads pointing outward. Roosting places are briar patches, tangled grass and brush. At dawn they move into the fields to feed on grain, soybeans, peas, weed seeds and berries.

When flushed, they practically explode into the air and they may all go in different directions, but at least some are almost certain to head toward heavy cover. Knowing this, as you approach a dog's point you can make a good guess about the direction of flight that will be taken by some of the birds, and you can be ready to swing your gun in that direction.

When the covey scatters, be sure to "mark down" some of the "singles"—which means to note where some of the individual birds fly.

Into the game pocket goes a ruffed grouse that was flushed in a patch of evergreen trees and birches

The well-camouflaged woodcock would rather eat worms than anything else, so look for these birds in spots where they can probe for dinner in soft earth

Then you can take your dog there to point the singles. Without a dog, incidentally, you could literally step on a quail and not know it. Hiding in tall grass, these birds flatten themselves against the ground and remain perfectly still until flushed. Their speckled brown plumage is an absolute camouflage even when you're only a couple of feet away.

Another well camouflaged bird is the long-beaked woodcock, which makes its home in alder runs, brushy pastures and young stands of birch and poplar, wherever rich black soil holds lots of earthworms to eat. Woodcock feed at night, and during the day they rest, usually on the ground. Even without a dog, you can often flush woodcock by walking slowly through the types of cover just described, searching the area thoroughly and pausing frequently. Look for chalky-white splashes on the ground; these are droppings. And look for concentrations of little round holes in the earth, where woodcock have used their long, thin beaks to probe for worms. These signs mean the area is worth exploring carefully. You may walk past a woodcock without knowing it and then, when you pause, the bird may become alarmed and fly up, giving you a chance for a fast shot. But nevertheless, you'll find more birds and have more sport if you take a good dog along.

Beagles are favorite dogs for hunting cottontail rabbits. These rabbits tend to run in large circles, so if you wait at a spot where your dog has jumped one, the rabbit is likely to streak past you again

Birds are by no means the only quarry hunted with dogs. Hounds are sometimes used to hunt many different kinds of mammals, including fox, raccoon, bear, cougar and rabbit. There are many species of rabbits and hares, all belonging to one great biological family called *leporidae*. North America has over seventy different varieties of cottontail rabbits, as well as jack rabbits, swamp rabbits, varying hares (also called snowshoe rabbits) and other species. Rabbits—particularly cottontails—are hunted more than any other kind of animal in America, and they continue to multiply as if no one ever shot at them.

When cottontails are hunted with rifles, dogs are not used. The object is to search until you see a rabbit sitting still within range and then try to hit it. But when cottontails are hunted with shotguns, hounds are often used, and the favorite breed is the beagle. The rabbits are then shot on the run.

With a pack of beagles in pursuit, a cottontail will often run in a huge, uneven circle, sooner or later coming back to where the chase started. Therefore, when hunting with hounds you can often wait for the pack of dogs to chase the rabbit back past you, instead of trying to run after the dogs or follow the sound of their distant barking.

Abandoned farms are probably the best of all places to hunt for cottontails. Search (or take your dogs searching) through run-down orchards, fence rows, thickets, the edges between fields and woods, weedy ditches, briar patches, brush and log piles. During the winter, rabbits spend much time huddling in their "forms," as their nests are called, and spots that may contain these forms include weed patches, briars, farm dumps or any handy windbreak. Relatively protected cropland such as a valley cornfield is also a good place to look. So are heaps of prunings or cornstalks, clumps of wild raspberries, strips of multiflora roses and sumac. If there's heavy undercover for protection, sumac makes a good winter habitat, and it has a high fat content that attracts rabbits during the cold, lean months. Hunting is almost invariably best during a sudden warm spell fol-

This rabbit is sitting in a raspberry patch which offers food and cover, and is therefore a good spot to hunt

The jack rabbit will often run a short distance and then pause. For a skilled rifleman, the moment the animal stops is the moment to shoot

lowing severe cold. On the other hand, if the weather is too cold for you to be comfortable, it will also be too cold for good hunting.

The little cottontail is plentiful in all regions, while the larger varying hare, or snowshoe rabbit, is found in the northern United States and Canada. Scientifically speaking, the animal is a hare, not a rabbit. Whereas the cottontail remains brown or greyish-brown all year, the varying hare's coat varies from camouflage-brown in the summer to camouflage-speckled in the fall and spring to camouflage-white in the winter. The name snowshoe rabbit refers to the animal's big hind feet, which spread out on the snow to make running easier during the winter.

In New England, the favorite way to hunt snowshoe rabbits is with dogs, but some sportsmen in that area, as well as in other northern

The ideal place to hunt bear is at a watering spot where signs show that a bear has been eating. The animal is likely to return to the same place before long

It is difficult to climb higher than mountain goats, but they should be stalked from above, when possible, because they tend to look for danger coming from below them

states, prefer to do their own trailing. In Canada, too, it is usually done without dogs. Rabbit tracks are easy to follow, and in spite of the varying hare's white winter fur this species is not completely invisible against the snow. Both the eyes and the ear tips are black. When stalking, be very alert and watch for those black spots.

In the West, jack rabbits are hunted a great deal, but not with dogs. A hound would probably get scratched badly on cactus and thorny brush, and the "jacks" are so abundant that they're easily found without dogs. Both rifles and shotguns are used. Jack rabbits are not supposed to be good table fare, but after eating all kinds of rabbits I can tell you that they all taste good. The biggest difference among the species is not in the taste but in the tenderness. The cottontail is the most tender, the snowshoe is a little tougher and the jack is tougher still.

Moose, like elk, can sometimes be attracted by bugling. They think what they hear is the challenging call of another moose so they approach, looking for a fight

Snowshoe rabbits are hard to see against the snow when their fur has turned winter-white, but an alert hunter can spot the black spots of their eyes and ear tips

Camouflage clothing may be red, spotted with grey and black to resemble foliage patterns. Most animals are color-blind and can't see your safety-red clothing

In long-range hunting for varmint species such as woodchucks, it is wise to scan the fields with binoculars. To steady your rifle, rest it over any natural support, and use a telescopic sight of fairly high power

When using a rifle to hunt rabbits, woodchucks and many other species, including big game, you will sometimes have to make long shots. For such shots, always use a rifle rest; that is, find a log or rock or hump of ground or tree crotch, or roll up a jacket on the ground, and rest your forward hand on it, under the rifle's stock.

Here are a few tips on hunting other animals: If you hear a squirrel scampering about on the other side of a tree, where you can't get a shot at it, throw a pebble or twig over to that side; the sound of it landing will send the animal running around to your side. If you're trying to hit a woodchuck but he's too low in the grass for a good shot, give a shrill whistle and he may sit up. If you're in the West or Southwest hunting antelope, don't shoot while the band is running at full speed; wait, and in a moment the last buck in the band—usually the biggest one—will often pause and look back, giving you time to take aim carefully and

The woodchuck has a strong streak of curiosity. If you frighten one into its burrow, wait a few minutes and it may come out again to see what's going on

fire. If you're hunting big game in Canada, and want to make a caribou come closer, gently wave a hat or handkerchief. Out of curiosity, the animal will sometimes take a few steps nearer. The same trick often works with antelope, too. And many antlered animals will come closer if you raise your arms in imitation of antlers. If you know for certain you'll be shooting at long range (as often happens in woodchuck hunting both in the East and West) buy a bipod—a two-legged shooting stand—and attach it to the fore-end of your rifle; it will help to keep the rifle steady for long, difficult shots, and sporting-goods stores sell bipods that will fit almost any rifle.

A list of tips could go on and on, but the best way to learn is by doing. One thing to do is to go hunting with someone who has had experience with the particular species that you're after. Another thing to do is to hunt by yourself and experiment with new ways of searching, tracking and stalking, using common sense and imagination to guide you. Now and then you'll make a mistake and come home without game, but you'll learn something on every hunt.

I'll end this chapter with just a few more tips for those who have always dreamed of hunting bear. In some states it is illegal to trail a bear with hounds, and I don't think there's enough sport in shooting down a bear that the dogs have treed. But after a snow you can follow a bear's tracks for long distances without hounds. Move silently and cautiously in the hope that you'll come upon the bear as it pauses to dig out a ground squirrel, a root, a patch of grass or some other food.

A surer method is to "still hunt"—waiting in a likely spot for a bear to come to you. A good place to do this is where there are lots of bear tracks, particularly at a watering place or where the signs show that a bear has been eating. A bear will come back to the same place to look for more food. When he does, you'd better be ready with a high-powered rifle.

* * *

INFORMATION SOURCES

For additional information on conservation, write to the Wildlife Management Institute, 709 Wire Building, Washington, D.C. 20005, and to the National Wildlife Federation, 1412 Sixteenth Street N.W., Washington, D.C. 20036.

For booklets of shooting and hunting tips, write to the following firearms manufacturers: Ithaca Gun Company, Ithaca, New York 14851; Marlin Firearms Company, 79 Willow Street, New Haven, Connecticut 06502; O. F. Mossberg and Sons, Inc., 7 Grasso Avenue, North Haven, Connecticut 06473; Remington Arms Company, 939 Barnum Avenue, Bridgeport, Connecticut 06602; Savage Arms, Westfield, Massachusetts 01085; and Winchester-Western Public Relations, 460 Park Avenue, New York, New York 10022.

A folding bipod makes an excellent rifle rest for long shots, either at big game or at varmints like chucks and prairie dogs

By listening to the calls of the dogs when hounds are chasing a fox, you can often judge which direction to take in order to head off the fox and get a shot

*Mountain-climbing is among the adventurous pursuits awaiting those who have kept fit and mastered many
outdoor skills*

23

BEYOND THE NEXT HILL

When you've gained some degree of skill in all of the outdoor activities discussed in this book, what next? There are many answers to that question, because there are many more activities to be explored once you've become an experienced outdoorsman. There are even additional aspects to the activities covered here.

For example, there's winter camping, which may require that you learn how to ski or how to use "Alaskan" snowshoes for long treks or the shorter, wider "bear paw" snowshoes for climbing. You might also want to learn how to drive a snowmobile. Winter camping requires heavier, better-insulated clothing and a cold-weather sleeping bag, as well as a knowledge of how to build a snow shelter and how to find dry wood in the deadfalls under drifts.

Then there's mountaineering, which demands special hobnail boots, spiked crampons to fit over these boots if the going is too slippery, Alpine rope, eyed spikes called pitons for attaching the rope to cliffs, a piton hammer, an ice axe and various other equipment. And you must not only have all the right gear but be taught how to use it by a qualified climber.

From the size of this marlin, you can envision the thrills of big-game fishing

There are beautiful caverns where you can take safe, guided tours as a prelude to learning the art of spelunking—exploring caves

Going from the heights to the depths, you might also want to try cave exploring, an art called spelunking, which can be more dangerous than mountaineering if you don't have the right kind of headlamp, rope, emergency rations and other gear—plus a knowledge of how to use all of this equipment.

Fortunately, you can find out whether caves fascinate you without doing anything dangerous. There are guided tours through many large, safe and eerily beautiful caverns where you can make your way from one end to the other without even smudging a newly cleaned business suit. This is not genuine spelunking—*exploring* caves—but it will give you a peek at underground streams and springs, fantastically colored rock walls, strange stalactites of limestone hanging from the cavern roof, stalagmites rising to meet them, echo chambers, natural bridges and other weird rock formations.

Nature photography has already been mentioned in this book as a fine outdoor activity, and since whole books are devoted exclusively to this subject I won't try to teach you the art of wilderness photography here. What those books don't generally tell you is how to know whether you're in danger while taking close-up pictures of certain animals. I will therefore give you a few tips here, regarding the moment to retreat.

Normally, most animals are not dangerous, but there are certain warning signs to watch for. To begin with, those that *may* be dangerous are usually sick, wounded, cornered or mean with old age. In addition, males of large species during mating season may be dangerous, and a mother guarding her young is often ready for a fight.

If you climb trees or cliffs to get close-up photographs of large birds, especially birds of prey, be alert. When such a bird is preparing to attack, it will circle and then swoop near you in a preliminary bluff. The next swoop may not be a bluff, so protect your eyes—a prime target for birds—and get down quickly.

Many animals will snarl, snort, hiss or make some other sound when getting ready to charge. A bobcat will hiss, snarl, spit and sometimes paw the air. In addition, the hair on its upper back and neck may rise. A bison may

It isn't easy to approach an osprey's nest, but this kind of nature photography provides opportunities for closely studying animals and birds

bellow and paw the ground; if he then humps up his back and lifts his tail erect, retreat, because that means he will definitely charge.

Horned animals will lower or thrust forward their heads when ready to fight. Antlered animals will wag their heads and sometimes paw the ground. Some, such as the moose, will often raise the hair on the back of their necks, as cat and dog species also do. If a moose shakes its head from side to side, then protrudes its tongue and bellows, that also means a charge is about to be made. Like many animals, a bull moose is usually easy to get along with except during the fall mating season.

A nature photographer (or anyone who stalks big game) should learn to recognize certain danger signals. For example, this elk, shaking his head and pawing the ground, is preparing to charge

Learning the ways of wildlife is a never-ending process. In time, you can gain an intimate knowledge of widely differing species such as the white-breasted nuthatch (above left) and the great horned owl (above right)

Many exciting skills can be learned in connection with outdoor pursuits. One of these hunters — a professional guide — flies his own light plane to reach otherwise inaccessible wilderness areas

If you make a hobby of observing animals, you will learn to understand their gestures. Usually if an animal begins to act nervous, the best thing to do is stay still and remain calm. But if the animal seems about to attack and you are unarmed, the only thing to do is to move off, watching the animal as you go in case there's a sudden need to get out of the way fast.

Wildlife photography is a safe enough hobby if you have a good knowledge of the animals you're stalking. It's also a very exciting pastime, especially if you try for close-up pictures.

Still other outdoor activities include archery (and bow-and-arrow hunting), trapping, big-game hunting, skin-diving, spear-fishing, horseback riding, target-shooting, sailing, ice-sailing, and even flying a motored airplane or sailplane. And sometimes you can combine activities—for instance, by trailer-camping at the edge of good sailing waters, or by flying to a remote fishing or hunting camp. When you've once felt the adventurous spirit of the outdoors, you may develop a curious wanderlust, a yearning to explore the world's possibilities. This is what makes some men and women great. Perhaps the most adventurous outdoorsmen in history are those gallant astronauts who have let their yearning to explore take them to the moon and who see no limit to future expeditions.

Of course, you may have the truly adventurous soul of an outdoorsman and still never explore space, but this little planet itself provides a miraculous kaleidoscope of discovery. There is a limitless, ever-changing horizon, and just beyond the next hill nature always holds more secrets waiting for discovery.

Skin diving, archery and skiing are among the many wonderful experiences awaiting the accomplished outdoorsman

INDEX